Contents

Social Theory and Modern Sociology

ANTHONY GIDDENS

Social Theory and Modern Sociology

Stanford University Press
Stanford, California

Stanford University Press
Stanford, California
©1987 Anthony Giddens
Originating publisher: Polity Press, Cambridge,
    in association with Basil Blackwell, Oxford
First published in the U.S.A. by
    Stanford University Press, 1987
Printed in the United States of America
Cloth ISBN 0-8047-1355-3
Paper ISBN 0-8047-1356-1
Original printing 1987
Last figure below indicates year of this printing:
00   99   98   97   96

Preface

Sociology, it would seem, is a discipline currently under strain. Never the least controversial of academic subjects, a decade or so ago it was nonetheless popular in terms of student appeal, and apparently in the vanguard of intellectual culture. The writings of the leading sociological thinkers were widely read and debated outside the sociological profession itself. Today student enrolments in sociology tend to be in decline world-wide, social research less well-funded than it was, while sociology might be thought to have lost its central position in respect of key intellectual developments and achievements. It would not appear to be the happiest of times for those who like to regard themselves as 'sociologists'.

How accurate is such a picture of the declining fortunes of sociology? Certainly in terms of student enthusiasm for the discipline and material support for research there is something to this view. In a period of tight labour markets students tend to turn their eyes towards what they might see as more vocationally rewarding subjects. Governments concerned to cut back on public spending are likely to see support for social research as among the more expendable items in their budgets. Such tends particularly to be the case where those governments are committed to policies substituting market relations for 'socially organized' provision for needs.

However these influences, which might be relatively transient in any case, have little to do with the intellectual status of sociology. As I seek to demonstrate throughout the essays in this book, sociology retains its focal importance for the social sciences — and indeed for anyone who seeks to study human beings and their cultural products. The domain of sociology does not correspond to that of social theory. The latter is much broader in scope than the former, dealing as it does with a whole range of issues to do with human action, social institutions and their mutual connections. But sociology, whose prime field of study is the social world brought about by the advent of modernity, has a peculiar and privileged relation to social theory. For modernity involves the systematic study of social relations as part of the forging and reforging of those relations, something integral to its dynamic character. The scope of the 'modern' can virtually be defined in these terms. Our understanding of ourselves, as discursively formulated and reflexively applied to transforming the conditions of our lives, is intrinsic to the nature of modern societies.

If in intellectual terms sociology remains just as important as it ever was, it has undergone very considerable changes over recent years. These in some part reflect developments in social theory, but are also bound up with potentially quite profound changes in the very 'object' of analysis — the modern social world. A series of transitions in social theory is traced out in the articles which comprise this book. These transitions have had both considerable impact upon sociology and been very directly influenced by the writings of sociologists. The period of the supposed intellectual decline of sociology has been enormously fruitful in respect of contributions to the recasting of social theory — a process now well advanced and whose main outlines are now reasonably clear. For a while it did seem that not just the theoretical frameworks of sociology, but those of the social sciences as a whole, stood in danger of complete disintegration amid a welter of divergent claims about their proper concerns. However today we can recognize that theoretical syntheses are emerging, sifting out what is valuable and closing off paths that have proved to be fruitless.

Such developments on the level of theory are in some degree related to the social transformations currently occurring in the social world. These concrete social changes offer a stimulus to sociological reflection at the same time as they demand a reorientation of the discipline. If it is not valid to speak of an intellectual diminishing of sociology over recent years, certainly sociologists face the need to elaborate new concepts and modes of analysis in order to confront a transmuted social universe. For a long while sociological thought has tended to draw too unabashedly upon nineteenth-century traditions in studying the twentieth-century world. We have to break more forcefully than hitherto with the 'endogenous models' of social organization and change characteristic of the preceding century. For we live in a world which is increasingly 'globalized' and from which such models are more and more distant. The origins and nature of new social movements, the shifting regionalization of social relationships and systems of production world-wide, changes brought about by the adoption of micro-electronics and information technology, plus the now ever-present potential for nuclear war — these all require sociological analysis. If sociologists are to meet the challenges posed by seeking to understand the world of the late twentieth century, they will have to place in question aspects of what often passes for the received wisdom of their subject. The discipline will thereby surely emerge only the stronger.

Anthony Giddens
King's College, Cambridge

1

What do sociologists do?

Sociology has been an established discipline — in most universities the world over — for many years.[1] Yet the subject is a worrying one to some people in a way that other academic endeavours are not. It would be overstating the case to say that it rouses the passions, but it would probably be fair to hold that it quite often produces feelings of disquiet which do not seem to attach to most other fields of academic enquiry. There is something about sociology that tends to raise hackles which remain undisturbed by most other academic pursuits. Disciplinary chauvinism is a familiar enough phenomenon in universities. One may legitimately suspect that it is rather rarely based upon a deep acquaintance with whatever areas of study happen to be the objects of disparagement. But there does appear to be something more involved in reactions to sociology than the commonplace expression of resentment and ignorance for which universities are unhappily on occasion the breeding-grounds.

What is the source of the unease which the presence of sociology in the academy in some degree creates? One rejoinder to such a question might be that there is no clear-cut field of study to which it corresponds — no subject-matter which can be definitely pointed to as delimiting its province of investigation. There is surely very little indeed in this view. Sociology is concerned with the comparative study of social institutions, giving particular emphasis to those forms of society brought into being by the advent of modern industrialism. There might be differences of opinion as to how modern societies should best be studied, but to suggest that such societies are not worthy of systematic enquiry seems more than faintly absurd.

[1] 'What sociologists do?' was an inaugural lecture delivered at the University of Cambridge on 29 January 1986.

In any case, there is more emotion involved in antagonistic responses to sociology than is compatible with an intellectual worry over how well-defined its field of study may be. Could the prompting impulse therefore be fear? Perhaps, however vaguely, there is some sort of threat implied in subjecting our own social behaviour to academic scrutiny? This is closer to the mark. If it is at all interesting, sociological work is bound to unsettle some people some of the time. Yet anyone who knows anything about sociology will affirm that it is very far from unsettling all of the people all of the time. There are some who naively associate sociology with political radicalism, with a shaggy horde pouring over the barricades to overturn all that every sensible citizen holds dear. However at least as many sociologists have been conservatives as radicals, and the probability is that most are political middle-of-the-roaders in much the same proportion as any other discipline. It would demand a piece of extended social research in its own right to validate this assertion properly. But no one having a developed familiarity with the subject is likely to suppose that its leading traditions of thought are located in a particular corner of the political spectrum.

No, it is surely not primarily a sense of brooding opposition to the *status quo* that can explain the attitude of reserve which sociology seems to provoke. Maybe it is that sociology is felt to be unenlightening? Perhaps we tend to feel that we already know enough about the sources of our own conduct, and that of others in societies like ours, not to need anything further? Let me put it in a provocative way. The sociologist, it might be said, is someone who states the obvious, but with an air of discovery. You might think it unlikely that anyone who would accept the designation 'sociologist' would be at all happy with this, because it would seem straight away to put him or her out of a job. In fact I think this is really the nub of the issue, and it gives particular cogency to the question: What do sociologists do? Putting the question in a slightly more elaborate form — What kind of enlightenment can sociologists offer about the origins and nature of our own social conduct? — turns up some very real problems. They are problems that are shared in some part by all the social sciences, and indeed the humanities too. But they are posed in a peculiarly acute way in sociology.

The matter can be put quite simply. One of the distinctive things about human beings, which separates us from the animals, is that normally we know what we are doing in our activities, and why. That is to say, human beings are concept-bearing agents, whose concepts in some part constitute what it is that they are up to, not contingently, but as an inherent element of what it is that they are up to. In addition, human actors have reasons for their actions, reasons that consistently inform the flow of day-to-day activities. Neither reasons nor act-identifications need be expressed discursively for them to govern the content of behaviour. Yet in general I think it valid to hold that agents virtually all the time know what their actions are, under some description, and why it is they carry them out. There is a further consideration. It is intrinsic to human action that, in any given situation, the agent, as philosophers sometimes say, could have acted otherwise. However oppressively the burden of particular circumstances may weigh upon us, we feel ourselves to be free in the sense that we decide upon our actions in the light of what we know of ourselves, the context of our activities, and their likely outcomes. This feeling is not spurious. For it is arguable that it is analytical to the concept of agency that the actor in some sense 'could have done otherwise' — or could have refrained from whatever course of action was followed.

These remarks seem doubly to compound the difficulties of sociology. For the persistent critic may push the argument beyond that mentioned previously. Not only are sociologists prone to state the obvious, but they tend to dress up what they have to say in terminology which seems to deny to agents the freedom of action we know ourselves to have. They may suggest that what we do is impelled by social forces, or social constraints, independently of our own volition. We believe ourselves to be acting freely, and in cognizance of the grounds of our actions, but really we are moved by compulsions of which we are quite unaware. This sort of claim does not ring true, for it transgresses what we feel ourselves to be — in my view rightly — as human actors. Sociology might therefore seem to be a doubly redundant discipline, not only telling us what we already know, but parading the familiar in a garb which conceals its proper nature.

However I am fairly confident that this is not all there is to it. I am not about to suggest that sociologists should all quietly pack their bags and slip away to pastures new. I am willing to accept, and even to accentuate, the claim that large segments of the discipline of sociology are concerned with things we think we know. But far from rendering the subject, or its practitioners, redundant, or their ideas without bite, this makes sociology in some ways the most challenging and the most intricately demanding of the social sciences. I do not want to say that there do not exist versions of sociology that I find either objectionable, or essentially uninteresting, or both. My speaking of 'what sociologists do' has something of an optative sense to it. I do not by any means approve of what all sociologists do. I wish only to give examples of what the discipline can accomplish, to show why, as an area of study, sociology is both intellectually compelling and of great practical importance.

Sociology and Lay Knowledge

In analysing what sociologists do, let me start from the observation that what seems obvious, or what 'everyone knows', may not only not be obvious at all, it might actually be wrong. Not many of us today belong to the flat-earth society, although it seems obvious enough when you look at it that the earth is as flat as any pancake. In the case of our presumed knowledge about social institutions, it might be argued, we are particularly inclined to error. At any rate, examples are very easy to find. It is commonly known — or believed — for example that there has been a steep rise in the number of 'broken homes' or one-parent families over the past century. Thus if we look back to Victorian times, we see a dramatic contrast between the stable, integrated families of that era and the disarray of the current period. In fact the proportion of one-parent families was possibly greater in the Victorian epoch than it is today — not as a result of divorce, but mainly as a consequence of higher rates of mortality in relatively youthful age-groups. Or again, it is common knowledge that the United Kingdom is particularly strike-prone, its tendency to industrial disruption even being taken by some to be the main origin of its shortcomings in respect of economic performance. However, in terms of any accepted measures, the incidence of strikes in Britain is not especially high as compared with various other industrially-developed countries. To take another example, it is well-known — or imagined — that Sweden has an extremely high rate of suicide. Something in the gloomy Nordic character, or the long years of having had to tolerate a socialist government, creates a disposition to melancholy or to despair. In actuality Sweden does not display a particularly elevated suicide rate, and never has done so.

One should not underestimate the contribution which social research can make to identifying false or slanted beliefs widely held about social phenomena. For such beliefs may often take the form of prejudices, and hence contribute to intolerance and discrimination, or might inhibit social changes that would otherwise be seen as desirable. It surely must be one of the tasks of the sociologist to seek to discover how far commonly-held views about given aspects of social life are in fact valid, even if they appear obvious to everyone else. And this is bound to mean that the results of social research may now and then seem uninspiring, since what is thought to be obvious may indeed prove to be the case. It should not be forgotten, moreover, that a good deal of what is now taken to be among the things everyone knows about social institutions is the result of sociological analysis and social research. An enormous amount of social research — often carried out by government bodies or survey agencies, not only by sociologists in a university context — goes into the routine running of a modern society. We tend to take this for granted, but without it much that is involved in what everyone knows would not be part of our awareness at all. We all know that rates of divorce in most Western countries are higher that they were two or three decades ago; but we tend to forget the very considerable amount of continuing social investigation involved in charting such trends.

If this were all there were to sociology, there would probably not be too much to get excited about. Sociology is not just in the business of correcting false beliefs which we may hold about social phenomena — although some of its advocates have in fact seen it only in this role. Let me return to the theorem I stated earlier. To be a human agent is to know, virtually all the time, under some description, what one is engaged in and why. There is a sense in which we cannot be wrong about what our actions are, or those actions would not exist. I cannot, for instance, write a cheque without knowing not only what it is I am doing, but without also knowing a complex array of concepts and rules, defining what 'credit' is, what 'having an account' is, what a 'bank' is, and so on. The formula that human agents always in a certain sense know what they are doing, and why, necessarily involves a range of elements in the broader institutional context within which a particular action is carried on. We do not need social research to tell us what these elements are, since not only do we know them already, we must know them already for the action in question to be possible at all.

This sort of knowledge — knowledge of the social conventions involved in the societies in which we live — cannot, therefore, be subject to illumination by sociology. Or so it might seem. Only a little reflection is required to see that such is not the case. I want to propose, in fact, that there are no less than four types of question that one might legitimately ask about social conduct, none of which contravenes the assertion that human individuals always know what their actions are and why they engage in them. These four kinds of enquiry, which have a logical unity with one another, supply the keys to understanding what sociologists do — to what the discipline of sociology is all about.

Consider again the example of signing a cheque. Everyone in a modern society knows what signing a cheque is, but someone from a culture in which there are no banks, and perhaps not even a monetary system at all, would not. What is familiar convention to one individual or group, in other words, is not necessarily so to another. This is true not only between different societies, or forms of society, but within them too. All of us live our lives within particular sectors of the societies of which we are members, and the modes of behaviour of those in other milieux may be largely opaque to us. Showing what it is like to live in one particular cultural setting to those who inhabit another (and vice versa) is a significant part of what the sociologist does. This might be called the anthropological moment of social research, and it is worthwhile noting some of its implications. Notice, for example, that the identification of the cultural diversity of social life is simultaneously often a means of disclosing the common rationality of human action. To provide an account of the conventions involved in a given cultural milieu, or a given community, allows a grasp of the intentions and reasons the agents have for what they do, which may entirely escape us in the absence of such an account.

There are complicated problems of a philosophical sort involved here, and I do not want to underestimate them. But it is fairly easy to develop the point. In a world riven with conflict and embedded hostilities, and yet increasingly interdependent, mutual comprehension across diverse cultural settings becomes of the first importance. The *sine qua non* of such cross-cultural communication is the effective prosecution of the ethnographic tasks of social research. This is just as true of the cultural distance which separates West Indian communities in Brixton from affluent white suburbs (and from Whitehall) as it is, for example, of that which separates the Islamic Revolution from the culture of the West. Of course, bridging the spaces of cultural dissimilarity does not inevitably lead to a reduction of pre-existing conflicts. The better one knows one's enemies, the clearer it may become that hostility towards them is justifiable or unavoidable. But this should not lead us to doubt what an elementary part the ethnography of culture plays in forging mutual understanding.

Its natural counterpart on the level of academic disciplines is the close meshing of sociology and anthropology.

Without seeming unduly mercenary, let me revert to the instance of signing a cheque. We all know what it is to sign a cheque, but this is not the same as saying we know all there is to know about it. Would a cheque be valid if I wrote it on the back of a bus ticket, rather than on the printed slips the bank so thoughtfully provides? Most of the knowledge we have of the conventions which define our actions is not only contextual, it is basically practical and *ad hoc* in character. In order to have a bank account, and cash cheques on it, we are not required to have an elaborate understanding of the banking system. Nor could everyone necessarily put into words what a 'cheque' or an 'account' is, if asked to do so. We all know (in modern societies) what money is in the sense that we have no trouble handling monetary transactions in our day-to-day lives. But as any economist will attest, giving a clear definition of what money is tends to be far from unproblematic. As St. Augustine remarked in the course of his celebrated observations about time, we all know what time is — until someone asks us.

Various inferences might be drawn from this, but I want to concentrate only upon one of them. This is that our discourse — what we are able to put into words — about our actions, and our reasons for them, only touches on certain aspects of what we do in our day-to-day lives. There is a highly complex non-discursive side to our activities which is of particular interest to sociology, and to other social sciences as well. It is not paradoxical here to say that sociology in this respect does study things we already know — although ordinarily we do not know them in the sense of being entirely aware of them. To put the matter another way, a good deal of our knowledge of social convention, as Wittgenstein famously observes, consists of being able to 'go on' in the multifarious contexts of social activity. The study of how we manage to accomplish this is a matter of great interest — and has potentially profound consequences, or so I shall try to indicate later.

We might offer as an illustration Erving Goffman's brilliant observations about body idiom.[2] To be a human agent, one must not only know what one is doing, but must also demonstrate this to others in visible fashion. We all expect each other to maintain a sort of 'controlled alertness' in our actions. We do this through the disciplined

[2] Erving Goffman: *Behaviour in Public Places.* New York: Free Press, 1963 and other writings.

management of bodily appearance, control of bodily posture and of facial expression. Goffman shows how dazzlingly intricate are the bodily rituals whereby we 'exhibit presence' to others, and thereby routinely and chronically defend our status as agents. The best insights into how tightly controlled our public exhibition of self ordinarily is can be gained by analysing circumstances in which it lapses. Thus we might investigate the behaviour of young children from this point of view, because it takes children years to acquire the controlled bodily idiom of their elders. Or we might study inadvertent interruptions in body management — slips of the tongue, lapses in control of posture, facial expression or dress. In this regard there are intriguing connections between Goffman and Freud, although I shall not pursue them here.

The social world never seems the same again after having read Goffman. The most inoffensive gesture becomes charged with potential associations, not all of them pleasant. But why should this be? What accounts for the fact that, for most of his readers, Goffman's writings tend to produce a feeling of privileged insight into the mundane? It is, I think, because they deal with what is intimate and familiar, but from its non-discursive side. They enhance our understanding of ourselves precisely because they reveal what we already know and must know to get around in the social world, but are not cognisant of discursively. There is from this perspective no paradox in saying that what we already know warrants detailed study, yet that the outcome of such study is far from self-evident. We could make the same point about the investigation of language. Linguists spend their professional careers studying what we already know, and indeed must know to be competent language speakers at all. But this in no way compromises the importance of linguistics, or makes it less demanding than other areas of research.

I have so far distinguished two qualifications to the proposition that we all know most of the time what our actions are, and why we perpetrate them — that all of us inhabit restricted milieux within a culturally variegated world, and that we are normally able discursively to identify only little of the complex conventional frameworks of our activities. To these we now have to add a third: that our activities constantly, I would even say routinely, have consequences that we do not intend, and of which we might be quite oblivious when undertaking the behaviour in question.

Let us trudge once more up the High Street to the bank. A modern monetary system depends upon public confidence in the exchange transactions it regularizes in order to keep going. At a given point of time banks only possess coinage to cover a small fraction of the deposits that are lodged with them. Therefore although every individual creditor can withdraw the whole of his or her deposit at will, the same is not true of all creditors. If there is a run on a bank, a spiralling diminution in confidence in the bank's ability to pay up may ensue, leading perhaps to its collapse. Now it will probably be the case that few, and perhaps none, of the bank's customers had the intention of initiating such a spiral. The outcome may be one that none of them wanted, even if it came about through their agency. It was an unintended consequence of a large number of intentional actions. The bank-run example is a special case, but it is not that special. There is, for example, a general category of unintended consequences that sociologists have often labelled 'perverse consequences'. Consider the following illustration. The state government in Florida made the shooting or trapping of alligators illegal, in order to rescue them from imminent extinction. But swampland areas that had been marginally profitable for farmers, when used for the cultivation of alligators for game hunting, then became uneconomic. As a result, the farmers began to drain the land, in order eventually to produce crops from it. The consequence was that the habitat of the alligators disappeared, and they were wiped out in the very region in which they were supposed to be conserved.[3]

Or consider an example taken from research carried out on urban renewal programmes. In some such programmes in the United States, legislation was introduced to force the owners of dilapidated buildings to bring them up to standard, especially where there were tenants in those buildings. As a consequence, some owners abandoned their buildings completely, while others only improved them insofar as they were able substantially to raise rents or turn them into non-rented accommodation. The end result was a diminution in the available amount of rented accommodation for low-income groups, coupled with a further deterioration in the housing stock in the areas involved.

Of course, not all unintended consequences are perverse. Schelling provides the following example. In the 1930s Federal deposit insurance was introduced to provide recompense for people losing their bank deposits.[4] By generating confidence, the effect of the insurance was

---

[3] Sam D. Sieber: *Fatal Remedies*. New York: Plenum Press, 1981, p. 59.

[4] Thomas C. Schelling: *Choice and Consequence*. Cambridge (Mass.): Harvard University Press, 1984, p. 8.

precisely to tend to obviate the behaviour that led to the problem. Similarly those who act purely selfishly may unintentionally contribute to the collective well-being. Those who act from base motives may contribute to the good of everyone. They echo Goethe's Mephistopheles, who is 'a part of that force which always intends evil and always does good.' Perverse consequences are a particularly significant and interesting class of unintended consequences, partly because they have a certain irony, tragic in some instances, deliciously comic in others; but mainly because the boomerang effect they express is a common feature of social policy-making. My point, however, is not just to suggest that one of the things sociologists can and should do is to study the perverse effects that attempts at social intervention frequently bring in their train. It is to emphasise how fundamental the analysis of the unintended consequences of intended actions is to the whole sociological enterprise. For it is this more than anything else that entails that, while as social agents we are necessarily the creators of social life, social life is at the same time not our own creation.

The examples of unintended consequences I have given this far are instances in which there is a discrete and singular outcome. And of course many of the unintended consequences which preoccupy us in social analysis are of this form. No one intended the overall sequence of events that led up to the Russian Revolution of 1917, not even Lenin and the Bolsheviks, anxious as they were to propel history along certain rails. It is surely always true of cataclysmic social events, like the outbreak of the World Wars, that they are only marginally the outcomes of design. But the unintended consequences of actions are not confined to sequences of events having discrete outcomes. When I speak English in a syntactically correct way, it is not my intention to reproduce the structures of the English language. Such is nonetheless a consequence of my speaking correctly, even if my contribution to the continuation of the language is a rather modest one. Generalizing this observation, we may say that unintended consequences are deeply involved in the reproduction of social institutions, however much such reproduction is also governed by intention and contrivance; and the study of the intertwining of what is intended and what is not is the fourth type of task that is of elementary importance in sociology.

This needs a certain amount of commentary, because it allows us in some part to link together each of the aspects of sociological study. As a way of thinking about what is involved, take the example of a poverty cycle. In the deprived areas of inner cities we may be able to trace a continuity in underprivilege across the generations. These areas tend to have badly-equipped schools, with teachers who have to spend more time maintaining some degree of order in the classroom than in the formal business of teaching, addressing pupils whose motivation to follow the academic syllabus is less than overwhelming. Children from such schools inevitably tend to have limited opportunities in job markets when they leave the place of education. Hence they are likely to live in similarly deprived areas to those of their parents. These areas will have badly-equipped schools . . . and so the cycle continues. Such a poverty cycle is not intended by any of those affected by it, or by anyone else either. It can be explicated via a 'mix' of intentional actions and unintended consequences, but it should be noted that these have a feedback effect, so that they become conditions of further action. This is pervasively true of social life as a whole, and forms a point of connection with the contextuality or cultural diversity mentioned earlier. Given that all action is situated in limited time-space contexts, it follows that all of us are influenced by institutional orders that none of us taken singly — and perhaps none of us taken collectively — intentionally established.

All I do under some description I do intentionally and knowledge-ably. However this scarcely makes me the master of my own fate. In following the routines of my day-to-day life I help reproduce social institutions that I played no part in bringing into being. They are more than merely the environment of my action since, as I have stressed previously, they enter constitutively into what it is I do as an agent. Similarly, my actions constitute and reconstitute the institutional conditions of action of others, just as their actions do of mine. The key concept tying together the several different endeavours of sociology which I have listed is that of what I like to call the recursive nature of social life. When I pursue the activities of my daily life, I draw chronically upon established convention — in a manner which is both largely tacit and at the same time extraordinarily complex — in order to do so. But this very process of drawing upon convention reconstitutes it, in some part as a binding influence upon the behaviour of others as well as that of myself. My activities are thus embedded within, and are constitutive elements of, structured properties of institutions stretching well beyond myself in time and in space.

In one of the most quoted methodological statements in sociology, Emile Durkheim observed: 'The system of signs that I employ to express my thoughts, the monetary system I use to pay my debts, the credit movements I utilise in my commercial relationships, the practices I follow in my profession, etc., all function independently of the use I make of them. Thus there are ways of acting, thinking and feeling which possess the remarkable property of existing outside the consciousness of the individual.'[5] There is nothing wrong with the general drift of the statement, but the conclusion is quite awry. For Durkheim was led effectively to deny that very sense of agency that all of us quite properly have. It is entirely possible to acknowledge the force of his point without drawing the implication that we are not after all the purposive reasoning agents we take ourselves to be.

Durkheim tended to argue as though only the study of the large-scale and the long-term were sufficiently important to warrant the attention of sociology. Yet — as a further element in drawing together the several strands of sociological endeavour I have identified — it can readily be demonstrated that the analysis of the apparently trivial or ephemeral can contribute in a basic way to understanding the more durable features of social institutions. Consider the following snippet of conversation. A husband and wife are conversing while idly watching television. The husband remarks that he is tired. After this, the conversation runs as follows:

> W: 'How are you tired? Physically, mentally, or just bored?'
> H: 'I don't know, I guess physically, mainly.'
> W: 'You mean that your muscles ache, or your bones?'
> H: 'What's the matter with you? You know what I mean.'
> W: 'I wish you would be more specific.'
> H: 'You know what I mean! Drop dead!'[6]

What is going on here? Well, what is going on is actually a piece of social research. The wife was a participant in a study designed to investigate the nature of ordinary language. Those involved in the study were asked simply to engage an acquaintance in conversation and to try to get the other to clarify the sense of commonplace remarks that he or she might make. On the face of things, it would be difficult to think of anything more trivial upon which to spend good research

---

[5] Emile Durkheim: *The Rules of Sociological Method*. London: Macmillan, 1982, p. 51.

[6] From Harold Garfinkel: 'A conception of, and experiments with, "trust" as a condition of stable concerted actions', in O. J. Harvey: *Motivation and Social Interaction*. New York: Ronald Press, 1963, p. 222. I have shortened the interchange slightly.

money, and indeed many within the sociological profession have concluded just that. I think such a judgement is quite wrong. The research is interesting from several different angles. The very severity of the responses elicited indicates that the deviation from certain accepted canons of small talk was perceived as a disturbing one. For breakdown in communication, and the assumption by the victim of what the researchers rather charmingly call a posture of 'righteous hostility', occurred very rapidly indeed. There is something in the tacit conventions of small talk which has a very powerful moral fixity. This something might be defined as unstated trust in the integrity of others, anchored in the assumed mutuality of what stays unsaid in the words of the conversation. The demand to supply precision of meaning was experienced as a breach of trust.

The apparent vagueness of ordinary language is expressive of the fact that it is geared to social practices, our tacit knowledge of the conventions that order those practices being the grounds of its meaningfulness. This is essentially the discovery that Wittgenstein made, by a very different route, when he forsook his earlier views in favour of the idea that language is what language does. Ordinary language cannot be tightened up and made into a simulacrum of scientific language. What remains unsaid — and, in a certain sense, unsayable — in day-to-day talk has largely to be taken on trust. For most of us this has become second nature. But imagine what the day-to-day social world would be like if no one ever felt secure that they could rely on the mutuality of the unstated conventions shared with others. That is to say, imagine a social universe in which every interaction was experienced by an individual as threatened by collapse in the manner brought about in the research setting. For how can I ever really be sure that the other party in a situation of interaction does not harbour malicious intentions towards me? Even the most harmless gesture may seem a possible threat. Now this is probably just how social life does look to some of those individuals whom we call mentally ill. There has been some very promising work done relating mental illness to the incapacity (or unwillingness) of certain types of person to take on trust what for most of us is only infrequently a source of serious worry. This connects back directly to Goffman's discussion of body idiom and its relation to continuity of self. Mental patients will often sit slackly, move jerkily rather than with the flow and control we ordinarily expect of agents, and may allow their clothing to become randomly disarrayed. They may avoid the gaze of another who talks to them, may flout the convention that one does not talk to oneself in public, and generally fail to observe other tacit conventions of talk and interaction.

The point is not that these characteristics are necessarily relevant in an aetiological sense to mental disorder, but that they drive home how important are apparently trivial features of micro-settings for broader institutions. The complex conventions we observe in day-to-day life are not just a superficial gloss upon large-scale social institutions, they are the very stuff of their continuity and fixity. That is why it is unsurprising that the French social historians, headed by Fernand Braudel, both concentrate upon the 'long duration' and are at the same time fascinated by the seemingly insignificant routines of mundane daily life. For the long-term institutional history that absorbs their interest is sedimented in the routine practices of day-to-day social activity. Among the things sociologists do, and must do, is to study long-term patterns of institutional stability and change. Although there may be differences of emphasis from the work of historians, with sociologists less concerned with recovering a sense of 'pastness' and more preoccupied with demonstrating the impact of the past on the present, the boundary-lines are, and should be, difficult to draw.

As an example, we may take the upsurge of recent work on the development of carceral institutions. This is one area among many others where there has been a marvellously fruitful cross-fertilization between sociology and history. In modern societies, certain categories of individuals are kept largely shut away from casual contact with the majority of the population. There are forms of structured concealment which separate from view a range of persons who in some way deviate from the normal run of activities in day-to-day life. These include the sick and the dying. The sight of death is not a common experience for the vast majority of those living in modern societies today. Ambulances typically have blacked out windows, concealing the potentially disturbing spectacle of injury or death from the onlooker:

> Closed like confessionals, they thread
> Loud noons of cities, giving back
> None of the glances they absorb.[7]

Sociologically most significant are prisons and asylums, 'total institutions' that sequester from the everyday world the criminal and

[7] Philip Larkin: *The Whitsun Weddings*. London: Faber and Faber, 1971, p. 33.

the mentally ill. These are substantially creations of the eighteenth century and after. Prior to this period, as Foucault and, following him, many more scrupulous but less innovative historians have shown, incarceration was relatively rare. Thus to take the influence of crime, far from being hidden away, punishment — including capital punishment — was a spectacle, an open display. The anonymous, impersonal discipline of the prison, where the main sanctions are no longer public humiliation or the marking of the body through the imposition of physical pain, but the loss of 'freely controlled time', is something very different. Where it remains, even capital punishment is really a 'maximal loss of time', in which far from publicly demonstrating the process of putting to death, there is a more or less private execution, where pain is minimized as far as possible.

Current Issues

So far, I have been analysing what sociologists do as if the discipline were an unchanging one, and as if there were complete agreement among its practitioners about its objectives and methods. Neither of these are the case, and in the next part of my discussion I want to indicate some of the changes going on in sociology today and where they look likely to lead us. Like the social sciences in general, sociology has undergone a considerable mutation in recent years — were the term not so over-used in the wake of Kuhn's writings in the philosophy of science, we could with some justification speak of the occurrence of a revolution in sociological thought. The changes involved are both substantive and methodological.

The late eighteenth and nineteenth centuries set the substantive agenda for, as well as the methodological content of, sociology in the current century. Sociology has its origins in the coming of modernity — in the dissolution of the traditional world and the consolidation of the modern. Exactly what 'traditional' and 'modern' should be taken to mean is a matter of chronic debate. But this much is plain. With the arrival of industrialism, the transfer of millions of people from rural communities to cities, the progressive development of mass democracy, and other quite fundamental institutional changes, the new world was savagely wrenched away from the old. What began as a series of transformations substantially internal to Europe and North America has increasingly traversed the globe. The lurching juggernaut of change which the West launched is still careering erratically over the surface of the earth. Sociology was born of the attempt to track its path, but until well into the twentieth century was itself rather too strongly stamped by the context of its own origins.

For one thing, in contrasting modernity with tradition, the dominant schools of thought in sociology have tended too forcefully to emphasize trends and mechanisms presumed to be inherent in the industrialized societies themselves. As a result, whether they have been swallowed up in history, or continue to exist in other parts of the world, traditional societies have too often been seen as essentially uninteresting. They have been regarded as no more than a foil to the development of a triumphant industrial order. There thus came about an unhappy disjuncture between sociology and anthropology; the fracturing clash between modern and traditional simultaneously became a disciplinary schism. But it has surely become apparent by now that anthropology can no longer confine itself to a preoccupation with otherness, any more than sociology can afford not to examine that destructive connection which binds the modern to other forms of society.

Modernity in the twentieth century demonstrably stands revealed as world-historical in the true sense of that term. At the same time as we have to recognize that the institutions created by the advent of modernity are not cut of whole cloth, we see more and more clearly that our lives today are dominated by influences no one living anywhere in the world can any longer entirely escape. Yet, together with the rest of the social sciences, sociology is only now starting to come to terms with an increasingly interdependent global system. Moreover, we seem to be living through an accelerated phase of social change. As the twenty-first century approaches, we are experiencing a period of social transformation as spectacular as anything that has occurred in earlier phases of the modern era. It seems certain that some of the leading sociological theories and concepts will have to be substantially overhauled if we are to seek to comprehend both this and the consolidation of something like a world society. Among the changes which might be singled out for mention are: exceptionally rapid technological innovation, coupled with the impact of the computer and of robotics; an apparent erosion of the established manufacturing base of Western economies, associated with a transfer of basic industrial production Eastwards; the deepening involvement of all the industrialised societies within an increasingly integrated global division of labour; widespread political disaffection within Western democracies, associated with realignments in patterns of voting and political support; and the looming threat of the proliferation of nuclear weapons, conjoined with the continuing application of science and technology to the intensification of weapons systems.

The list is a formidable one, and I certainly do not want to claim that sociology is the only discipline relevant to tackling it. But daunting though the intellectual and practical problems facing us in the late twentieth century may be, it is surely indisputable that they are above all organizational and institutional in character. That is to say, they are in a fundamental sense sociological. The sociological enterprise is now even more pivotal to the social sciences as a whole, and indeed to current intellectual culture generally, than it has ever been before. We live today, not to put too fine a point on it, in a world on a knife-edge between extraordinary possibility and global disaster. We cannot even say with confidence which of these alternatives is the more likely. This is the residue of modernity for us all, and it is distant indeed from the scenarios laid out by the more optimistic of the eighteenth- and nineteenth-century founders of sociology. For they expected modernity to culminate, one way or another, in a humane and rational social order. In the light of trends of development in the current century, we must see these anticipations as at best premature and rash.

Nonetheless we must sustain the practical intent that underlay their writings. We must defend the ambition of sociology in a practical fashion to influence for the better the human condition. This thought both allows me to fashion a conclusion and also to return to the themes with which I opened. For in some degree the unsettling character of sociology derives from the special position it has in respect of the practical governance of social change. Sociology occupies a tensed zone of transition between diagnosis and prognosis; and this is another area in which a spate of controversies over the past few years has allowed us eventually to clarify what the role of sociology can and should be.

These controversies cannot be comprehended without an analysis of methodological problems in sociology — concerning which, it would be fair to say, sociologists recently have been rather radically reappraising what they themselves do. The majority of the early founders of sociology, in the late eighteenth and the nineteenth centuries, sought to derive the logic and the method of their field of study from the natural sciences. This view certainly never went unchallenged, for such an idea is difficult to reconcile with those features of human agency that I have discussed. Consequently the discipline — and in some considerable degree the whole of the social sciences — tended to be divided between the notion that a natural science of society is possible and the opposing view that sociology is essentially a type of humanism. For advocates of the former standpoint, everything short of a precisely specified corpus of laws about social life is a disappointment. In the eyes of the anti-naturalists on the other hand, the claims of sociology to emulate natural science are spurious and misleading. This methodological division was for many years given conceptual form by the contrast, drawn from German traditions of historiography, between *Verstehen* and *Erklären* — understanding versus explanation. It was accepted by both sides that the natural sciences have to do with explanation. The differences of opinion concerned whether the realm of *Erklären* could also be extended to the explication of human social institutions.

We know today that the separating of *Verstehen* from *Erklären* was a misleading way to characterize both social and natural science. Summarizing complicated matters briefly, advances in the philosophy of the natural sciences have made it plain that understanding or interpretation are just as elemental to these sciences as they are to the humanities. On the other hand, while generalizations in the social sciences are logically discrepant from those of natural science, there is no reason to doubt that they involve causal attributions. We must therefore discard the conceptual clothing of the *Verstehen* versus *Erklären* debate. There is no harm done, and there are positive virtues, in continuing to use the phrase social 'sciences'. The social sciences share with natural science a respect for logical clarity in the formulation of theories and for disciplined empirical investigation. But social science is not a battered tramp steamer chugging along vainly in the wake of the sleek cruiser of the natural sciences. In large degree the two simply sail on different oceans, however much they might share certain common navigational procedures. There are thus profound differences between the social and natural sciences, but they do not concern the presence or absence of interpretation as such. Rather, they are bound up with what I have elsewhere, no doubt rather clumsily, called a 'double hermeneutic'.[8] As I have been at pains to emphasize earlier, the subjects of study in the social sciences and the humanities are concept-using beings, whose concepts of their actions enter in a constitutive manner into what those actions are. Social life cannot even be accurately described by a sociological

[8] Anthony Giddens: *The Constitution of Society*. Cambridge: Polity Press, 1984.

observer, let alone causally elucidated, if that observer does not master the array of concepts employed (discursively or non-discursively) by those involved.

All social science, to put the issue bluntly, is parasitic upon lay concepts, as a logical condition of its endeavours. Sociologists invent their own conceptual metalanguages, and have to do so for reasons described earlier — that they seek to grasp aspects of social institutions which are not described by agents' concepts. However, unlike in natural science, in the social sciences there is no way of keeping the conceptual apparatus of the observer — whether in sociology, political science or economics — free from appropriation by lay actors. The concepts and theories invented by social scientists, in other words, circulate in and out of the social world they are coined to analyse. The best and most original ideas in the social sciences, if they have any purchase on the reality it is their business to capture, tend to become appropriated and utilized by social actors themselves. John Barnes expressed this aptly when he wrote that sociology makes it possible for us 'to take a more informed and more far-seeing view of the social scene' than is available to those 'who have not been trained to take a detached view of their own social institutions and who lack the opportunity to compare these carefully with alternative arrangements found in other societies'. Remarking that sociology is 'concerned with the regularities and the lack of regularity in institutions', he added: 'There is a two-way or dialectical relation between the conceptual apparatus of the sociologist and the world view of the people whose actions, sentiments and beliefs he [or she] seeks to understand.'[9] This two-way relation, however, deserves careful consideration, for grasping its nature leads us to a major reappraisal of the practical influence of sociology upon modern societies.

It is often thought that the social sciences — not only sociology — have been unsuccessful as policy-making aids. Perhaps this is even one final reason why their critics have found them wanting. After all, consider the impact that natural science has had, via the implementation of technology, in shaping our interactions with the material world. The natural sciences have plainly increased our capabilities of controlling the material contexts of our activities. For surely one cannot make a parallel claim for social science? For there just are not

[9] J. A. Barnes: *Sociology in Cambridge.* Cambridge: Cambridge University Press, 1970, p. 19.

the social technologies that would allow us to control social life in the manner in which material technology permits us to harness the forces of nature.

However we can see the issue in an entirely different light if we follow through the implications of the double hermeneutic. Those who have discussed this problem, particularly philosophers of the social sciences, have tended to concentrate their attention upon the manner in which lay concepts obstinately intrude into the technical discourse of social science. Few have considered the matter the other way round. But the concepts of the social sciences are not produced about an independently constituted subject-matter, which continues regardless of what these concepts are. The 'findings' of the social sciences very often enter constitutively into the world they describe. Let me give examples from several of the social sciences to show how significant this point is.

When, in the early fifteenth century, Bodin, Machiavelli and others invented some novel ideas about political power and government, they did not simply describe an independently occurring series of social changes. They helped constitute the state forms that emerged from those changes. Modern states could not exist at all were not concepts such as 'citizen', 'sovereignty', and 'government' itself, mastered by the individuals who administer them and those subject to their rule. Political theory has ever after been reflexively tied to what it is about: the elucidation of the mechanics of government within modern states. Something very similar is true from the late eighteenth century onwards of both economics and sociology. The discourse of economics has not only made it possible for us to understand — within limits — the workings of modern economies, it has become basic to what those economies are. Shifts in the usage of terms like 'economic', or 'industrial' were in some part fostered by the writings of academic economists, helping to introduce into the newly-forming fields of economic activity the concepts that constitute what those fields have become. Economics has thereafter been reflexively implicated in processes of continuity and change in modern economic systems.

The same can be said of sociology in respect of a whole spectrum of modern social institutions. One of the best illustrations that can be given of this is the collation of social statistics. For statistical surveys might seem on the face of things to be furthest removed from incorporation into what they are about. Statistics on the distribution of population, patterns of birth and death rates, or marriage and the family, all might appear to be simply quantified analyses of objectively-given sets of phenomena. So, of course, in a sense they are. But as I emphasized at the beginning, the gathering of social statistics also enters in a fundamental way into the constitution of modern societies. Modern societies could not exist were their demographic characteristics not regularly charted and analysed. In the study of class divisions, bureaucracy, urbanism, religion, and many other areas, sociological concepts regularly enter our lives and help redefine them.

The inferences to be drawn from this are far from simple, but they are of very considerable importance. On the one hand we are able to see why even the most brilliantly innovative ideas in the social sciences risk becoming banal. Once they become constitutive of what we do, after all, they are part of the patterns of our daily activities and may become almost numbingly familiar. Every time I use a passport to travel abroad I demonstrate my practical grasp of the concept of sovereignty; far from being novel any longer, it has become an entirely routine part of modern life. Precisely because of its adoption within society itself, knowledge generated by the social sciences does not have a neatly cumulative form. By this I do not mean that we do not progressively learn more about social institutions than we knew before, or that there is not continual conceptual and theoretical innovation. But the achievements of the social sciences tend to become submerged from view by their very success. On the other hand, exactly because of this we can in all seriousness make the claim that the social sciences have influenced 'their' world — the universe of human social activity — much more strongly than the natural sciences have influenced 'theirs'. The social sciences have been reflexively involved in a most basic way with those very transformations of modernity which give them their main subject-matter.

There are no options in this regard. The practical impact of social sciences is both profound and inescapable. Modern societies, together with the organizations that compose and straddle them, are like learning machines, imbibing information in order to regularize their mastery of themselves. Because of the perversity of unintended consequences, and the very contingency of social change, we may presume that such mastery will always be less than complete. Yet upon our capabilities for social learning, in the world that is the legacy of modernity, we predicate our future. Only societies reflexively capable of modifying their institutions in the face of accelerated social change will be able to confront that future with any confidence. Sociology is the prime medium of such reflexivity. The degree, therefore, to which a society fosters an active and imaginative sociological culture will be a measure of its flexibility and openness.

2

Nine theses on the future of sociology

In some quarters sociology has lately had a bad press.[1] This might be thought unsurprising in a subject which has after all had to suffer probably more than its fair share of opprobrium. If it is at all well-practised, sociology is bound to be in some part an unsettling subject, ill-designed to pander to the prejudices which an unreflective citizenry might intuitively defend. However some of the scepticism about sociology comes from those involved in the discipline itself, who feel that it has not delivered upon promises held out by its leading figures of a generation ago. To them it appears all was set fair in sociology until some ten to fifteen years back, but since then the subject has lost its way. Whereas the prominent sociological thinkers at that time were in the vanguard of important developments in intellectual culture generally, it might seem that sociology has now retreated more to the periphery of the social sciences. Small beer indeed when compared with the claims of some of the early founders of the subject, anticipating that sociology would be the central and unifying discipline for all those engaged in the study of human beings and their creations.

Of course, these sentiments of mild or more intensive disillusionment to an extent reflect the relatively unpropitious material climate in which most of those working in sociology now exist. Just at the time when it might appear that innovative social research and sociological thought is most urgently needed — in a context of global recession, far-reaching social and cultural change, and a crisis in

---

[1] A version of this essay was given as a plenary lecture at the meetings of the Eastern Sociological Association in New York, April 1986.

welfare institutions in Western countries — in many universities the world over enrollments in sociology have declined, and funding for empirical work has been cut back. Although in this respect it is like most of the other social sciences, sociology is in a literal sense rapidly becoming a subject taught by the grey middle-aged, the embattled inheritors of a period of university expansion which now seems entirely remote. If this should be combined with an intellectual decline within sociology the outlook for the discipline looks bleak indeed.

Should those of us who like to call ourselves sociologists thus succumb to doom and gloom? I think not. For although the material travails of sociology in many countries are real, the intellectual decline is not. The view that such a fall from grace has occurred, I think, is a result of a misinterpretation of the development of the social sciences over the past few years. It is almost an inversion of what has actually happened. In the first place, what has occurred, and is continuing, is the incorporation of sociological thinking and a sociological outlook into disciplines that had previously kept their distance from them. These influences are by no means uncontentious in their consequences, but they can quite easily be traced in history, philosophy, political science, human geography, international relations, and other areas of study also. One must give special mention to social anthropology. Although it frequently remains split off from sociology in the departmental structure of universities, the intellectual merger long heralded between these two subjects has recently advanced at an accelerating rate. Of course, the intellectual traffic flowing between sociology and all these subjects has not been proceeding down a one-way street. Sociology has profited from these encounters as well as contributing to them.

To pick an example, chosen more or less at random, one could mention developments in the study of the family. Here the application of sociological ideas, and research methods borrowed both from sociology and social anthropology, have in some part created a substantially new sub-area within social history, and in some part revitalized pre-existing interpretations. We now know an enormous amount more about the family than we did. We have been led radically to reappraise our understanding of the nature of family institutions in the present as a result of our more systematic and adequate grasp of how things were in the past. The study of the family used to seem to many one of the dullest of endeavours. Now it appears as one of the most provocative and involving.

In the second place, sociology over recent years has been enlivened and enriched by being confronted by a range of social movements that have thrown down a gauntlet to its interpretative capabilities. Although some such social movements are long-standing, they have tended to gain a renewed importance in the current period. I have in mind particularly the women's movement, ecological and peace movements. These have of course taken varying forms in different areas and countries of the world and the challenge they pose is from one angle simply to understand how and why they developed as they have. But they have also helped to identify considerable weaknesses in established frameworks of sociological reasoning. The women's movement, for instance, has had a far-reaching — and surely mostly fruitful — impact upon both the substance and the concepts of sociology during the past two decades. If one wanted an illustration, one could again turn to the study of the family. The women's movement has helped to give a particular cogency to the analysis of family institutions, at the same time as it has made clear that the study of the family and the study of gender are very far from being one and the same thing.

In the third place, not independently of these processes, major advances have taken place in our understanding of sociological work itself. There has occurred a methodological transformation of sociology over that very same period which might seem to mark the declining fortunes of the discipline. For some years, the violence thus wreaked upon prior modes of thinking was easier to recognize than the fruitfulness of its outcome. During the period of pre-eminence of what I have elsewhere called the 'orthodox consensus' — naturalism combined with functionalism — there seemed at least to be some overall coherence to sociology. Its dissolution was accompanied by the emergence of numerous theoretical schools, each engaged in talking past the others. As I would see things, at any rate, that moment is now over. While for reasons I shall go on to mention it is not in the nature of sociology to generate anything like complete professional accord either about its theories or methods, some general lines of agreement are developing as to how human social life and social institutions should best be understood. It is undeniable that sociology emerges from these debates considerably more sophisticated than when they first began.

These processes have not occurred without costs to what some might see as the desirable drawing of clear-cut boundaries between sociology and its neighbouring disciplines in the social sciences. Many have liked to see the distinctiveness of sociology in a particular type of explanatory apparatus held to be lacking elsewhere. That is to say, what characterizes the sociological perspective is supposed to be the demonstration that much (most, all?) of our activity, although we might not suspect it, is determined by social influences, rather than being a matter of our own volition. The developments in social theory of which I have just spoken substantially dissolve this viewpoint. Some have discerned the specificity of sociology in its pre-eminent concern with a particular object — 'society'. How far this is meaningful is again dubious. For in spite of the ubiquity of its usage, the term 'society' has figured largely as an unexamined one in sociological discourse. 'Societies' in the modern world are nation-states, bounded by other nation-states in a global system.[2] However we might think it best to conceptualize nation-states, they are obviously territorial and political formations, not the particular province of one discipline, be it sociology, political science, or economics.

We should recognize that it is not possible, and even positively undesirable, to preserve an absolutely clear-cut and inviolable domain for sociology. This was only plausible when the alliance of naturalism and functionalism held sway. Then it could be held that sociology was on the one hand 'scientific', and thus plainly distinct from the humanities; and on the other that its object of study was 'society', as a cleanly delimited unity, providing a bounded subject-matter. As I see it, sociology involves a disciplinary concentration upon those institutions and modes of life brought into being by 'modernity' — that massive set of social changes emanating first of all from Europe (and which today have become global in scope) creating modern social institutions. Sociology has a range of concepts and theories which tend to be distinctive to it, but methodologically it is not as separable from the rest of the social sciences — and indeed the humanities — as many have been prone to claim.

The observations made so far cover the past and the present of sociology, and in this discussion I am committed to appraising its likely future. As the preceding remarks suggest, sociology has been undergoing some rather substantial changes and I expect some of these to continue. But the future is unlikely to be a pure extrapolation of trends in the present — as sociologists should know better than anyone. Guesses about the future are hazardous, and I shall not

[2] cf. Anthony Giddens: *The Nation-State and Violence.* Cambridge: Polity Press, 1985.

attempt any long-term predictions. I shall therefore be concerned only with what is likely to happen over the next decade or ·so. A further rider has to be added. In discussing a topic such as the title of this essay the urge is irresistible to suggest that what is likely to happen is what one wants to see happen. In most of what I shall have to say I am rather unashamedly portraying the directions I would like to see sociology taking. What I shall offer is an endeavour modestly to influence the future of sociology as much as a demographic projection about the overall make-up of the discipline in the years to come. I want to propose nine theses on the future of sociology — in some part these will develop remarks I have just made.

1 *Sociology will increasingly shed the residue of nineteenth- and early twentieth-century social thought*

Sociology is bound up with the 'project of modernity'. This has supplied, and will continue to supply, the core of its substantive preoccupations. But the most common ways in which we seek to understand the trajectories of development of modern societies have been strongly influenced — and limited — by the contexts of their origin in nineteenth- and early twentieth-century Europe. 'Classical social theory' has continued to hold sway well beyond the circumstances of its first formation. The key period in the intellectual development of sociology was the nineteenth century. The first emergence of the subject in recognizable form can be traced to an earlier period, and it has achieved its fullest prominence only in the twentieth century. Nonetheless throughout most of its history in the current century sociology has borne the stamp of the contexts in which its outlines first took shape.

This has many ramifications, and I shall only trace out certain of them. One pervasive legacy of nineteenth-century thinking over the subsequent development of sociology has been the idea that the basic dynamic forces at work in the modern world are economic — that they are to do with infrastructural changes which have dragged along changes in other institutions in their wake. The most long-standing debate in sociology concerns how far the modern world is a result of the expansion of *capitalism*, or how far alternatively it is the outcome of the spread of *industrialism*. One group of theories, including particularly Marxist or neo-Marxist theories, essentially equate modernity with capitalism. Capitalist institutions are believed to provide the dynamic of modern history, based upon the tendency of capitalist enterprise to be constantly in restless expansion world-wide. For the proponents of such theories, industrialism is simply an extension of capitalism. Capitalism precedes the origins of industrialism in time, and industrialism is regarded as the outcome of pressures to the maximization of production generated by capitalistic mechanisms. On the other hand, those who see industrialism as the leading force moulding modern institutions reverse this position. For them we live in industrial (or perhaps now 'post-industrial') societies; capitalism is merely a particular way of organizing industrialism, and one that was only of relatively short duration.

The participants in this debate are in considerable degree all prisoners of a shared style of reasoning, marked by the strong impress of nineteenth-century social thought. The debate is probably largely a misconceived one even in its own terms. Rather than seeking reductively to explain industrialism in terms of capitalism, or the other way around, we should recognize that these are partly independent and increasingly separate influences on modern social development. But more importantly we should reject the economic reductionism which, however sophisticated it may be, each of these approaches involve. Modernity is very much more complex than either of these viewpoints tend to assume, and the future development of sociology will surely recognize this to be the case. To the impact of capitalism and industrialism we must add the influence of at least three other major parameters of modernity.[3] One, brilliantly analysed by Foucault, is the development of administrative power.[4] What sociologists call 'societies' are, as I have mentioned, also states. The intensifying of the administrative power of the state, involving especially the harnessing of informational resources, is one of the most characteristic features of the modern epoch. Modern states, and the modern world system as a whole, involve a tremendous acceleration in the production and organization of information. Although it is commonly supposed that we are only now in the late twentieth century entering the era of information, modern societies have been 'information societies' since their beginnings.

A further dimension of modernity, largely unrecognized in most traditions of sociological thought — for reasons that again have their origin in the nineteenth century — concerns military power and war.

[3] Ibid., chpt. 5.
[4] cf. particularly *Discipline and Punish*. London: Allen Lane, 1977.

It is surely obvious that modern states have been shaped substantially by their association with military power and by the wars in which they have been involved. But such matters have not usually formed part of the main body of sociological thinking and research (nor have they in the rest of the social sciences, with the exception of international relations). Twentieth-century sociology has here again sustained a pervasive theme of the earlier development of social thought. For the nineteenth-century social thinkers, capitalism or industrialism were to replace the military societies of previous epochs. Military power was presumed above all to be associated with traditional societies, not with modern ones. The economic transformations that shape modernity are essentially pacific in character. That is to say, it was supposed that economic exchange transactions, leading to economic interdependence, would replace the militaristic societies of the past. Yet in some basic respects this has proved to be quite out of kilter with the modern world, in which the continuing significance of military power and of armed violence is there for all — save apparently social scientists — to see. We can summarize this in a single but effective way as follows. The dissolution of the traditional world under the impact of modernity is not the result of capitalism, or of industrialism, or even of the concentration of administrative resources in modern states. It is the result of all of these in co-ordination with modern means of using military strength and making war.

Finally, there is the cultural dimension of modernity — something obviously highly complex in its own right. In some guises, the analysis of this dimension has long been a preoccupation of sociology. Sociologists have understood the emergence of their own discipline against the background of the rise of 'rationalism' and the 'disenchantment of the world' attendant upon secularization. But once more it would probably be true to say that the culture of modernity has been understood largely as the reflex of capitalism or industrialism. Even Max Weber's famous attempts to claim an independent role for 'ideas' concentrated upon the conditions that initially gave rise to capitalism, rather than proposing a continuing role for a partially autonomous modern culture.[5] Current controversies about what many have labelled 'post-modernity' should perhaps rather be seen as the first real initiatives in the ambitious task of charting the

---

[5] Max Weber: *The Protestant Ethic and the Spirit of Capitalism*. London: Allen & Unwin, 1976.

cultural universe resulting from the ever-more complete disintegration of the traditional world. At a minimum they surely express the strong sense that pre-established models of cultural analysis were radically defective.

Wrestling free from the frameworks of nineteenth-century social thought means abandoning the idea that a continuing critical encounter with Marxist thought somehow supplies the central focus of sociological concerns. Insofar as that has been the case, it was produced by the very limitations in the understanding of modernity just noted. Marxism has a vitality that has enabled it — in its multifarious versions — long to survive the repeated announcements of its demise. But the future of sociology will not be bound up with a preponderant concern with the organizing concepts of Marxist thought. Or if such should prove to be the case, the range of analyses of modernity made available by the sociological imagination will be much more feeble than they should be.

2 *A theoretical synthesis will emerge giving a renewed coherence to sociological debates*

The idea of achieving a unified theoretical language for sociology is an old one, more or less convergent with the first springs of development of the discipline. It tends to follow rather directly from the premises of naturalism, since the various natural sciences are normally held to have achieved distinct conceptual unity within themselves. If Comte's hierarchy of the sciences, with sociology at the apex, is its most characteristic expression in the nineteenth century, in the twentieth its most influential advocate — certainly in the English-speaking world — has been Talcott Parsons. Notwithstanding his sensitivity to 'voluntarism' in human action, Parsons's system represents easily the most advanced formulation of that marriage of naturalism and functionalism of which I have spoken. What he explicitly sought to achieve was the construction of a unified conceptual language not only for sociology but for the whole of the social sciences. The model of classical mechanics — which also inspired Comte — was early on taken by Parsons as a guideline for the proper aspirations of sociology.

The disintegration of the 'orthodox consensus' — in its Parsonian form and in its other less sophisticated guises — opened the way for the squabbling diversity of schools of social theory to which I have previously alluded. On the whole it would probably be true to say that the majority of these schools of thought have tended to emphasize subjective aspects of human behaviour. They have reacted against what was seen as an exaggeration of the hold social institutions have over the conduct of the individual agent. Such a reaction was by no means universal — structuralist accounts of the 'decentring of the subject', even in the extreme form postulated by Althusser, have found their adherents. But for the most part a common thread in the variety of competing versions of social theory was a reaction against what was widely regarded as an illegitimate sociological determinism.

There have always been many who regard the achievement of a unified theoretical framework for sociology as the *sine qua non* of the reputability of the subject. There have been others — sometimes enthusiastic converts from the first view — who have welcomed the new abundance of theoretical standpoints. Whether or not directly influenced by the ideas of Feyerabend in the philosophy of natural science, they have tended to argue that pluralism in theory is desirable; if ever a unified theoretical perspective were generally accepted in sociology it would signal for them an authoritarian exclusion of competing points of view, since social reality is multifaceted.[6] A common perspective on social reality, it has been said, would only be possible in a totalitarian order. A society in which a variety of outlooks and styles of life are allowed to flourish is one in which sociology — and no doubt the other social sciences also — would be variegated in nature.

This is a position that must be taken seriously. The notion that there is a straightforward road to 'theory-building' in sociology, which will take us towards the theoretical consensus found (so it is believed) within the natural sciences, is surely misconceived. It is another view which falls casualty to the dissolution of naturalistic conceptions of sociology. Sociology does not, and cannot, consist of a body of theory and research built up and kept insulated from its 'subject-matter' — the social conduct of human agents. There is only a 'single hermeneutic' in natural science. Scientists construct theories about a 'given' world, however much the technological applications of their theories allow us to change and control that world. The social sciences operate within a double hermeneutic, involving two-way ties with the actions and institutions of those they study. Sociological observers depend upon lay concepts to generate accurate descriptions of social processes; and agents regularly appropriate theories and concepts of social science

[6] Paul Feyerabend: *Against Method*. London: New Left Books, 1975.

within their behaviour, thus potentially changing its character. This introduces an instability into sociological theorizing which inevitably takes it some distance from the 'cumulative and uncontested' model that naturalistically-inclined sociologists have in mind. There is more, however. The social world is an internally contested one, in which dissensus between actors and groups of actors — in relation to divergent world-views or clashes of interest — is pervasive. The ties which connect the social sciences constitutively to the social world inevitably mean that these divisions tend to shape strongly the theoretical perspectives sociological observers assume (this is *not* merely a matter of deficiencies in their 'objectivity'). If all this is seen in conjunction with the traditional difficulties of replication and control of variables in the empirical testing of theories, we surely must be sceptical of the ambition to achieve a professionally agreed-upon schema of theories and concepts in sociology.

But it does not follow that the only alternative is a deliberately cultivated diversity of theoretical standpoints. Different theoretical frameworks can be assessed in terms of their fruitfulness and accuracy; and theories can always be in some degree evaluated in terms of observations generated by empirical research. The proliferation of theoretical traditions noted earlier was a response to the decline of the 'orthodox consensus', but is unlikely to be in such an extreme form a persistent feature of sociology in the years to come. As I have mentioned, we are moving out of that phase of development. The time when it seemed that the advocates of the competing theoretical schools simply inhabited different universes, hermetically sealed off from one another, is now surely past. The new synthesis which is likely to emerge will differ from the old not only in its content, but in respect of its recognition that key aspects of the interpretation of social life are likely to remain contested. However a certain degree of 'closure' of the diversity of standpoints will no doubt generally be accepted as desirable and possible. It is already fairly clear what such a synthesis will look like. In discarding naturalism, it will accept that sociology is not a purely 'interpretative' endeavour, but involves the formulation of accounts of social life which differ from those offered by social agents themselves. Generalizations suggested by social research have to be validated by reference to detailed empirical observation, but such generalizations are in principle capable of being modified by their incorporation within the tissue of social life itself. The new synthesis will reject all forms of explanation which suggest that human behaviour is in a direct sense the result of social causes (*one* sense which determinism can assume in the social sciences). At the same time, it will acknowledge the significance of institutional constraints and parameters forming both the condition and outcome of individual action. All this will alter the self-perception of sociology, because in this emergent standpoint emphasis is placed upon a relation between social science and the subjects of its study. The concepts, theories and findings generated by sociology 'spiral in and out' of social life, they do not form an ever-growing corpus of knowledge.

3 *The dominant object of analysis of sociology will be substantially rethought*

Sociologists have traditionally thought of their subject as concerned with the study of 'society'. Now 'society' is an ambiguous term. It can mean 'social association' or 'social interaction' in general, or it can mean a clearly delimited overall social system. Although sociologists have sometimes deliberately exploited the ambiguity, probably for the most part when they have held themselves to be concerned with 'society' they have had in mind the second sense of the word. This applies across the various different genres of sociological thinking, although sometimes what has been suggested is a conception of a functionally integrated system, and at other times a more internally divided 'social formation'.

Treating 'society' as the prime object of analysis with which sociology is concerned has several implications. First, it has encouraged a preoccupation with endogenous models of social change. By this I mean accounts of change supposing that the primary impelling influences towards social transformation derive from 'inside' societies. Societies contain a 'logic', as it were, which drives them along certain paths in virtue of the structural potentialities they embody. But the limitations of such a view are severe. All types of social system, from small oral cultures and agrarian states to modern social orders, have existed in the context of inter-social systems that have influenced their nature and their trajectories of development in very basic ways. Second, the idea that the prime objects of study of sociology are clearly distinguishable 'societies' is not consistent with the character of pre-modern oral cultures and agrarian states — those 'societies', in other words, in which human beings have lived for by far the greater period of their history. Agrarian states were normally heavily segmental, internally heterogeneous, and had diffusely shaded 'frontiers', rather than 'borders' in the modern sense. In the case of most oral cultures — in spite of traditions in anthropology that have identified 'society' with the bounded local community — it is usually very difficult to say with any precision where one cultural unit ends and another begins.

When sociologists speak of 'societies', they are characteristically referring — as I have said — to modern nation-states. Nation-states do have clearly delimited borders, to which the administrative purview of the state apparatus corresponds. They do in greater or lesser degree appear as integrated overall systems, often having a fairly homogeneous general cultural identity separating them from surrounding states. But in spite of the fact that 'society' in this sense is usually taken to be the dominant focus of investigation of sociology, the nation-state remains essentially untheorized in sociological discourse. Nation-states, as the term suggests, are largely constituted politically, and they are territorial formations, gaining their identity not only by what goes on within them but by their involvement in a nation-state system. Partly because of the disciplinary divisions which suggest that political science monopolizes concern with mechanisms of government, while international relations specializes in the study of the 'outside' context of states, sociologists have failed to come to terms conceptually with fundamental factors which make the societies they analyse 'societies' at all.

Finally, although nation-states mostly are far more internally unified in some respects than prior types of social order, they are still more regionalized than many have tended to assume. Ethnic diversity has long been a prominent concern of sociology, but sociologists have tended until recently largely to ignore the strong regional differentiation most nation-states display, in terms of, for example, the distribution of industry, class structure and other patterns of social organization. The 'systemness' of modern societies is often more defined by the administrative unification of the state administration than by the infrastructure of the social order. Moreover, the forms of regionalization and networks of culture and social relations that diversify societies internally also stretch across the borders of states. This is recognized by writers in international relations when they talk of the role of 'non-state actors' and 'inter-governmental organizations' in the settings of modern social life, but is as yet underplayed in most forms of sociological analysis.

All this alters how we should think of 'societies' in sociology. Sociologists will surely have to become more sensitive to geo-political influences affecting modes of social organization or social change in which they are interested. We will have to bring the theoretical analysis of the nation-state, and the nation-state system, more into the centre of the discipline than they have been before. And we shall have to pay more attention than hitherto to the internal regionalization of even the most coherent of modern states, as well as to the interlacing of such regionalization with ties and modes of organization that cross-cut national perimeters.

4 *Sociology will become much more concerned than hitherto with the study of the world system*

The embeddedness of societies and cultures within inter-societal systems has always been of more pronounced significance than sociologists have tended to recognize. It has been left to historians like Toynbee or Braudel to emphasize the importance of larger geographical connections — although they have often simply substituted more encompassing 'societies' (civilizations) for the smaller units upon which others have concentrated.[7] The increasingly interconnectedness of the modern world is not like that involved in traditional civilizations, since these held sway only over certain areas of the globe. Today, many of the connections that span states are truly global in character. To say this is commonplace, yet because of the concentration upon endogenous models, and because of the disciplinary severance of sociology from international relations, it continues largely to pass sociology by.

Certain traditions in sociology, most notably Marxism, have long emphasized the expansionist character of Western modes of economic production and culture. They have also stressed that characteristics of the 'less developed' sectors of the world are brought about in some part by the spreading dominance of Western capitalism. In this respect Marxist thought has not placed so much emphasis upon societies (social formations) as the prime focus of sociology as have other schools of sociological thought. There is indeed a fairly recent type of work explicitly represented as a Marxist standpoint — although strongly influenced by Braudel — which takes the world system as its

---

[7] Arnold Toynbee: *The Present-Day Experiment in Western Civilisation.* Oxford: Oxford University Press, 1962; Fernand Braudel: *The Mediterranean and the Mediterranean World in the Age of Philip II.* London: Fontana, 1973 (2 vols).

pre-eminent concern: the writings of Wallerstein and his followers.[8]

Wallerstein's work is important exactly because he breaks away strongly from the endogenous concentration upon 'societies' that has pervaded so much of sociology. But 'world system studies' have unfortunately become much too closely identified with his work. One less than happy result of this is that the old division between international relations and the concerns of the rest of the social sciences has thereby reappeared. But in addition the manner in which Wallerstein has formulated the concept of the world system, and pursued its study empirically, is unsatisfactory. In reacting against endogenous conceptions of change he moves too far in the opposite direction. The world system, even from its relatively early origins, is presented as though it were as coherent and all-enveloping as most sociologists' pictures of individual societies tend to be. Developments within particular states, or even in the heartland of Western capitalism more generally, tend invariably to be attributed to the workings of the world system. Moreover, his work firmly continues the 'reductive' interpretation of modernity that should come to be seen as wanting. Everything is treated as bound up with the expansion of capitalistic relations world-wide, and the categorization of the world system that is offered, into core, semi-periphery and periphery, is almost wholly one of economic power. Just as in more conventional schools of sociology, but for contrasting reasons, no adequate explanation is given as to why distinctive 'societies' exist at all, as discrete nation-states.

One major problem that must attract the attention of sociology in the future is that of assessing in just what the 'systemness' of the world system consists. Not only in Wallerstein's writings but in sociology more generally the concept of social system has frequently been used to suggest a set of mutually interdependent parts — each part connected in some way with every other within the whole. But it is often more accurate to portray social systems as like networks, in which 'systemness' does not imply complete mutual connectedness. This makes it possible to identify several interlacing yet partly independent sets of relations within what nevertheless remains distinctively a 'system'. I have no doubt in my own mind that it makes sense to speak of the existence of a world system today, and one that

---

[8] Immanuel Wallerstein: *The Capitalist World Economy*. Cambridge: Cambridge University Press, 1979.

has quite long-standing historical roots. However the components of its 'systemness' include all those dimensions that I indicated as centrally involved with modernity.

The dimensions of the world system that will need careful investigation, and conceptual interpretation, are at a minimum the following. First, the burgeoning complexity of the international division of labour, draining autonomy away from many national economies, and influencing in particular the shifting regionalism of manufacturing production on a global level. This is fuelled by the expansion of capitalistic markets, and by the activities of the transnational corporations. But it is also something strongly influenced by the hegemonic position in the global economy which the United States has been able to sustain in the post-Second World War period, guided by political convictions that freedom of international trade is by and large beneficial to those who participate in it.[9] This is one — although obviously only one among many — point of connection between the international division of labour and the global distribution of power in the nation-state system, the second fundamental axis of the world system. A third is the global military order, a network of alliances and security communities. Although military power necessarily stands in close connection to levels of economic development, there is by no means a complete correspondence between the two.

In claiming that sociologists will have to become more and more concerned with the world system, I do not want to suggest that sociology appropriates the whole of the field of study of international relations. There must be academic areas of concentration of effort, which hence tend to define the major preoccupations of the related disciplines comprising the social sciences as a whole. It is entirely appropriate for sociologists to be concerned predominantly with tracing some of the key ways in which the involvement of particular societies, or types of society, in the world system influences their trajectories of development. But it will become increasingly difficult to ignore these influences, both in social theorizing and in empirical work, and those who do so will risk either substantially weakening, or altogether undermining, the validity of their ideas.

[9] Robert Keohane: *After Hegemony*. Princeton: Princeton University Press, 1984.

5 *Pre-existing disciplinary divisions within the social sciences
will become progressively less sharply-defined than at present*

To repeat, there obviously must be areas of concentration and
specialism within the social sciences, which taken collectively cover
vast ranges of subject-matter. But the recent shifts in boundaries
between sociology and the other social sciences show some quite
significant changes in intellectual structure and substantive concerns.
The distinctions that currently exist between the social sciences, as
they have come to be institutionalized in the curricula of universities,
derive once more primarily from the nineteenth century. Sociology
developed in large part through a critique of political economy,
including both its 'political' and its 'economic' dimensions. So far as
the former of these is concerned, the discipline achieved its self-
identity via the demonstration that forms of government or state
rested upon — and, in some versions, were virtually epiphenomena of
— an institutional infrastructure of civil society. In relation to
economics, sociology was shaped through showing that economic
action and market relations presume a broad institutional and
normative framework. Although this was always questioned within
Marxism, with its more encyclopaedic vision, what emerged was an
object of study defined as a cluster of institutions forming a system of
civil society. 'Society', defined as the disciplinary centre of sociology,
has largely been understood in terms of 'civil society' since that time.

The relations between sociology and history, and sociology and
anthropology have been complicated and shifting. Probably the
predominant view as regards sociology and history (shared by many
within both disciplines) has been that sociology deals with the general,
history with the particular; and that the former concentrates upon the
present-day, the latter on the past. These perceived divisions have
sometimes taken a very sharp form, particularly when naturalistic
versions of sociology have been counterposed to detailed narrative
history. The period of the ascendancy of the 'orthodox consensus',
with some qualifications, can be said to be that at which the general
separation of sociology from history was most severe. In some contexts
— for example, in France, where the historians of the *longue durée*
preserved and developed a tradition of sociological history — contacts
between the disciplines were intimate. But very frequently, where
sociologists concerned themselves with the past in any depth, they did
so under the aegis of evolutionism. The identification of evolutionary
stages of development is not at all necessarily conducive either to the

detailed study of history, or to an appreciation of historical contingency. Where sociologists broke with evolutionism, they normally did so in the guise of pursuing the goal of developing sociology as a generalizing science. In neither case was any close attention to the work of historians encouraged.

Sociology and anthropology similarly have enjoyed closer contact of a continuing sort in some countries and traditions than in others. Again one might take the case of France as demonstrating fruitful and long-standing connections between the two disciplines from the time of Durkheim onwards — although in spite of the prominence of Lévi-Strauss and some others, anthropology has not been as intensively developed a subject there as in the English-speaking world. No great subtlety is needed to see that the origins of modern anthropology, and its separation from sociology, are bound up with colonialism, in Britain in respect of its imperial domains externally, and in the United States the internal conquest and displacement of the indigenous peoples. Neither sociology nor anthropology, of course, has been squarely ethnocentric, although the fact of their separation certainly creates an impetus in this direction — one subject being concerned with 'us' (or the whites) and the other with 'them' (or the non-whites). Anthropologists have charted a disappearing cultural universe at the same time as they have shown how important is the preservation of an understanding of the diversity of authentic styles of human existence.

Once established, disciplinary divisions stabilize different frameworks of training, which tend to have such an influence over educational socialization that those whose thought is framed in terms of them often find it extraordinarily difficult to communicate with one another. No one should therefore underestimate the difficulty of transcending disciplinary divisions or altering the present disciplinary organization of the social sciences. Yet it surely is evident that, given some of the social and intellectual developments mentioned earlier, shifts will occur — in large part furthering already existing trends — in the relationship between the various social sciences.

If there ever was an intellectual case for separating sociology from anthropology, it has surely today disappeared. The division of departments within the teaching structure of universities may persist for a good while yet and where they are attempted, mergers might not always be happy. But unless anthropology is going to be a sort of special cultural history, its concerns must necessarily become the same as those of sociology. Who is to say which is the best name for the outcome of this inevitable disciplinary unification? Since 'sociology' has, as it were, pre-empted the study of the 'advanced' sectors of the world, it might seem to have the overriding claim. Yet the term was always a bastard one, and 'anthropology' has the purer etymological lineage as the study of human social institutions. What would be difficult to dispute is that each discipline can only gain from an assimilation of the traditions of thought and methods of the other. Even if it were true, following Lévi-Strauss, that the concepts and modes of study appropriate to small oral cultures have to be distinct from those applied to larger, class-divided civilizations — and especially modern societies — the contrasts involved will be all the more illuminating for being directly analysed and detailed.[10]

There will no doubt not be such an overall merging between sociology and history. Given that the present is forever shading into the past, we cannot merely say that the sociologist is concerned with the former, the historian with the latter. Nor can sociology operate 'out of time', while the historian specializes in handling the temporal. But the 'recovery of the past' that is the preoccupation of the historian involves tasks of retrieval which sociologists do not normally have to master. The sociologist is mainly concerned with the pastness that lingers in the present and has entered formatively into its character. There is thus an intellectual division of labour here, but it cannot in any way be made precise, and it does not imply any logical or even major methodological differences between sociology and history. Historians are right to object to the 'sociologizing' of history where this means the naive importation into historical study of the former 'orthodox consensus'.[11] But such objections cannot justifiably form the basis for insisting upon a clearly distinct disciplinary identity for history, in which cause they have sometimes been invoked. The introduction of sociological notions into history cannot be assessed in terms of the debate between 'institutional' and 'narrative' versions of historical method. The issues involved in this debate are of as much relevance to sociology as to history, and have been explored precisely in the discussions that have ensued in the former discipline in the wake of the demise of naturalism and functionalism.

Sociology will not absorb political science and economics into some

---

[10] Claude Lévi-Strauss: *Structural Anthropology*. London: Allen Lane, 1968.

[11] Cf. G. R. Elton: *The Practice of History*. London: Fontana, 1967.

sort of all-enveloping social science. But the division which separated sociology, as the study of the (non-economic) infrastructure, from the analysis of the mechanisms of government, now appears almost wholly untenable. In the first place, if they are the prime objects of concern of sociology — something that I have sought to question — 'societies', as nation-states, are in large part politically ordered. They are delimited by the geo-political distribution of territory, and their internal cohesion is in greater or lesser degree brought about by, or dependent upon, political power. Second, it has long since been obvious to everyone, except for a substantial proportion of the sociological profession over whom nineteenth-century traditions still have a strong hold, that government and the state are at least as influential upon other institutions as vice versa. The long conceptual detour that had to be taken within modern Marxism to discover that the state has even a 'relative autonomy' from its supposed 'economic base' demonstrates what a struggle it is to break free from the dead weight of ideas inherited from previous generations!

Political science has its own internal tensions and problems. It continues to be divided between those who see the subject as concerned with the empirical study and theoretical interpretation of comparative systems of government, on the one hand, and those on the other who would see its main centre of conceptual gravity in normative political philosophy. In so far as the advances in social theory discussed earlier involve overturning the ambitions of 'behavioural political science' as a model for the first of these views, they serve to diminish the distance between these two conceptions. Distinctions between 'political science' and 'political sociology' become difficult to make. If they are not likely to become one and the same thing, it is just because government and politics are so distinctively important and influential in social life as a whole that they warrant a concentration of attention not demanded elsewhere. It will not do for sociologists to take an imperialistic attitude towards political science in a period of shifting disciplinary divisions. For given that political power is so manifestly of key significance in the shaping of modern social institutions, such an imperialistic stance could just as well be reversed.

The most complex problems concerning disciplinary differentiations in the social sciences probably are those to do with the relation between sociology and economics. Modern economics has become the most insulated of the social sciences, at least in the shape of its dominant neo-classical standpoint. The pervasive use of mathematical modelling also tends to distinguish the discipline rather clearly from most other areas of the social sciences, into which either mathematics has not penetrated or where claims for its usefulness are rather more obviously gratuitous than they are in economics. Claims of neo-classical economists for the distinctiveness of their discipline should not be seen as resting mainly upon the institutional separation — in capitalist economies — of markets from other segments of social activity. Rather they rest upon the more embracing theoretical position that the allocation of goods and resources is most effectively analysed at the margins of the preferences of producers and consumers. The analysis of marginal preferences or decisions can largely 'bracket' their origins and their extra-economic consequences.

Although attempts have been made to extend this viewpoint into broad sectors of social science, for the most part its pre-eminence within economics has tended to give the subject a more marked conceptual distinctiveness than any of the other social sciences. How far economics will continue to occupy its position of rather splendid isolation will presumably depend in substantial part upon the degree to which the neo-classical view remains dominant. Economic theory is at the moment in a disarray not far removed from that found in social theory a few years ago. Whether this will lead to a toppling of economics' own 'orthodox consensus' is difficult to say, but if so it is surely likely that the discipline will move back in a more 'institutional' direction. Without such an internally-propelled change of orientation any *rapprochement* between sociology and economics, outside Marxist economics, which has always remained exceptional in this respect, will be more muted than elsewhere in the social sciences. But that various sorts of renewed contacts between the two disciplines will be explored in the immediate future certainly seems more than likely.

6 *Sociologists will redevelop a concern with large-scale, long-term processes of social transformation*

One reaction to the embattled circumstances in which sociology has found itself over recent years has been a turn to an emphasis upon detailed empirical research. This may be seen also as a reaction to what has seemed to many to be the irremediable discordance between vying theoretical positions. If the proponents of different theoretical standpoints seemingly can reach little agreement over even the most basic concepts of social analysis, why not ignore theoretical debates and get on with the concrete study of the social world? There has consistently been a strong strain within sociology of what C. Wright

Mills disparagingly called 'mindless empiricism'; but rather than succumbing to his critique, in the United States in particular it has if anything grown stronger in the current period.[12]

Probably considerably more important, however, is the call to 'theory-building' promoted by Merton's celebrated declaration in favour of developing generalizations of the 'middle range' in sociology.[13] Merton's manifesto was originally part of a general reaction to what was seen as the over-ambitious endeavours of the classical founders of sociology to produce general theories of social transformation. Merton was just as critical as Mills of attempts to consolidate social research without the intrusion of theoretical thinking. But a sober approach is called for if empirical work is really to be integrated closely with, and properly informed by, such thinking. The speculative ideas of those interested in more embracing theories are too closely involved with philosophies of history, which are by definition refractory to empirical testing, and can at most be plundered for ideas that can be scaled down to something respectably modest.

Now no doubt there is something entirely salutary and sensible in all this. Merton's own writings were justifiably an inspiration to a whole generation of sociologists. Yet I want unashamedly to reclaim for sociology the grand questions. Here perhaps more than anywhere else I am imposing what I should like to see happen upon a prognosis of the future. Admirable though Merton's strictures may on the whole have been, it was a mistake to suppose that the study of the large-scale and the long-term has much to do with a philosophy of history — where that phrase is taken to mean a proclivity for arm-chair doctrines comfortably detached from the details of empirical research. It was also an error to presume that theories of a 'middle range' sort are more eminently open to test, in such a way as to build up a body of theoretically sophisticated work accepted by the sociological profession, than more encompassing theoretical ventures. In the wake of recent controversies in the philosophy of science, we know that 'testability' is much more complex than used to be assumed. The notion that the testable can be identified with what is limited in scope carries a definite residue of empiricism (understood in more of a technical philosophical sense than is involved in Mills's attribution of the term).

---

[12] C. Wright Mills: *The Sociological Imagination*. Harmondsworth: Pelican, 1970.

[13] R. K. Merton: *Social Theory & Social Structure*. Glencoe: Free Press, 1963, Introduction.

Let us by all means rid ourselves of our arm-chairs, or at least regularly issue forth from them into the realities of the outside world. But having previously endorsed a movement to break free from the traditions of nineteenth-century social thought, I want on this point to defend them — or, more accurately, some of the ends to which they aspired. We live in a world in which the pace of social change, if anything, has accelerated since the turn of the present century. It is a world increasingly defined by its overall 'systemness'. How can we hope to come to terms with the nature and implications of these phenomena if we try to refrain from any portrayals of social institutions save miniatures painted with a fine-grained brush?

For logical reasons, I have considerable reservations both about the notion of 'theory building' and the idea that the prime concern of theory in sociology is the construction of generalizations about the social world, whether of the 'middle range' or of any other variety. 'Theory-building' carries with it an imagery of the careful construction of layers of generalizations, firmly cemented together by accumulated empirical observations. How far such a view is appropriate even in the natural sciences might justifiably be doubted. It is naive to suppose that it has much relevance to social science. This is in some part because of the traditional problems of control of variable influences, replication of observations and so on, but mainly because of the reflexive relation in which the social sciences stand to the human activities they analyse. Save for those that are firmly limited in their application to the past, generalizations made by sociological observers — if they are at all interesting or novel — are likely to become known to lay actors, thus probably altering the conditions initially involved. Moreover, large tracts of the predictability of social life do not demand that the observer introduce any new knowledge to explain them. Such predictability is brought about by generalizations (normally in the form of taken-for-granted conventions) that agents apply in the course of their conduct. Conceptual innovation (coupled to empirical research) is at least as important in social science as is the formulating of novel generalizations. For such innovation opens up 'ways of seeing' that do not exist within the perspectives of lay actors, disclosing unsuspected aspects of, and potentialities within, a given set of institutions.

If we do not ask, and seek to answer as well as we can, questions like — how should we best characterize modernity? What were its origins? What are the major transformations currently influencing the trajectories of development of world history? — most of the intellectual challenge of sociology is lost. This is not in any way to question the need to continue detailed and rigorous research into a host of less awesome problems. But such research will not automatically become aggregated in such a way as to become of relevance to larger issues. If the idea of 'theory-building' is defective, we cannot expect that we shall be able to clamber up a growing pyramid of middle range generalizations eventually confidently to approach more ambitious endeavours.

These things having been said, I do think we can expect a re-evaluation of the relation between the study of the small-scale, on the one hand, and the large-scale on the other. Merton's 'generalizations of the middle range' did not have much to do with the distinction ordinarily drawn between micro- and macro-sociological studies. The opposition usually thought to exist between these poses not entirely dissimilar issues. Those who have concerned themselves with the study of the immediate contexts of interaction have often been sceptical of how 'real' are more inclusive forms of social organization or types of social change. *Per contra*, those preoccupied with larger institutional orders have tended to dismiss as trivial the work of the 'micro-sociologists'. However, in the wake in particular of the impact of phenomenology and ethnomethodology, we now understand more clearly the shortcomings in each of these rival positions. Far from being uninteresting and inconsequential trivia of day-to-day life, some of the features of mundane social activity are deeply implicated in the long-term (and large-scale) reproduction of institutions. At the same time, 'macro-structural' properties of social systems are embedded in the most casual or ephemeral local interactions. There are some complicated theoretical and empirical problems to be worked upon here. But it can be said with some confidence that their resolution is involved with analysing the recursive nature of social life.[14]

7 *There will be a deepening involvement of sociology with the formation of practical social policies or reforms*

How can one make such an assertion at a time at which sociology seems largely to have failed as a source of guidance for policy-making? There is (what I imagine to be) a short-lived series of considerations and a more intricate set of issues involved here. What is likely to have

[14] *The Constitution of Society*. Polity Press, 1984, chpt. 5 and *passim*.

only a limited life is the current vogue for a particular sort of economics — based on a view of the omniscience of markets — in some Western government circles. Insofar as markets are believed to provide both the most economically rational and morally optimal distribution of resources, the role of social research and of sociological thinking is substantially diminished in respect of social policy. If this means practical and deliberate intervention in a given state of affairs so as to produce desired forms of change, 'social policy' becomes irrelevant to those large swathes of social life left open to the play of market forces.

I do not believe that markets are thus omniscient, and I find it hard to suppose that government policies based upon this viewpoint will prove at all durable. The blunt and sometimes quite abrasive prejudices which those policies fostered surely will largely evaporate with their demise. This does not mean there will simply be a return to pre-existing views of the relation between sociology and social policy. For this relation needs to be rethought in the light of previously described changes in our understanding of the nature of sociology itself.

The idea that systematic social research could in a direct fashion contribute to bringing about a more desirable social order — however that be defined, from the revolutionary scenarios of Marxism to the melioristic aspirations of more conventional forms of social science — was one of the main factors influencing the burgeoning of sociology (and the other social sciences) in the post-Second World War period. This mushrooming of social science tended to go hand-in-hand with the altered role of government signalled by the extension of the welfare state and by increasing state intervention in industry. Among non-Marxist writers at least, effective research in sociology, political science and economics was expected to turn into informed policy-making in government and administration, this then furthering social progress and economic prosperity. The relation between research and policy was presumed to be an instrumental one, the former being a means to a practical end of controlling social organization and social change in an effective manner.

For the most part, this type of orientation in practice has tended to place an emphasis upon research work often not far removed from Mills's 'mindless empiricism', geared to known and restricted policy objectives. The point of doing social research, from a practical angle, is simply to allow policy-makers better to understand the social world, and thereby to influence it in a more reliable fashion than would otherwise be the case. From this standpoint research does not play a significant part in shaping the ends of policy-making, but serves to provide efficient means of pursuing already formulated objectives.

No doubt sociological research has played an effective part in the achievement of policy objectives in many areas. At the same time, however, there is widespread disillusionment with the outcome of social research programmes in this respect, a disillusionment deriving not only from the rise of the 'market models' mentioned above. It is a familiar enough tale that those who wish to derive practical guidance from social science research infrequently find the clear recommendations they seek; and sociologists for their part discover that their work is ignored or trivialized by those whose concerns are primarily organizational and practical. A series of recent studies of attempts to link social science to practical goals has turned up depressingly negative conclusions. Thus looking at research work in the United States Weiss concludes that, among the cases he analysed, there were only a small number of instances in which research conclusions substantially informed and facilitated practical courses of action. As another observer puts it, 'sometimes scholarly communities have simply failed to respond to urgent calls for policy-oriented knowledge. And when they have, their response has been belated, inadequate or irrelevant. When there has been something for policy-makers to utilise, they have often failed to take notice of it.'[15]

Now of course these dislocations are in some degree endemic. There is a whole body of work ('implementation analysis') devoted to considering problems involved in matching research to practical imperatives. But most such work presumes that research generates 'findings' neutral in respect of their interpretation, the difficulties concerning only how they are utilized; and it tends to suppose that the environment of action is static, such that the conditions of implementation can be specified in a generalized fashion. While these emphases are inevitable if we understand the relation between research and practical goals as a merely instrumental one, a different conception can be developed if we move away from what might be called a 'control' notion of the practical implications of sociology towards a 'dialogical' model. Such a movement, I would say, is inherent in the transition in social theory referred to earlier; it recovers a more

[15] C. H. Weiss: *Social Science Research and Decision-Making*. New York: Columbia University Press, 1980, p. 47.

fundamental practical role for social analysis than was possible according to the prior type of viewpoint.

A dialogical model introduces the notion that the most effective forms of connection between social research and policy-making are forged through an extended process of communication between researchers, policy-makers and those affected by whatever issues are under consideration. Such a model tends to reverse the traditional view that specified policy objectives should determine the character of research carried out. Primacy instead tends to be given to the process of research over the formulation of policy objectives, which this influences as much as the other way around. In a rapidly changing world, continuing processes of social research help indicate where the most urgent practical questions cluster, at the same time as they offer frameworks for seeking to cope with them.

Three suppositions, all closely integrated with developments in social theory, might be said to underlie a dialogical model. First, social research cannot just be 'applied' to an independently-given subject matter, but has to be linked to the potentiality of persuading actors to expand or modify the forms of knowledge of belief they draw upon in organizing their contexts of action. This is only secondarily because policies might be ineffective otherwise. It is mainly because of the acknowledgement that all agents are (in principle) capable both of grasping the new knowledge generated by social research and of inferring its implications for their activities. Connecting social research with practical policies may not imply a full-blown 'ideal speech situation' in Habermas's sense. But it involves at a minimum the counterfactual of assessing what courses of action relevant individuals would have taken if in possession of the research in question; and, most desirably, direct consultation of a prolonged kind wherever feasible.

Second, we should affirm that the 'mediation of cultural settings', coupled with conceptual innovation, are at least as significant for the practical outcomes of social research as is the establishing of generalizations. By the former of these, I mean the communication, via social research, of what it is like to live in one cultural setting to those in another. The practical implications of this 'anthropological moment' of social research should not be underestimated. As the condition of establishing a dialogical relation between researchers, policy-makers and those whose behaviour is the subject of study, it is inevitably one of the main contributions social research can make to the formulation of practical policy. Since the will to change things for the better involves positing 'possible worlds' of what might become the case via programmes of social reform, it is easy to see why conceptual innovation is of essential importance. Novel conceptual frameworks open up possible fields of action previously unperceived either by policy-makers or by the agents involved.

Third, the practical implications of the double hermeneutic should be underscored. The most far-reaching practical consequences of social science do not involve the creation of sets of generalizations that can be used to generate instrumental control over the social world. They concern instead the constant absorption of concepts and theories into that 'subject-matter' they seek to analyse, constituting and reconstituting what that 'subject-matter' is. Nothing confirms more completely the importance of a dialogical model, for only such a model incorporates the attention to reflexivity thus entailed.

8 *Social movements will continue to be of prime significance in stimulating the sociological imagination*

Organizations and social movements, it might be argued, are the two ways in which reflexive appropriation of knowledge about the social life is mobilized in the modern world. In organizations, information is systematically gathered, stored and drawn upon in the stabilizing of conditions of social reproduction. Social movements have more dynamism, and in some ways greater transformative potential, because they are specifically geared to the achievement of novel projects, and because they set themselves against the established order of things. If they are not always the harbingers of the future states of affairs they announce, they are inevitably disturbing elements in the present. Hence — as I have mentioned previously — social movements not only are sources of tension and change that sociologists are called upon to analyse, they may identify previously undiagnosed characteristics of, and possibilities within, a given institutional order. Various social movements have traditionally figured prominently in the domain of sociological discourse — in particular, labour, political and religious movements. But some of the most important sources of stimulus to sociological reflection today are provided by social movements which, if they are not necessarily of recent provenance, are particularly significant in the current period. As I have stressed earlier, particularly important here are ecological, peace and women's movements.

Ecological and peace movements help compel us to confront those dimensions of modernity which tend to have been poorly analysed in sociology. The debate about whether capitalism or industrialism has been the prime mover in shaping the modern world until relatively recently ignored the destructive effects that modern production systems may have upon the environment. Being prompted to consider how far such effects exist, and what these effects are, leads to the disclosure of a whole range of issues of sociological concern. At the same time as we must face the question — Can modes of economic and social development under way for two centuries or more continue for much longer? — we are led to re-examine existing institutions. Thus sociological accounts of 'work' and 'unemployment' may very often have been overly influenced by accepted economic definitions, neglecting both other forms of labour that are unpaid and other modes of organizing paid labour than those involving full-time careers. Ecological movements have also of course sensitized us to subtleties in the relation between human beings and nature that would otherwise remain unexplored. We have to look again at the character of the built environment in the light of just these subtleties.

Peace movements are, as it were, the other face of the process of the industrialization of war. In forcing upon public consciousness the potentially devastating implications of the arms race they help to make plain that sociologists can no longer leave aside the analysis of military power as one of the parameters of modernity. Peace movements have become a significant influence upon the nature and distribution of military power, and naturally merit study in their own right. How far they are effective in seeking to achieve their aims, limited and more ambitious; how far the preservation of 'peace' depends in the foreseeable future upon a stable balance of deployment of military forces on the part of the super-powers — these are not questions devoid of sociological interest. On the contrary, sociologists can scarcely not become involved with what is plainly *the* overriding issue now affecting all our futures — can humanity survive a period which seems certain to witness a further escalation in weapons development world-wide?

If the issues brought to the fore by the women's movement are less obviously dramatic in their implications, the rethinking which is being forced upon the social sciences is nonetheless profound. The domination of women by men is certainly not something brought into being by modernity, although there are peculiarly modern expressions of such domination. Since asymmetries of power between the sexes are so deeply engrained historically and cross-culturally, attempts to eradicate them are likely to come up against extraordinary resistance.

The material success of the women's movement in diminishing inequalities is again separable from the bringing of novel issues to the forefront of sociological debate. Once more we need to acknowledge both the emergence of a field of study and a set of intellectual challenges. 'Women's studies' have become an accepted part of most sociology programmes — although, of course, these endeavours also stretch well beyond the confines of such programmes. Just as significant is the challenge thrown down to orthodox sociological standpoints. How should we think about gender sociologically? What connections can and should be made between gender and notions such as class? How far has social research unthinkingly been preoccupied with male experience? These and other parallel questions have by no means been satisfactorily answered as yet, and we may expect a concern with them to be of major importance to the future development of sociology.

In making these observations, I do not want to claim that other types of social movement are no longer of much interest. Social movements are expressive of sites of conflict, and the 'traditional' sites of conflict have quite evidently not disappeared. It has become apparent to even the most committed Marxist that the labour movement is not going to play the world-historical role that Marx attributed to it. But there is no denying that labour movements have significantly altered pre-existing patterns of capitalist development, and that industrial conflict tends to be more or less chronic in industrialized countries. Contrary to what some others have claimed, I am not persuaded that the 'newer' forms of social movement are increasingly replacing the labour movement as frameworks of struggle. Moreover, seemingly 'traditional' types of social movement may provide food for sociological thought. In a discipline dominated by the idea of secularization, the occurrence of the 'Islamic Revolution' was certainly something quite unanticipated.

9 *Sociology will remain just as controversial a subject as it ever was*

By this I mean two things. One is that within the discipline of sociology we will not achieve the cherished goal of a consensus over theories and the interpretation of research findings. The second is that externally the discipline will continue to have its detractors and opponents. The first I have already sought to explain. But will sociology persistently be as controversial externally? In one sense, I hope (and think) not; in another I think (and hope) so. Sociologists have not been particularly popular in recent years, in some degree because of the disfavour into which social research has fallen. As I have said, I do not suppose that this will last. But there is another kind of enduring unpopularity of sociology which, perhaps paradoxically, we should look to preserve. This is the unpopularity of those who are not afraid to disclose unpleasant truths, or assert views about an existing order of things that contravene those held by the powerful. Not for nothing is sociology a poorly developed subject in the Soviet Union.

3

The social sciences and philosophy — trends in recent social theory

---

In the English-speaking world, the social sciences — particularly sociology — have changed quite dramatically over the past ten to fifteen years.[1] It will be one of my objectives in this discussion to document what these changes have been and where they are currently tending. But there can be no doubt that they derive in part from the impact of philosophy upon theorizing in social science. In return it can be said with some plausibility that it is probably those working in social theory who have contributed most to the *rapprochements* between Anglo-American philosophy and Continental traditions of thought that seem now to be taking place.

There is one fairly obvious reason for this. Those concerned with social theory in the English-speaking world have long been accustomed to regarding their main forbears as Continental. Marx, Durkheim and Weber tend to be regarded as the 'classical three', certainly by sociologists.[2] Partly as a result of the impact of these authors, social theory early on broke very substantially, and it seems irretrievably, with the perspectives of political economy and utilitarianism with which at least some main branches of Anglo-American philosophy have maintained ties. The essential 'Englishness' of English philosophy,

[1] This essay derives from a lecture at the University of Chicago in May 1984.

[2] See Anthony Giddens: *Capitalism and Modern Social Theory*. Cambridge: 1971.

and the indigenous 'Americanness' of philosophy in the United States have, of course, been 'interrupted' — but only in a really significant way by the relatively short-lived prominence of Idealism. Diffuse Continental influences of various kinds have chronically influenced philosophy in the USA, while Wittgenstein — whose thought undoubtedly was more steeped in Continental traditions than either he or his close disciples were wont to admit — has had an enormous impact upon philosophy on both sides of the Atlantic. Nonetheless, one can without difficulty trace direct continuities in Anglo-American philosophical thought from even the late eighteenth century to the present day. The same is not true of sociology. Spencer is not today regarded on a par with the above-mentioned sociological authors. Those working in social theory have not lost contact with Continental social thought in the way in which many analytical philosophers have tended to do. Since the boundaries between social theory and philosophy are fuzzy, it is not surprising that social theorists have had a good deal to say about recent developments in Continental philosophical thought, and have helped to act as catalysts in relating these to analytical philosophy.

A more interesting reason for the phenomenon might be stated as follows. Social science and philosophy, particularly certain forms of Continental philosophy, have over the past several decades been drawn closer together, such that problems and questions of mutual concern are more apparent than they ever were before — even if the solutions to these remain clouded and indeterminate. It is often said that social theory has become more 'philosophical' in recent years and that it has become preoccupied with issues of epistemology in particular. This is probably in some degree the case. But at the same time philosophy has become much more 'sociological', and it is in its increasingly 'sociological' nature that there are to be found some of the main meeting-points between Anglo-American and Continental philosophy. Matters which once were seen as inevitably epistemological in character now tend to be regarded instead as resting on social convention. The problems that used to preoccupy metaphysicians are held to be falsely posed, at least in the manner in which they construed them. Not in the unquestioned basis of transcendental knowledge, but in the shifting social arrangements of forms of life are to be found the clues that will cast light on difficulties that have perennially worried philosophers in the West.

Developments in social theory

Some of the key changes occurring in social theory over the past decade and a half can be fairly readily described, although tracing out their implications is a different matter, and in various respects a formidably complicated affair.[3] Up to something like the early 1970s (I speak only of the English-speaking world) the social sciences were dominated by the view that the objectives and logic of social science are more or less the same as those of natural science. Such a standpoint, of course, was not uncontested, and alongside the naturalistic outlook there existed certain alternatives emphasizing the distinctive qualities of human beings and their action as compared to the movement of objects and events in nature. Ranged against 'the orthodox consensus' there existed such schools of thought as symbolic interactionism and more latterly ethnomethodology. The idea of *Verstehen* was known through the writings of Max Weber, although it was generally thought to be a discredited notion. Very few sociologists had any familiarity with the hermeneutic tradition from which the concept of *Verstehen* originated, nor did they have anything beyond the most elementary understanding of the differences between the concept as employed in that tradition and the rather attenuated version adopted by Weber.

Proponents of the orthodox consensus conceived of the aims of the social sciences in relation to a definite model of natural science. That is to say, especially in the United States, they thought of natural science in terms of one or other version of logical empiricism. The model of natural science worked out within logical empiricism has often been referred to as the received model, but most social scientists 'received' it in a fairly untutored way. The idea of natural science to which they tied the aspirations of social science was not seen as a particular philosophical interpretation of natural science, but as an unquestioned picture of the essential character of the natural sciences. Although the received model has some while since been abandoned by the vast majority of philosophers of science, its residues linger on in sociology. Somewhat paradoxically, it is most particularly in those texts which are regarded as accounts of 'methodology' in the social sciences that a naive acceptance of the logical empiricist model of

[3] For a fuller analysis, see Anthony Giddens: *Central Problems in Social Theory*. London: Macmillan, 1979, especially chpt. 1.

science still tends to appear. Of course, even within the orthodox tradition there were very few writers who supposed that the social sciences could match the achievements of natural science in its most developed and mathematicized areas.

Although it was common to make some sort of diffuse appeal to physics as a model for social science — recapitulating Comte's idea of social physics — the more prevalent type of perspective tended to link the social sciences to biology. In other words, a naturalistic perspective converged with an advocacy of functionalism in social science, informed by the general notion that the mechanics of biological systems have close affinities with the operation of social systems. It is true that some writers of a naturalistic persuasion had feelings of disquiet about suggesting too close an affinity between sociology and biology. For after all, although there seem to be sets of established laws in certain other areas of natural science, in biology the prevalence of functionalist-style concepts tends to inhibit the formulation of law-like generalizations. Yet if it was never an entirely trouble-free alliance, the relation between naturalism and functionalism for a considerable period defined what was regarded by proponents and critics alike as the 'mainstream' version of social science.

On the level of the practice of the social sciences — that is to say in the more heavily and determinedly empirical areas of research — the 'mainstream' view has still not been discarded. Although its acceptance is very often implicit rather than explicit, such research still tends quite frequently to follow the basic presumptions of the pre-established perspective I have just described. In other sectors of social science, however, particularly in social theory, the orthodox model lies in ruins. Just as the 'received model' of natural science has been discarded by most philosophers, so there is no longer anything which is clearly definable as 'mainstream' social science.[4] What was something of a consensus, an acknowledged terrain over which intellectual and conceptual battles were fought out, now appears riddled with chasms across which the advocates of different perspectives find it difficult to stay in communication with one another. A measure of the changes that have occurred over the past few years can be gleaned by looking at the fate of Peter Winch's celebrated little book *The Idea of a Social Science.*[5] When it was first published, some quarter of a century ago,

[4] See Richard Bernstein: *The Restructuring of Social and Political Theory.* Oxford: Basil Blackwell, 1976.
[5] Peter Winch: *The Idea of a Social Science.* London: Routledge, 1958.

it received a good deal of attention from philosophers. In fact, they took sufficient notice of the book to subject it to a barrage of critical appraisals. But most practising social scientists displayed little interest in the work and it was not widely reviewed in the professional journals of sociology. Those who were aware of it inclined to dismiss the book as of little interest — as preaching an unacceptably subjectivist version of what social science should be about. It was seen as a somewhat eccentric statement of an essentially untenable position. Today, however critical sociological writers might be of the book, both friend and foe would tend to see it in a different light. Even those who oppose the views Winch adopts would recognize that the standpoint expressed in the book is to be taken seriously.

The outcome of the fading fortunes of naturalistic versions of social science has been the appearance of an apparently bewildering variety of schools of social theory. Some of the styles of thought that have become prominent are directly philosophical in origin and include English-speaking as well as Continental philosophies. Wittgenstein, to repeat, was hardly a born and bred Anglo-Saxon philosopher; nevertheless, his ideas have been most influential in the Anglo-Saxon world. Conjoined with the ordinary language philosophy of Austin, Wittgensteinian themes have surfaced strongly in social theory. Winch has played his part in this, of course, but the influence of Wittgenstein has been much wider than that represented by Winch's particular interpretation. Some of the most influential uses of Wittgensteinian notions, in fact, have come from Continental social theorists. If English-speaking philosophers have not thus far been prone to take the writings of their Continental counterparts too seriously, the reverse has by no means always been true. Habermas and Apel are among those whose writings involve a self-conscious attempt to draw upon the work of Wittgenstein, and analytical philosophy more generally, in conjunction with other streams of thought, to attempt a reconstitution of social theory.[6] 'Hermeneutics' is no longer a term unfamiliar to English-speaking social scientists; indeed the recovery of the hermeneutic tradition is one of the most significant occurrences in recent trends of development. There are however numerous other schools of thought that have come to the fore in recent years, including critical theory, particularly as practised by Habermas, and various

---

[6] Jürgen Habermas: *The Theory of Communicative Action*, vol. I. London: Polity, 1985; K. – A. Apel: *Analytic Philosophy of Language and the Geisteswissenschaften*. New York: Reidel, 1967.

versions of Marxism and neo-Marxism. To these one must add the impact of the newer philosophy of science associated with Kuhn and others. Here again there is a 'Continental connection', although not one which has been explored as thoroughly as it might have been — to Bachelard and Canguilhem, for example.

Many social scientists, especially those working on more empirical issues, do not at all welcome this situation of apparent disarray. It seems to them simply to interfere with the prosecution of empirical work, because there is no clear and obvious theoretical orientation into which such work can be placed. If they retain an interest in social theory at all, such researchers prefer it to be one of the old naturalistic type. Hence the aforementioned phenomenon that those who produce texts on research 'methodology' are the last to linger in the old ways. For many empirical researchers, the apparently chaotic state of social theory today substantiates traditional prejudices. Suspicious of theoretical endeavours anyway, they find their view confirmed that the only worthwhile type of social science keeps its nose firmly to the empirical grindstone. If the practitioners of social theory are in such complete disagreement with one another, why not ignore the more theoretical segments of social science altogether? If this is one reaction to the disintegration of 'mainstream' social science, there is something of an opposite standpoint quite often adopted by those working in social theory. For members of this second group, the appearance of numerous vying theoretical traditions signals a welcome pluralism in social science. They see any attempt to effect a closure of divergent perspectives as producing a renewed dogmatism. It is obvious enough that the issues posed by this view are part and parcel of the very debates that the advent of new philosophical positions in social theory (and in the philosophy of natural science) have stimulated.

Although I shall not attempt to discuss the matter in detail, I think each of these positions is misconceived. The retreat to 'mindless empiricism' surely has nothing to commend it. While it might be the case that some debates in social theory do not effectively alter the practice of social research, it can be demonstrated that questions of social theory often intrude very deeply into the nature of the tasks which empirical researchers undertake. The view which argues for unconstrained theoretical pluralism is surely not defensible either. We must accept that there exist criteria relevant to the evaluation of divergent truth-claims, or the whole enterprise of social science would be dissolved. While there is bound to be a diversity of variant perspectives in social theory, this does not imply the abandonment of attempts to mediate and in some part reconcile differing viewpoints. There does seem to be something of a reconstruction of social theory currently occurring, and some of its main lines of development can be identified. It was a progressive move in social theory to abandon naturalism and functionalism; and a more satisfactory synthetic standpoint is currently well on the way to fruition. It is an emergent perspective that integrates strands from English-speaking and Continental philosophy. If it is unlikely that such a synthesis will entirely recapture the middle ground occupied by the orthodox consensus, it nonetheless promises to command a fairly wide range of agreement.[7]

The issues raised here go beyond what could be covered adequately within the confines of a relatively concise analysis. I shall therefore concentrate upon a limited range of themes, although each of these is arguably quite vital to the rethinking of the social sciences now in progress. We should first of all raise the question of the nature of human action. Here is one area, basic to philosophy and social science alike, to the understanding of which philosophers have in recent years made important contributions. This leads on to discussion of the twin problems of subjectivity and meaning. In analysing these issues we must confront a further set of Continental philosophical influences — those associated with structuralism and post-structuralism. In general, English-speaking philosophers have regarded these schools of thought with the greatest suspicion, where they have given any time to them at all. Nonetheless, they raise questions directly relevant to themes characteristically pursued in ordinary language and Wittgensteinian philosophy.

Having looked at these problems, we are led to raise certain matters to do with the relation of social science to 'common sense'. For sociologists writing in naturalistic traditions, the question of the connection of social science to common sense appears relatively unproblematic. The point of social science, like natural science, is to improve upon the presumptions of commonsense beliefs, correcting them when they happen to be false and remodelling them when they are expressed in an imprecise fashion. One feature which most of the theoretical perspectives that have recently come to the fore share is that they all (in some guise or another) regard the relation between social science and common sense as intrinsically interesting, and as

[7] Anthony Giddens: *New Rules of Sociological Method*. London: Hutchinson, 1976, chpt. 2.

posing questions of considerable significance. Phenomenology, critical theory in Continental philosophy, Wittgensteinian and ordinary language philosophy in the Anglo-Saxon world — all these involve a defence of the mundane. The 'sociological' orientation of a good deal of recent philosophy is not so much a concern with matters that have typically preoccupied naturalistic sociologists, but rather an understanding of the importance of lay practices and lay beliefs both for philosophy and social analysis.

Action

First, then, the problem of action. In respect of the concerns of sociologists the issue of the nature of human action has to be understood in the context of a traditional division in social theory, a dichotomy between objectivism and subjectivism. By the former of these notions I mean that perspective in social theory according to which the social object ('society') has some sort of priority over the individual agent and in which social institutions are regarded as the core concern of social analysis. Subjectivism essentially means its opposite. The human agent is treated as the prime focus of social analysis. That is to say, the main concern of the social sciences is held to be the purposeful, reasoning actor.

Each of these standpoints has its attractions. On the one hand, those who belong to objectivist traditions — both inside and outside the orthodox consensus — have surely been correct in arguing that 'society' or 'social institutions' have structural properties stretching 'beyond' the activities of individual members of society. Those who veer to the subjectivist side — the majority of the newer or newly rediscovered schools of social theory — have quite rightly seen us as beings capable of understanding the conditions of our own action, as acting intentionally and having reasons for what we do.

However if each perspective has its attractions, each also has its shortcomings. Those who tend to the objectivist perspective have typically not been very adept at capturing the qualities which quite definitely have to be attributed to human agents, that is to say, self-understanding, intentionality, acting for reasons. Those on the subjectivist side of the fence, on the other hand, have failed to analyse adequately just those phenomena which the objectivists rightly see as so essential in the study of human conduct. Subjectivism has tended to skirt issues concerned with long-term processes of change and the large-scale organization of institutions.[8]

In spite of the pre-eminence once held by the orthodox consensus, the dualism between objectivism and subjectivism is deeply embedded in social analysis. Many of the controversies which dominate social theory turn upon issues raised by this division. In the approach to social theory which I have worked out over the past several years — structuration theory — I have proposed that this seeming opposition of perspectives actually disguises a complementarity. This dualism should actually be represented as a duality, the duality of structure.[9] In order to understand the importance of the notion of the duality of structure in social theory we have to look at the concepts both of structure and action. In those approaches which treat human agents as purposive, reasoning beings, the notion of action is often understood as though it were composed of an aggregation of intentions. That is to say, the agent is not placed in the unfolding of the routines which constitute day-to-day life. This unfolding is a duration, as Schutz put it, a continuity which persists throughout the waking life of the individual. Action in other words has an essential temporality which is part of its constitution.[10]

Interpreting agency within the context of its duration helps link the notion of action to those concepts — that is, structure, institutions and so on — which have been so important to objectivist social scientists. To see how these connections might be made, we have however to consider afresh the concept of structure. Among English-speaking social scientists, the concept of structure has ordinarily been a received notion. In contrast, for example, to the concept of function, the idea of structure has received remarkably little discussion. Why should this be so? The reason is probably that most English-speaking social scientists have a clear idea of how the concept of structure should be understood. When they talk of structure, or of 'the structural properties of institutions', they have in mind a sort of visual analogy. They see the structural properties of institutions as like the girders of a building, or the anatomy of a body. Structure consists of the patterns or relationships observable in a diversity of social contexts.

---

[8] For further development of the above points, see Giddens: *Central Problems in Social Theory*. London: Macmillan, 1979, chpt. 1.

[9] Ibid., chpt. 2.

[10] Alfred Schutz: *The Phenomenology of the Social World*. London: Heinemann, 1972.

Now this notion of structure needs to be examined just as closely as the idea of action.

In the traditions of structuralism and post-structuralism, the concept of structure is used in a fashion quite divergent from that characteristic of Anglo-Saxon social science and philosophy. The easiest way to indicate this is by reference to Saussure's classic discussion of the structural qualities of language. Structural features of language do not exist as patterns situated in time and space, like patterns of social relationships; they consist of relations of absences and presences embedded in the instantiation of language, in speech or in texts.[11] Structure here presumes the idea of an absent totality. To understand a sentence which a speaker utters means knowing an enormous range of rules and strategies of a syntactical and semantical kind, which are not contained within the speech act, but are nevertheless necessary to either understand it or to produce it. It is such a notion of structure (as an absent totality) which I hold to be important as a concept for the social sciences as a whole and basic to the notion of duality of structure. The problem with conceptualizing structure as a set of relations of 'presences', is that structure then appears as a constraint which is 'external' to action.[12]

If we conceive of structure in this fashion, it is not surprising that action appears to be limited by structural constraints which have essentially nothing to do with it. For structures limit behaviour, although it may be that within those limits — so one would have to presume — the agent is capable of acting freely. According to the notion of the duality of structure, by contrast, structure is not as such external to human action, and is not identified solely with constraint. Structure is both the medium and the outcome of the human activities which it recursively organizes. Institutions, or large-scale societies, have structural properties in virtue of the continuity of the actions of their component members. But those members of society are only able to carry out their day-to-day activities in virtue of their capability of instantiating those structural properties.

[11] Ferdinand de Saussure: *Course in General Linguistics.* London: Fontana, 1974.

[12] Emile Durkheim: *The Rules of Sociological Method.* London: Macmillan, 1982.

Subjectivity

One of the problems with subjectivist approaches in the social sciences and elsewhere is that subjectivity is taken as a given, not as a phenomenon to be explicated. In structuration theory the agent is not understood as 'pre-constituted' subjectively. In this respect we should recognize the importance of the critique of subjectivism developed in structuralism and post-structuralism. However the 'decentring of the subject' in structuralism and post-structuralism leads to the 'insertion' of the subject in language, conceived of in a particular way — signs constituted through difference. This methodological tactic follows very directly from the premises introduced by Saussure and accepted even by many subsequent writers who were critical of that author. Structuralism and post-structuralism promote a 'retreat into the code'. For example, it is pointed out that the term 'I', while referring to the most essential conditions of human subjectivity, is in fact a linguistic term like any other, which therefore has to be understood in relation to the remainder of language. The 'I' is in linguistic terms a 'shifter', which has no content in relation to its referent any more than the term 'tree' has in relation to the object which it 'stands for'.

Now this critique of object theories of meaning or theories of ostensive reference is in its main lines valid. However, what tends to happen in structuralist and post-structuralist traditions of thought is that the referent disappears altogether. The meaning is not the referent; but we cannot do without an account of reference, without showing how language relates to aspects of the external world. As regards the terminology of human subjectivity, the fact that the 'I' is constituted in language, and does not 'mean' the body or the acting self, should not lead to a methodological disappearance of the agent. Terms like 'I' and 'me' may not have as their meaning the object (the body) to which they relate, but they nevertheless gain their significance from the context of activities in which human agents are implicated. They are part of the practical mastery of social relations which human agents display, and of the continuity of social contexts in which they act.

There are two basic shortcomings in structuralist and post-structuralist accounts of agency: no analysis is provided of what I call 'practical consciousness' and it is not possible to generate an interpretation of meaning as the use of 'methods' embedded in such practical consciousness. It is to ordinary language philosophy and to phenomenology that we owe an analysis of practical consciousness in human day-to-day affairs. Agents can sometimes express their reasons for what they do in verbal or discursive form. Human beings can in some degree — fluctuating according to historically given social circumstances — give accounts of the circumstances of their action. But this by no means exhausts what they know about why they act as they do. Many most subtle and dazzlingly intricate forms of knowledge are embedded in, and constitutive of, the actions we carry out. They are done knowledgeably, but without necessarily being available to the discursive awareness of the actor. To speak a language, an individual needs to know an enormously complicated range of rules, strategies and tactics involved in language use. However, if that individual were asked to give a discursive account of what it is that he or she knows in knowing these rules etc., he or she would normally find it very difficult indeed. Any analysis of social activity which ignores practical consciousness is massively deficient.

Practical consciousness is in a certain sense unconscious. That is to say, it consists of forms of knowledge not immediately available to discourse. But it is not unconscious in the same way as symbols and modes of cognition subject to repression are unconscious. For these latter forms of cognition cannot be translated into discourse without the influence of some kind of distorting mechanism. The unconscious has a definite role in human social activity, and it is reasonable to argue that one can at least make headway in understanding what the unconscious is by following the line of thought that the unconscious 'is structured like a language'. But intervening between the unconscious and the conscious is practical consciousness, the medium of human practical activity. Here there is a complex relation not just between discourse and 'the other side of language', but between the individual as an agent and the institutions which the individual constitutes and reconstitutes in the course of the duration of day-to-day activity. A good deal of what we do is organized knowledgeably in and through practical consciousness; it follows that the way in which we make sense of our own actions and the actions of others, and the ways in which we generate meaning in the world, are 'methodological'. The meanings of words and of actions do not originate solely in the differences created by sign codes, or more generically by language. They derive in a more basic way from the 'procedures' which agents use in the course of practical action to reach 'interpretations' of what they and others do.

To say that all social activity, and indeed all interpretation of meaning, is 'procedural' is to accept the significance of ethno-methods in social life.[13] The origins of meaning are not to be traced to the referent, or to the system of differences that constitutes language as a semiotic system, but to a 'methodological apparatus' embedded in a practical consciousness of the routines of day-to-day social life.[14] Wittgenstein's writings are an essential source for explicating the nature of this apparatus. What Wittgenstein provides is essentially a theory of *Praxis*, elucidated in the context of the use of ordinary language on the one hand, and the enactment of the ordinary practices of day-to-day social life on the other. Language is the medium of social practice and it follows that there is no essence to language — even if one should seek this essence in the differences which constitute a code.

Let me sum up so far. I think it necessary to accept certain of the insights of structuralism, and particularly post-structuralism, in understanding the relation between the conscious and the unconscious in action. Subjectivity does indeed hinge upon the use of the deictic terminologies of 'I', 'me' etc. as linguistic shifters. The unconscious can profitably be regarded as the 'other side' of language, that which cannot be said in language because it is the foundation of linguistic usage. But there is another sense of what cannot be said, and that is what has to be *done*. There is a vast conceptual arena here for the re-introduction of the skilled and knowledgeable subject, whose activities are geared to the continuities of day-to-day social life and whose knowledgeability is expressed in practice.

At this point we may move to the implications of this analysis for the understanding of meaning. As I have indicated previously, in structuralism as well as in post-structuralism, meaning is understood essentially in terms of the play of difference within linguistically constituted codes. Meaning is located in a system of signs, syntagmatically organized in the flow of language use, and paradigmatically organized in terms of their association within language as a whole. Here we find a quite direct line of continuity from Saussure to Derrida. But if by contrast meaning is taken to be (a) contextual and (b) procedural, quite a different conception emerges. There is a contrast between the 'fuzzy' nature of ordinary language terms and their precision in use. Words when taken in isolation or considered lexically seem to have only vague meanings as utilized in day-to-day

[13] Harold Garfinkel: *Studies in Ethnomethodology*, Cambridge: Polity Press, 1984.
[14] Anthony Giddens: *Central Problems in Social Theory*, chpt. 1.

discourse. In fact if we examine sequences of talk we find that the meanings involved in such talk are normally quite precise. The participants in a conversation are ordinarily able to follow what each other says and relate what is said to its referential properties. This precision is impossible to understand without seeing practical consciousness as a medium of the constitution and re-constitution of meaning in day-to-day contexts of activity, and without accepting the 'methodological' nature of the knowledge involved.

This means revising the approach deriving from structuralist and post-structuralist thought. Such a view sees the text, or more generically writing, as the 'carriers' of meaning. Meaning is constituted through difference, and difference derives from the overall nature of the code. It was therefore quite logical for Derrida to take the step of regarding writing as the prime modality of signification. However if the approach I have suggested here is correct we have to accept that it is temporally and spatially situated conversation, not the text, and not writing, which is most essential to explaining language and meaning.

Common sense and mutual knowledge

The 'sociological' direction of modern philosophy involves a recovery of the everyday or the mundane. Our day-to-day activities are not merely inconsequential habits, of no interest to the student of more profound matters, but on the contrary are relevant to the explication of quite basic issues in philosophy and in social science. Common sense is thus not to be dismissed as merely the inertia of habit or as a set of semi-formulated ideas of no importance to social analysis. To develop this observation further, however, we have to enquire a little more deeply into what common sense is. We cannot necessarily understand the term 'common sense' in a common-sense way.

Although no doubt more finely-honed distinctions could be made, I shall distinguish two basic meanings of 'common sense'. One of these I call 'mutual knowledge' and separate from what can simply be called 'common sense' understood generically. By mutual knowledge I refer to knowledge of convention which actors must possess in common in order to make sense of what both they and other actors do in the course of their day-to-day social lives. Meanings are produced and reproduced via the practical application and continued reformulation in practice of 'what everyone knows'. As I would understand it, the programme of ethnomethodology consists in the detailed study of the nature and variations of mutual knowledge. Mutual knowledge refers to the methods used by lay actors to generate the practices which are constitutive of the tissue of social life. It is in substantial part non-discursive. That is to say, to use Wittgenstein's phrase, it consists of the capability to 'go on' in the routines of social life.

Not having any place for a concept of mutual knowledge, naturalistic social science presumes that the descriptive terminology of social analysis can be developed solely within professionally articulated theories. But in order to generate valid descriptions of social life, the sociological observer must employ the same elements of mutual knowledge used by participants to 'bring off' what they do. To be able to generate veridical descriptions of social activity means in principle being able to 'go on' in that activity, knowing what its constituent actors know in order to accomplish what they do. Winch was surely right about this, whatever misleading conclusions to which it may have led him in some respects. The implications of the point are rich. All social analysis has a 'hermeneutic' or 'ethnographic' moment, which was simply dissolved in traditional mainstream social science.

There is one way in which a grasp of the inescapably hermeneutic character of social science provides an answer to the question of its enlightening possibilities. That is to say, we might suppose — as Winch seemingly did — that what is 'new' in social science concerns only descriptions of forms of life (either in unfamiliar settings in our own culture, or in other cultures). In the view of the naturalistic social scientist, of course, the claim that social analysis can be no more than ethnography is absurd — this was one of the reasons why Winch's work was so little regarded within mainstream social science when it first appeared. But it is a proposition that deserves to be taken seriously. For there is a sense in which lay agents must always 'know what they are doing' in the course of their daily activities. Their knowledge of what they do is not just incidental but is constitutively involved in that doing. If they already not only do know, but in at least one sense *must* know what they are doing, it might seem that social science cannot deliver 'findings' with which the actors involved are not already familiar. At a minimum we must accept that the conditions under which the social sciences can deliver enlightenment to lay actors are more complex than was presumed in naturalistic social science.

What forms, then, might such enlightenment assume? The following considerations provide the basis of an answer.

1) It has to be accepted that the ethnographic tasks of social science are indeed fundamentally important. That is to say, all of us live within specific cultures which differ from other cultures distributed across the world, and from others 'recoverable' by historical analysis. In modern societies we also all live in specific contexts of larger cultural totalities. The 'news value' of the ethnographic description of culturally alien settings is certainly a significant element in social science.

2) Second, social science can 'display' — that is, give discursive form to — aspects of mutual knowledge which lay actors employ non-discursively in their conduct. The term 'mutual knowledge' covers a diversity of practical techniques of making sense of social activities, the study of which is a task of social science in its own right. As I have already mentioned, it can be construed as the task of ethnomethodology to provide such a 'display' of the taken-for-granted practicalities of our conduct. We might also instance, however, the writings of Erving Goffman as of singular importance in this respect. Perhaps more than any other single writer, Goffman has made clear how complicated, how subtle — but how routinely managed — are the components of mutual knowledge. We might also remark that the whole of linguistics is concerned with the 'display' of mutual knowledge. Linguistics is about what the language user knows, and must know, to be able to speak whatever language is in question. However most of what we 'know' in order to speak a language, we know non-discursively. Linguistics tells us what we already know, but in a discursive form quite distinct from the typical modes of expression of such knowledge.

3) A matter of very considerable significance — social science can investigate the unintended consequences of purposive action. Actors always know what they are doing (under some description or potential description), but the consequences of what they do characteristically escape what they intend. A nest of interesting problems and puzzles is to be found here, and I shall only discuss them briefly. Naturalistic versions of social science depend for their cogency upon the observation that many of the events and processes in social life are not intended by any of the participants involved. It is in the 'escape' of social institutions from the purposes of individual actors that the tasks of social science are discovered. In this respect we must in some part continue to defend the version of social science advanced by the 'mainstream' against more 'interpretative' conceptions. A characteristic failing of those traditions of thought which have done most to bring into focus the significance of mundane social practices is that they

have ignored altogether the unintended consequences of social activity. But it would be futile to imagine that the issue was adequately handled in naturalistic social science. For the naturalistic sociologist, the unintended character of much social activity is wedded to the view that social life can be analysed in terms of the operation of factors of which social actors are ignorant. But it is one thing to argue that some of the main parameters of social activity are unintended by those who participate in that activity; it is quite another to presume that consequently individual agents are acted upon by 'social causes' which somehow determine the course of what they do. Far from reinforcing such a conclusion, a proper appreciation of the significance of the unintended consequences of action should lead us to emphasize the importance of a sophisticated treatment of the purposive nature of human conduct. What is unintentional cannot be even characterized unless we are clear about the nature of what is intentional; and this, I would argue, also presumes an account of agents' reasons.

There are several different types of inquiry that relate to the role of unintended consequences in human action. For example, we might be interested in asking why a singular event occurred in spite of no one's intending it to occur. Thus a historian might pose the question: why did the First World War break out, when none of the main parties involved intended their actions to produce such an outcome? However, the type of question with which naturalistic social scientists have traditionally been preoccupied concerns the conditions of social reproduction. That is to say, they have sought to demonstrate that social institutions have properties which extend beyond the specific contexts of interaction in which individuals are involved. The connection between functionalism and naturalism has specific application here. For the point of functional explanation has normally been to show that there are 'reasons' for the existence and continuance of social institutions that are quite distinct from the reasons actors might have for whatever they do.

   In recent years, partly as a result of a renewed critical examination of functionalism, it has become apparent that an account of institutional reproduction need not, and should not, have recourse to functional interpretations at all. Human social systems do not have needs, except as counter-factually posited 'as if' properties. It is perfectly appropriate, and often necessary, to enquire what conditions are needed for the persistence of a given set of social institutions over a specified period of time. But such an enquiry invites analysis of the mechanics of social reproduction, it does not supply an explanation for them. All large-scale social reproduction occurs under conditions of 'mixed intentionality'. In other words, the perpetuation of social institutions involves some kind of mix of intended and unintended outcomes of action. What this mix is, however, has to be carefully analysed and is historically variable. There is a range of circumstances which separate 'highly monitored' conditions of system reproduction from those involving a feedback of unintended consequences. The monitoring of conditions of system reproduction is undoubtedly a phenomenon associated with the emergence of modern society and with the formation of modern organizations generally. However the intersection between intended and unintended consequences in respect of institutional reproduction is variable and in all instances needs to be concretely studied. A double objection can be made to explaining social reproduction in terms of statements of the form 'the function of x is . . .'. The first is, as already stated, that such a statement has no explanatory value, and can only be rendered intelligible when applied to social activity in the form of a counter-factual proposition. The second is that the statement is ambiguous in respect of intentionality. In conditions in which reproduction is 'highly monitored', the tie between purposes (of some agents) and the continuity of social institutions will be direct and pervasive. Where an unintended feedback operates, the mechanics of the reproduction process will be quite different. It is normally essential to distinguish the difference.

Practical connotations

These considerations have significant, although complex, implications for analysing the practical impact of the social sciences. Mainstream social science tended to operate with a defective view of the corrigibility of common sense. Common sense here refers to propositional beliefs that actors hold about social life and the conditions of social reproduction. Given their naturalistic presumptions, the proponents of the orthodox consensus assumed that the practical connotations of social science have a 'technological' form. The social sciences correct false beliefs that agents have about social activity or institutions. As we get to know the social world better, just as in the case of the natural world, we are in a position to change it. Such a view has a deeply founded ancestry in the social sciences, dating back at least to Montesquieu, reiterated by Comte, Durkheim and by all naturalistic versions of Marxism. If the arguments set out earlier are valid, however, such a viewpoint cannot be sustained — at least, in anything like the form in which it is developed by these authors and by many others. Social science does involve the attempted critique of false beliefs about the social world held by lay actors. But the context in which these critical ideas and theories are formulated, and their practical implications, are quite different from what is involved in natural science. Social science is concerned with concept-bearing and concept-inventing agents, who theorize about what they do as well as the conditions of doing it. Now natural science, as has been made clear in the 'newer philosophy of science', involves a hermeneutic. Science is an interpretative endeavour, in which the theories comprise meaning-frames. Unlike natural science, however, the social sciences involve a double hermeneutic, since the concepts and theories developed therein apply to a world constituted of the activities of conceptualizing and theorizing agents. The social scientist does not have to interpret the meanings of the social world to actors within it. To the contrary, the technical concepts of social science are, and must be, parasitical upon lay concepts. This is exactly the sense in which, as Winch says, technical social science concepts are 'logically tied' to those of the 'common-sense world'. Generating veridical descriptions of human action presumes that the sociological observer has access to the mutual knowledge whereby actors orient what they do. The condition of being able to describe what actors are doing, in any given context of action, is being able to 'go on' with the 'form of life' in question. What Winch does not consider at all is the reciprocal 'absorption' of social scientific concepts into the social world they are coined to analyse. The concepts and theories of natural science are entirely insulated from 'their' world, the object-world of nature. This absorption process, I want to maintain, helps explain the apparent banality of social scientific findings as contrasted with what appear to be the far more innovative findings of natural science.

The banality of social science was a major source of worry to practitioners of mainstream sociology. Why have not the social sciences generated discoveries about the social world which parallel those of natural science? If such discoveries are not made, we would seem to lack the capability of producing the 'technological' control upon which the practical connotations of social science (in the orthodox model) depend. If social science is apparently in a relatively primitive state, compared with natural science, it might simply be because the former developed at a considerably later date than the latter, and consequently has a large amount of catching up to do. Such was the usual view of the proponents of the orthodox consensus, but it is surely not one that has anything to commend it. Both social and natural science, in their modern guises, can be traced back in their origins to the Renaissance, and while the character of their development differs, one would be hard put to it to assign either a general temporal priority over the other. Understanding the social sciences to be implicated in a double hermeneutic, in the manner I have proposed, allows us both to explain the apparent banality of the social sciences — and at the same time shows that this banality is only apparent.

From its first inception in modern times social science has had, and continues to have today, a very far-reaching practical impact upon the social world. It could be argued that the transformative consequences of social science for the social world have been considerably greater than those of the natural sciences for 'their' world. But the practical impact of social science has not primarily been a 'technological' one. It has proceeded by the absorption of social scientific concepts into the social world, of which they have become in some part constitutive. As they become taken over by lay actors and incorporated into the practices of social activity, they of course become familiar elements of social routines. Their originality becomes lost even though when first constructed they might have been as brilliantly innovative as anything that has existed in natural science.

If the ideas and knowledge-claims of social science cannot be kept insulated from the social world itself, we reach a new appreciation of the significance of critical theory. Social science does not stand in a neutral relation to the social world, as an instrument of 'technological change'; critique cannot be limited to the criticism of false lay beliefs. The implication of the double hermeneutic is that social scientists cannot but be alert to the transformative effects that their concepts and theories might have upon what it is they set out to analyse. Critical theory is not an option for social science, which can either be taken up or left alone; it is inherent in its nature. I do not think any existing versions of critical theory — those associated with the Frankfurt School, for example — can be deemed satisfactory. Thereby, however, hangs a tale I shall not seek to relate here.

Conclusion

Over the past ten to fifteen years, as I have tried to indicate, social theory has both drawn profitably from current developments in philosophy and also made some contributions in return. The 'sociologizing' of philosophy has led many philosophers more directly to discuss problems of immediate relevance to social science than probably was the case before. At the same time, the social sciences have been passing through a period of transition, particularly marked in social theory, in which their concerns have also shifted. There is a range of issues — to do with agency, intentionality, structure and meaning — about which it would be difficult to say whether they should properly be called 'philosophical' or 'sociological'. I have sought to indicate what some of these look like from the sociological side. But I do not think, as Winch has asserted, that social science is in some general sense a philosophical endeavour. While interchange may be rewarding and important, the concepts and theories of social science are in the end only of enduring value if they usefully help guide the practice of empirical research.

4

Structuralism, post-structuralism and the production of culture

Structuralism, and post-structuralism also, are dead traditions of thought.[1] Notwithstanding the promise they held in the fresh bloom of youth, they have ultimately failed to generate the revolution in philosophical understanding and social theory which once was their pledge. In this discussion, I shall not so much seek to write their obituary as to indicate what they have bequeathed to us today in respect of intellectual possessions which still might be put to good use. For although they did not transform our intellectual universe in the manner which was often claimed, they nonetheless drew to our attention some problems of considerable and durable significance.

Of course, many have doubted that there ever was a coherent enough body of thought to be designated by the name 'structuralism', let alone the even vaguer appellation 'post-structuralism'.[2] After all, most of the leading figures ordinarily lumped under these labels have rejected these terms as applying meaningfully to their own endeavours. Saussure, commonly regarded as the founder of structuralist linguistics, barely uses the term 'structure' at all in his work.[3] Lévi-Strauss at one time actively promoted the cause of both 'structural

---

[1] Delivered as lectures at the University of Melbourne, Australia, in August 1986.

[2] See W. G. Runciman: 'What is structuralism?' in *Sociology in its Place*. Cambridge: Cambridge University Press, 1970.

[3] Ferdinand de Saussure: *Course in General Linguistics*. London: Fontana, 1974.

anthropology' and of 'structuralism' more generally, but has become more cautious in characterizing his approach in these ways over the latter part of his career. Barthes may have in his early writings drawn fairly heavily from Lévi-Strauss, but later on any such connections became quite remote. Foucault, Lacan, Althusser and Derrida diverge radically both from the main ideas of Saussure and Lévi-Strauss and from one another. The homogeneity needed to speak of a distinct tradition of thought might appear to be almost completely lacking.

But for all their diversity there are a number of themes that crop up in the works of all these authors. Moreover, with the exception of Saussure, all are French and have been involved in networks of mutual influence and contact. In using the terms 'structuralism' and 'post-structuralism' in what follows, I have in mind Saussure and Lévi-Strauss as belonging to the first category, with the others in the second. 'Post-structuralism' is admittedly a fairly loose label for a cluster of authors who, while reacting against some of the distinctive emphases of earlier structuralist thought, at the same time take over some of those very ideas in their own work. Thus while they handle these themes in diverse ways, the following can be said to be persistent, and definitive, characteristics of structuralism and post-structuralism: the thesis that linguistics, or more accurately, certain aspects of particular versions of linguistics, are of key importance to philosophy and social theory as a whole; an emphasis upon the relational nature of totalities, connected with the thesis of the arbitrary character of the sign, together with a stress upon the primacy of signifiers over what is signified; the de-centring of the subject; a peculiar concern with the nature of writing, and therefore with textual materials; and an interest in the character of temporality, as somehow constitutively involved with the nature of objects and events. There is not a single one of these themes which does not bear upon issues of importance for social theory today. Equally, however, there is not one in respect of which the views of any of the writers listed above could be said to be fully acceptable.

Problems of linguistics

Structuralism was of course originally a movement within linguistics, at the same time as it was an endeavour to demonstrate the significance of concepts and methods of linguistics for a wide variety of issues in the humanities and social sciences. Saussure's distinction between *langue* and *parole* may justly be regarded as the key idea in structuralist linguistics. The distinction removes the study of 'language' from the sphere of the contingent and the contextual. As an overall structural form, language is to be separated from the multifarious uses to which particular speech acts may be put. *Parole* is what Saussure calls the 'executive side of language', while *langue* is 'a system of signs in which the only essential thing is the union of meanings and acoustic images'.[4] Language is thus an idealized system, inferred from, but nevertheless independent of, the particular uses to which speech is put. The actual sound contents of language are in a way irrelevant to the analysis of *langue*, because the concern is with the formal relations between sounds, or marks, not with their actual substance. Although in Saussure a certain mentalism and reliance upon psychology remain, in principle linguistics becomes clearly separable from other disciplines concerned with the study of human activity. Phonemics becomes also cleanly differentiated from phonetics, the latter being of relatively marginal importance to the main core of linguistic analysis.

There is an inconsistency at the heart of Saussure's conception of *langue*. On the one hand language is regarded as ultimately a psychological phenomenon, organized in terms of mental properties. On the other — as Saussure's seeming indebtedness to Durkheim would indicate — language is a collective product, a system of social representations. As critics have pointed out, if language is essentially a psychological reality, signs are no longer arbitrary. Since the relations that constitute language would be patterned in terms of characteristics of mind, they would have a determinate form controlled by mental processes. 'Thus if language is looked at as a mental reality the sign is by no means arbitrary and its meaning is by no means defined by its relations with contemporaneous elements of the language.'[5]

Broadly speaking, most forms of structuralist linguistics have opted for the 'psychological' rather than the 'social' version of *langue*. It was by adopting this approach that Chomsky was able to effect a fusion of ideas drawn from Continental linguistics with notions taken from the 'behaviourist structuralism' of Bloomfield, Harris and others within linguistics in the United States. Bloomfield and Harris sought to separate linguistics completely from any kind of mentalism or

---

[4] Ibid.
[5] Simon Clarke: *The Foundations of Structuralism*. Sussex: Harvester, 1981, p. 123.

psychology.[6] For them the aim of linguistics is to analyse language as far as possible solely as sequences of regularized sounds. Attention is not to be concentrated upon the interpretative involvements of speakers with language-use. While this standpoint at first sight seems substantially distinct from Saussurian linguistics, and while indeed its leading advocates rejected the differentiation of *langue* from *parole*, there are certainly some underlying affinities, which Chomsky was able to bring out. Redefining the distinction of *langue* and *parole* as one of competence and performance, and dissociating himself in a radical way from the behaviourism of Bloomfield and Harris, Chomsky was able to reconnect a mentalistic basis for language with an elaborated model of formal linguistics. Given the differentiation which is made between competence and performance, Chomskyian linguistics necessarily accords a central significance to syntax.[7] Its objective is not to explicate all utterances of the speakers within a particular language community, but only the syntactical structures of an idealized language speaker. Chomsky's theory reintroduces interpretation, because the identification of syntactical correctness depends upon what is deemed acceptable by language speakers. It also gives a certain priority to the creative components of language, in the sense that the competent speaker is able to generate an indefinite corpus of syntactically acceptable sentences. It is arguable that the Chomskyian competence/performance distinction is in major respects superior to the *langue/parole* differentiation, because Chomsky at least has a model of the linguistic agent. As Chomsky points out, criticizing Saussure, the latter treated *langue* mainly as a repository of 'word-like elements' and 'fixed phrases', contrasting it to the more flexible character of *parole*. What is missing is an account of the 'mediating term' between *langue* and *parole*. The agent is for Chomsky the locus of what he regards as the 'rule-governed creativity' of language as a system.[8]

Chomsky's transformational grammar is one approach influenced by some of the emphases of Saussure; another is the linguistics of the

---

[6] M. Bloomfield: *Language*. London: Allen & Unwin, 1957; Z. Harris: *Methods in Structural Linguistics*. Chicago: University of Chicago Press, 1951.

[7] See, for example, Noam Chomsky: *Language and Mind*. New York: Harcourt Brace, 1968.

[8] Noam Chomsky: *Current Issues in Linguistic Theory*. The Hague: Mouton, 1964, p. 23.

Prague School, which via Jakobson was the main influence upon Lévi-Strauss. Broadly speaking one can say that the Prague group followed the 'social' conception of *langue* rather than the 'psychological' one. Whereas Chomsky's linguistics focuses upon the competence of the individual speaker, the linguistics of the Prague School concentrates above all upon language as a communicative medium. Thus semantics is not completely severed from syntactics, and the nature of *langue* expresses relations of meaning. As Trubetzkoy claims, linguistics should investigate 'which phonic differences are linked, in the language under consideration, with differences of meaning, how these differentiating elements or marks are related to one another, and according to what rules they combine to form words and phrases'.[9] Stress upon the use of language as communication, combined with an emphasis on meaning, would seem to compromise the autonomous character of linguistics as specified by Saussure (and Chomsky). For it would appear that language would then have to be analysed in connection with the institutions of social life. Certainly the Prague linguists dissociated themselves from the inflexible distinction between *langue* and *parole* drawn by Saussure, and the associated division between the synchronic and the diachronic. In spite of this, the distinctive emphasis of the Prague group tended to be concentrated upon phonology, in reference to which the sound system of language can be studied without attention to the external connotations of meaning. Jakobson's early work in particular pursued the idea that a 'phonological revolution' (Lévi-Strauss's term) could be produced by analysing phonemes in terms of oppositions which are the constituent features of language as a whole. Although this was justified on methodological rather than epistemological grounds, the result was again to return linguistics to the study of the internal structures of *langue*.[10]

Lévi-Strauss and Barthes have each at various times seen the main basis for structuralism as consisting in the application of procedures of linguistics to other areas of analysis. Lévi-Strauss regards structuralist linguistics as both supplying modes of analysis that are applicable elsewhere and as providing substantive clues to the nature of human mind. In *The Elementary Structures* he explicitly compares his objectives with those of phonological linguistics, and adds that

[9] N. Trubetzkoy: *Principles of Phonology*. Berkeley: University of California Press, 1969, p. 12.
[10] Roman Jakobson: *Word and Language*. The Hague: Mouton, 1971.

linguists and social scientists 'do not merely apply the same methods, but are studying the same thing'.[11] For structural linguistics allows us to discern what he later came to regard as 'fundamental and objective realities consisting of systems of relations which are the products of unconscious thought processes.'[12] As Culler points out, regarding linguistics as of central importance to structuralism generally carries several implications. First, linguistics seems to provide a rigour lacking elsewhere in the humanities and social sciences. Second, linguistics offers a number of basic concepts which seem to be capable of much wider application than that involved in the framework of their origin — *langue* and *parole* in particular, perhaps, but also the associated distinctions of the syntagmatic and the paradigmatic, signifier and signified, the idea of the arbitrary nature of the sign and so on. Third, linguistics appears to provide a series of general guidelines for the formulation of semiotic programmes. Such a notion was of course sketched out by Saussure and developed in some detail by Jakobson and others.

Because of the connections between structuralist linguistics and structuralism more generally, it is often held that structuralism has participated in the general 'linguistic turn' characteristic of modern philosophy and social theory. However, this is a specious conclusion, for reasons I shall go on immediately to indicate. On the one hand, the hopes that were pinned on linguistics for providing general models of procedure that could be applied very widely now quite plainly appear to be misplaced. On the other the 'linguistic turn', at least in its most valuable forms, does not involve an extension of ideas taken from the study of language to other aspects of human activity, but rather explores the intersection between language and the constitution of social practices. The relevant considerations here concern both the critique of structuralist linguistics as an approach to the analysis of language itself, and the critical appraisal of the importation of notions taken from this version of linguistics into other areas of the explication of human behaviour.

Many criticisms, of course, have been made of Saussure's version of linguistics — or at any rate, that portrayal of it which has come down to us through the medium of his students — including those offered

[11] Claude Lévi-Strauss: *The Elementary Structures of Kinship*. London: Eyre and Spottiswoode, 1969, p. 493.

[12] Claude Lévi-Strauss: *Structural Anthropology*. London: Allen Lane, 1968, p. 58.

cogently by Chomsky. There is no point in rehearsing these in any detail here. Most significant for the lines of argument to be developed later in this discussion are shortcomings shared by virtually all forms of structuralist linguistics, including that of Chomsky. These concern above all the isolation of language, or of certain features taken to be fundamental to the structure and properties of language, from the social environments of language use. Thus, while Chomsky recognizes, and even accentuates, the creative capabilities of human subjects, this creative quality is attributed to characteristics of human mind, not to conscious agents carrying on their day-to-day activities in the context of social institutions. As one observer puts it, 'the creative power of the subject has to be taken away as soon as it is acknowledged and given to a mechanism inscribed in the biological constitution of the mind'.[13] Although it is in many ways the most developed and sophisticated form of structuralist linguistics, Chomsky's theory of language has proved essentially defective in respect of the understanding of quite elementary features of language. These defects do not centre so much upon the unsatisfactory nature of the division drawn between syntactics and semantics, as the identification of the core features of linguistic competence. In Chomsky's view, the idealized language speaker is able unconsciously to grasp rules making possible the production and understanding of any or all grammatical sentences in a language. But this is not really an appropriate model of competence. Someone who might in any given context produce any sentence at all, however syntactically correct it might be, would be treated as distinctly aberrant. Linguistic competence involves not only the syntactical mastery of sentences, but mastery of the circumstances in which particular types of sentence are appropriate. In Hymes's words: 'he or she acquires competence as to when to speak, when not, and as to what to talk about with whom, when, where, in what manner'.[14] In other words, mastery of the language is inseparable from mastery of the variety of contexts in which language is used.

The works of authors as diverse as Wittgenstein and Garfinkel have made us aware of what this involves, both for understanding the nature of language and for grasping the character of social life. Knowing a language certainly means knowing syntactical rules but, equally importantly, to know a language is to acquire a range of

[13] Clarke: *Foundations* . . . . p. 171.
[14] D. H. Hymes: 'On communicative competence', in J. B. Pride and Janet Holmes: *Sociolinguistics*. Harmondsworth: Penguin, 1972, p. 277.

methodological devices, involved both with the production of utterances themselves and with the constitution and reconstitution of social life in the daily contexts of social activity.[15] It is not just that to know a language is to know a form of life, or rather a multiplicity of interweaving forms of life; to know a form of life is to be able to deploy certain methodical strategies geared to indexical qualities of the contexts in which social practices are carried on. In this understanding of language, linguistics neither has the degree of self-sufficiency which Saussure, the Prague Group, Chomsky and others have claimed, nor does it make much sense to hold, as Lévi-Strauss has sometimes asserted, that social life is 'like a language'. Linguistics cannot provide a model for analysing either the nature of agency or of social institutions, because it is in a basic sense only explicable via an understanding of these. The 'linguistic turn' is in a sense a turn away from linguistics, conceived as an independently formed discipline, towards examining the mutual co-ordination of language and *praxis*.

The relational nature of totalities

In Saussure's doctrines, the relational character of *langue* is closely connected with the thesis of the arbitrary character of the sign, and with a stress upon the significance of signifiers as compared with the more traditional preoccupation with signifieds. It is often remarked that Saussure's differentiation of *langue* from *parole*, according priority to the former over the latter, reflects Durkheim's assertion that the qualities of social wholes are more than the sum of their parts. This is surely wrong, and underestimates the subtlety with which Saussure designates the systematic form of *langue*. In explicating *langue* as a system of differences, Saussure reformulates both the nature of what the 'whole' is and what its 'parts' are, indicating that each is only defined in terms of the other. To say that language is a system without positive terms, that is, formed through the differences recognized to exist between sounds or marks, shows that the 'parts' are only such in virtue of the self-same characteristics that compose the 'whole'. The insight is a fundamental one insofar as it demonstrates that the

[15] Anthony Giddens: *The Constitution of Society*. Cambridge: Polity Press, chpt. 1.

linguistic totality does not 'exist' in the contexts of the use of language themselves. The totality is not 'present' in the instantiations which are its traces.

The tie between this view and the notion of the arbitrary character of the sign is easily specified. The assertion of the arbitrary nature of the sign can be read as a critique of object theories of meaning and of theories of ostensive reference. But this critique does not stem from the sorts of demonstration which Wittgenstein, Quine and other later philosophers were to make that the use of lexical items cannot be said to 'correspond' to objects or events in the world. Saussure's criticism is based wholly upon the idea of the constitution of *langue* through difference. Because a word only derives its meaning from the differences established between it and other words, words cannot mean their objects. Language is form, not substance, and is only able to generate meaning by the internal play of differences. This is therefore just as much the case with the relation between words — or sentences — and the mental states which might accompany them, as it is with the relation between words and external objects or events.

The emphasis upon the constitution of the totality through difference might appear to lead away from signifiers rather than towards them. For what matters is not whatever is used to signify, but only the differences that create the 'spacing' between them. However a concentration on the properties of signifiers in fact tends to flow rather readily from Saussure's views, because of the rejection that there is anything 'underneath' language which explains its character (apart from the vague presumption of some kind of innate mental qualities). While the actual substance comprising signifiers is unimportant, without the differences which sounds, marks or other material differentiations create, no meanings of any kind could exist. The programme of semiotics is hence certainly not just an adjunct to linguistics in the Saussurian formulation, but is necessarily coextensive with the exploration of *langue* itself.

The relational character of wholes, the arbitrary nature of the sign, and the notion of difference are concepts which run through structuralist and post-structuralist perspectives as a whole. At the same time they are the source of some of the main features which tend to separate the structuralist authors from their post-structuralist successors. Jakobson and Lévi-Strauss provide clear cases of the direct utilization of the Saussurian idea of the relational character of totalities. For the former, structuralism is defined in terms of the study of phenomena 'treated not as a mechanical agglomeration, but as a structural whole'.[16] Lévi-Strauss writes even more emphatically when he claims: 'authentic structuralism seeks . . . above all to grasp the intrinsic properties of certain kinds of order. The properties express nothing which would be external to them.'[17] However, Jakobson's own criticisms of Saussure make it clear that the principle of the identification of relations through difference is separable from the assertion that *langue* is a clearly definable whole. The boundaries of the 'whole' that is Saussure's *langue*, or that is Chomsky's linguistic corpus known to a competent speaker, are exceedingly difficult to draw. It can therefore be argued that more important than the principle of the establishing of the coherence of the totality is the endeavour to examine the nature of difference itself. Within linguistics, Jakobson already established the beginning of such an endeavour in his attempt to focus upon the basic structuring properties of codes rather than on the parameters of these codes themselves.

Derrida's philosophy radicalizes this much further. His disavowal of the 'metaphysics of presence' derives directly from his treatment of the idea of difference as constitutive, not only of modes of signification, but of existence in general.[18] Derrida will have nothing of the search for universal properties of mind, or indeed of any attempt to construct a systematic philosophy at all. In his discussion of Lévi-Strauss and structuralism in the social sciences, Derrida emphasizes the unrealizable character of Lévi-Strauss's programme, deriving this from contradictions supposedly immanent in Lévi-Strauss's own text. Lévi-Strauss's exploration of oral cultures is paradoxically itself a form of western 'logocentrism'. Derrida's critique of the metaphysics of presence is derived more or less directly from an exploration of the implications of the idea of difference — first of all as indicated by Saussure, and contrasted with notions of negation involved in the work of Hegel, Freud and others. Because of his distinction between *langue* and *parole*, Saussure was able to treat the idea of difference as involved with a 'virtual system' out of time. The transmutation of the Saussurian version of difference into Derrida's *différance* is made by introducing the temporal element. To differ is also to defer. If this is so, Derrida asks, how can anything, such as forms of signification, be considered as presences? Saussure's writings already contain the notion of the

16 Jakobson: *Word* . . . . p. 711.
17 Claude Lévi-Strauss: *L'homme nu*. Paris: Plon, 1971, pp. 561—2.
18 Jacques Derrida: *Of Grammatology*. Baltimore: Johns Hopkins University Press, 1976; *Writing and Difference*. London: Routledge, 1978.

'absent totality' which is language. In this idea of totality, however, there is still in Derrida's view a lingering nostalgia for presence. All signification operates through traces; memory traces in the brain, the fading of sounds as they are uttered, and the traces that writing leaves.

Derrida's reversal of the usual priority accorded to speaking over writing vigorously pursues a preoccupation with signifiers at the expense of the signified. This is also in some part derived from an immanent critique of Saussure. Speech, Derrida claims, seems to represent a moment in which form and meaning are present simultaneously. Once we see, however, as Saussure himself demonstrates, that this cannot be so, then we are led to question the presumption that speech is the most elemental expression of language. As I hear myself speak, it seems as though the words uttered are simply vehicles for my thoughts, consciousness being clothed in and given expression by language. Access to the inner contents of consciousness is regarded as the real basis of the meanings inherent in language, which writing can only hope indirectly to recapture. At key parts in his arguments about the structuring of language through difference, however, Saussure abandons sound units in favour of taking examples from writing. Thus for instance any particular letter of the alphabet, he points out, may be written in varying ways; all that matters is that it is distinct from other letters which potentially could be confused with it. Writing turns out in fact to be the best illustration of difference. The characteristics of absence and deferment involved in the nature of written texts indicate the conditions of signification in general. Speech 'personalizes' language by connecting it with the thoughts of the speaker. In fact language is essentially anonymous, being never the property of individual speakers and depending for its form upon its recursive properties. Of course, Derrida does not intend by this to accord a primacy to actual writing over instances of speech, which would make little sense, even if only for the reason that writing is in historical terms such a relatively recent development compared with the prevalence of oral cultures. Rather, language is a 'proto-writing' (*archi-écriture*), a process of the temporal spacing and repetition of signifying phenomena. Proto-writing, Derrida argues, 'is *invoked* by the themes of the arbitrariness of the sign and of difference', but it 'can never be recognised as the *object of science*'.[19]

[19] In Jonathan Culler: 'Jacques Derrida', in John Sturrock: *Structuralism and Since*. Oxford: Oxford University Press, 1979.

That is to say, it is not to be the object of investigation of a sort of non-logocentric linguistics.

The notion of the arbitrary character of the sign is responsible both for some of the strengths, but also of enduring weaknesses, that run through structuralist and post-structuralist traditions of thought. As formulated by Saussure, the doctrine of the arbitrary character of the sign itself has a fairly heavily arbitrary aspect to it. One can accept that the term 'arbitrary' is not a particularly happy one for the phenomenon at issue. That is to say, as Saussure himself fully accepted, the conventions involved in language-use are certainly not arbitrary in the sense that the language user is free to choose whatever utterances he or she might care to make. On the contrary, accepted usage has a strongly binding force. More important is that the thesis of the arbitrary nature of the sign is in the end rather obscure, especially in so far as it bears upon the nature of the signified rather than upon the signifier. If Saussure merely meant to claim that words have only a conventional connection with whatever objects they might be used to designate or refer to, it is so obvious as to be uninteresting. If — as quite often seems to be the case in Saussure's argument — the arbitrary nature of the sign is the same as the idea that language is constituted through difference, it is true that this has implications for the nature of meaning, but these implications are not pursued because the nature of signifieds is left largely unexplicated. Saussure evidently wished to claim that the meaning of a word is not the object to which that word might be used to refer, but since he nowhere analyses what reference actually is, this claim remains essentially unelucidated philosophically. The result is the confusion noted by Benveniste. As Benveniste observes: 'even though Saussure said that the idea of "sister" is not connected to the signifier s-ö-r (soeur), he was not thinking any less of the *reality of the notion*. When he spoke of the difference between b-ö-f (boeuf) and o-k-s (ox), he was referring in spite of himself to the fact that these two terms apply to the same *reality*. Here, then, is the *thing*, expressly excluded at first from the definition of the sign, now creeping into it by a detour . . .'.[20]

Saussure's writings promoted a 'retreat into the code' which has ever after been characteristic both of structuralist and post-structuralist authors. That is to say, the discovery that the component elements of *langue* only have identity through their differentiation within the

[20] Emile Benveniste: 'The nature of the linguistic sign', in *Problems in General Linguistics*. Florida: University of Miami Press, 1971, p. 44.

overall system serves to drag language away from whatever connections of reference it might have with the object world. Structuralist and post-structuralist thought alike have consistently failed to generate an account of reference, and it is surely not by chance that these traditions of thought have concentrated their attention so much upon the internal organization of texts, in which the play of signifiers can be analysed as an inside affair.[21] It is important to see that while the 'retreat into the code' was promoted by the Saussurian emphases, as these were modified and adapted by subsequent authors, this 'retreat' was never really established by philosophical argument. It derived from the assimilation of the doctrine of the arbitrary nature of the sign and that of the role of difference.

Derrida's writings are in some ways the most sophisticated outcome of the transition from structuralism to post-structuralism. Although Derrida's works seem on first contact to be quite alien to Anglo-Saxon eyes, there are some rather close affinities between them and views expressed by the later Wittgenstein. Derrida's disavowal of the 'metaphysics of presence' is by no means entirely dissimilar, either in its objectives or in its methods, from Wittgenstein's attempt to puncture the aspirations of metaphysics in *Philosophical Investigations*.[22] For both authors the goals of metaphysics cannot simply be re-examined, or somehow brought up to date; they have to be 'deconstructed' rather than 'reconstructed' because they rest upon mistaken premises. In both cases it is suggested that this is because of a misapprehension about the nature of reality. There are no essences to be captured by appropriate linguistic formulations. Wittgenstein is as firm as Derrida that neither words nor sentences involve some sort of corresponding mental images which supply their meaning, any more than the objects or events in the external world to which words can be used to refer. While Wittgenstein would no doubt protest against Derrida's ambitious extension of the concept of writing, he would agree with the latter author that language is not to be interpreted in terms of the subjective meanings of individual agents. Wittgenstein's rejection of the private language argument is obviously not directly an analogue of Derrida's embrace of the idea of writing, but in both

[21] See Anthony Giddens: *Central Problems in Social Theory*. London: Macmillan, 1979, chpt. 1 and following.

[22] Ludwig Wittgenstein: *Philosophical Investigations*. Oxford: Basil Blackwell, 1953.

instances language is necessarily an 'anonymous' production and thus in an important sense 'subject-less'.

Whether Wittgenstein would have had much regard for the idea of difference is, to say the least, debatable. Nonetheless, in his elaboration of the notion of language-games the 'spacing' of utterances and activities is plainly central. Both the recursive and the relational character of language are stressed. However it seems indisputable that the main lines of development of Wittgensteinian philosophy are more defensible than those worked out within post-structuralism. Rather than promoting a 'retreat into the code' Wittgenstein seeks to understand the relational character of signification in the context of social practices. His resolute preoccupation with ordinary language tends to inhibit a concern with poetics, art or literature. But there do not seem to be any distinctively logical barriers to extending Wittgenstein's ideas into these domains, while the account of language and meaning which can be generated from Wittgenstein's philosophy (or at least from certain basic notions contained within it) are more sophisticated than those available within structuralism and post-structuralism (a matter I shall develop further below).

The unsatisfactory character of the thesis of the arbitrary form of the sign, as diffused into structuralist and post-structuralist traditions, has radically impoverished the accounts of meaning such traditions have been able to offer. A preoccupation with signifiers at the expense of the signified is in large part an emphasis enforced by this circumstance. For Wittgenstein the meaning of lexical items is to be found in the intermeshing of language and practice, within the complex of language-games involved in forms of life. While no doubt this view, as formulated by Wittgenstein himself, leaves aside certain fundamental problems of meaning — in particular in what sense, if at all, the understanding of meaning implies a grasp of the truth-conditions of certain classes of assertions — it is surely a perspective of considerable fruitfulness.

The decentring of the subject

Although the phrase 'the decentring of the subject' has come to be peculiarly associated with structuralism and post-structuralism, the ideas involved derive from wider sources. As structuralist and post-structuralist authors themselves are fond of pointing out, psycho-analysis already showed the ego not to be master in its own home, its characteristics only being uncovered via a detour through the unconscious. Although this was not the interpretation which Sartre made, Heidegger's writings from *Being and Time* onwards can be taken to assert the primacy of being over consciousness.[23] Moreover, there is more than a diffuse connection between Freud, Heidegger and Nietzsche. Indeed, of course, the writings of each of these authors tend to figure prominently in the work of those associated with post-structuralism. This having been said, it is evident that we can discern the origins of the notion of the 'decentred subject' in Saussure.

According to Saussure, language is a system of signs, constituted by differences, with an arbitrary relation to objects. If this includes objects in the external world, it also must embrace the characteristics of the producer of language — the speaker. Just as the meaning of 'tree' is not the object tree, so the meaning of terms that refer to human subjectivity, most particularly the 'I' of the thinking or acting subject, cannot be the states of consciousness of that subject. Like any other term in a language, 'I' is only constituted as a sign in virtue of its differences from 'you', 'we', 'they', etc. Since the 'I' has sense only in virtue of being an element in an 'anonymous' totality, there can be no question of according it some distinctive philosophical privilege. In Saussure this idea is not developed in a direct way; moreover Saussure's own views are somewhat confusing in the light of the persistence of a certain mentalism in his writings. It was therefore left to others to develop what Saussure left largely implicit, and they did not hesitate to do so; there is probably no theme which more persistently appears in the literature of structuralism and post-structuralism.

Lévi-Strauss has written less in the explicit way about the decentring of the subject than have most of his successors. Nonetheless in certain respects his writings have been the main mediating link between Saussure and criticisms of 'humanism' in post-structuralist philosophy. Referring to his analysis of myths, Lévi-Strauss observes in a celebrated statement that he claims to show 'not how men think in myths, but how myths operate in men's minds without their being aware of the fact'; or again: 'myths signify the mind which evolves them by making use of the world of which it is itself a part'.[24] There is

---

[23] Martin Heidegger: *Being and Time*. Oxford: Basil Blackwell, 1978.

[24] Claude Lévi-Strauss: *The Raw and the Cooked*. London: Cape, 1969, pp. 12 and 341.

no 'I think' in this characterization of human mind. The unconscious categories of mind are the constitutive backdrop against which sentiments of selfhood exist. Consciousness is made possible by structures of mind not immediately available to it.

The decentring of the subject emerges in various guises in the post-structuralist literature. In Foucault's discussion of the beginnings and end of the 'age of man' it is primarily a set of historical observations about the development of Western philosophy and of Western culture as a whole. In Barthes, it is a series of claims about the nature of authors in relation to their texts. In Lacan, it is part of an attempt to rework the main concepts of psychoanalysis, giving of course especial attention to the idea that the unconscious exemplifies certain features of language. All these clearly share in common a critical attitude towards Cartesianism and to every philosophy (such as certain versions of phenomenology) which treats consciousness as a datum upon which the foundations of claims to knowledge may somehow be established. 'I think, therefore I am' is disqualified on a number of grounds. The 'I' is not immediately available to itself, deriving its identity as it does from its involvement in a system of signification. The 'I' is not the expression of some core of continuous selfhood that is its basis. The 'being' suggested in the 'I am' is not given via the capability of the subject to use the concept 'I'. What Lacan calls the 'discourse of the Other' is taken to be the source both of the capability of the subject to employ 'I' and the assertion of existence in 'I am'. As Lacan puts it: 'the Other is, therefore, the locus in which is constituted the I who speaks to him who hears, that which is said by the one being already the reply, the other deciding to hear it whether the one has or has not spoken.'[25]

All the above authors agree upon the irrelevance of the author to the interpretation of texts. The writer is not a presence somehow to be uncovered behind the text. Just as the primacy accorded to the author is an historical expression of the individualism of the Age of Man, so the 'I' of the author is a grammatical form rather than a flesh-and-blood agent. Since the text is organized in terms of the internal play of signifiers, what its originator or originators intended to put into it is more or less irrelevant to our understanding of it. Authors are to be found everywhere in their texts and consequently nowhere; as Barthes puts it: 'a text is . . . a multi-dimensional space in which a variety of

25 Jacques Lacan: *Écrits*. London: Tavistock, 1977, p. 453.

writings, none of them original, blend and clash.'[26] Once more, of course, this is not a conclusion which is specifically the province of structuralism or post-structuralism. The view of the 'autonomy' of texts reached by Gadamer, drawing primarily upon Heidegger, is in some respects directly comparable with that reached within the French traditions of thought.[27] In neither case is it believed that the author has some kind of privileged relation to his or her text. Both textual analysis and literary criticism therefore must break in a clear-cut fashion with 'intentionalist' perspectives.

The theme of the decentring of the subject is without doubt one which must be taken seriously by anyone interested in modern philosophy or social theory. But while the basic perspective surely must be accepted, the particular mode in which it is elaborated within structuralism and post-structuralism remains defective. To reject the idea that consciousness, whether consciousness of self or the sensory registering of the external world, can provide a foundation for knowledge, is to participate in one of the major transitions in modern philosophy. Those forms of philosophy, and therefore modes of social analysis based on them, which presume an unmediated access to consciousness are by now thoroughly discredited. Since some schools of philosophical thought, most notably phenomenology, have been closely associated with such philosophical standpoints, the rejection of those standpoints unavoidably compromises those schools of thought also. But structuralist and post-structuralist accounts of the decentring of the subject are inevitably closely tied to the versions of language and the unconscious associated with structuralist linguistics and its influence. The detour needed to recover the 'I' is not only taken very largely through language, but is in addition filtered through a particular theory of language as well. If we regard language as situated in social practices, and if we reject the distinction between consciousness and the unconscious followed by the structuralist and post-structuralist authors, we reach a different conception of the human subject — as agent. Again, this is a theme I shall pursue in what follows later.

[26] Roland Barthes: 'The death of the author', in *Image-Music-Text*. Glasgow: Fontana, 1977, p. 146.

[27] Hans-Georg Gadamer: *Truth and Method*. London: Sheed and Ward, 1975.

Writing and the text

Comparing Wittgenstein and Derrida, it is worth considering why the latter gives such a fundamental priority to the theme of writing, whereas in the former a concern with the significance of writing is largely absent. Derrida's preoccupation with writing is closely connected with his rejection of the metaphysics of presence. In Derrida's words:

> . . . no element can function as a sign without relating to another element which itself is not simply present. This linkage means that each 'element' — phoneme or grapheme — is constituted with reference to the trace in it of the other elements of the sequence of system . . . Nothing, in either the elements or the system, is anywhere ever simply present or absent.[28]

Thus, in Derrida's view, it is mistaken to suppose that writing is a particular mode of giving expression to speech. Writing — in the extended sense which Derrida attributes to the term — expresses more clearly than does speech the relational nature of signification as constituted both in space and in time. We might more accurately speak of the timing and spacing of signification, rather than its 'occurrence' in a given context. There are similarities with what Wittgenstein has to say here, both in respect of the 'deconstruction' of metaphysical questions about time and space, and the mode in which it is suggested that time-space is constitutive of the identity of objects or events. In commenting critically upon St Augustine's reflections on the nature of time, Wittgenstein argues that the puzzles with which Augustine grappled are empty of content, because they rest upon the mistaken attribution of an essence to temporality. It is actually the 'grammar' of time that needs elucidating. Time has no essence, and there is no abstract formulation that can therefore convey its nature. We can only experience and observe temporality in the unfolding of events. It might be argued that Wittgenstein does not in fact take the next step, and like Derrida (and before him Heidegger) treat time-space as constitutive of events and objects. But I think in fact there is no other way of making sense of Wittgenstein's philosophy save by presuming this to be intrinsic to the analyses he develops.

[28] Jacques Derrida: *Positions*. London: Athlone, 1981, p. 92.

Wittgenstein's struggles with form — his disinclination to write in a narrative style, and the seemingly disorganized character of the *Philosophical Investigations* — have a definite affinity with Derrida's use of various sorts of graphic innovations. For both writers wish to give expression to views that are refractory to being 'described'. Both assert that it is not the presence of some sort of reality, physical or mental, which serves to anchor the meaningful components of systems of signification.

The limitations of Derrida's view of writing can be understood when we consider what is involved in his 'timing' and 'spacing'. 'Writing', as Derrida conceives of it, is a direct development out of the separation of the signifier from an external world of objects and events which was established by Saussure. Derrida participates in the 'retreat into the text', the universe of signifiers, characteristic of structuralist and post-structuralist traditions of thought as a whole. His 'text' is that of the play of differences intrinsic to signification as such. Although the notion of *différance* makes it possible for Derrida to comprehend temporality, his treatment of space is purely nominal. Or to put things another way, although he talks of 'timing' and 'spacing', to all intents and purposes these are the same. The 'extending' of writing is involved in the spacing of sounds or marks, but this is the very same phenomenon as their temporal differentiation. Wittgenstein's portrayal of the relational character of signification as expressed in the organization of social practices, however, does not involve the collapsing of time into space. Time-space enters into the structuring of signification not via the 'flat' dimension of writing — even conceptualized as proto-writing — but via the contextuality of social practices themselves. For a long while, philosophers influenced by Wittgenstein were misled by the idea that the meaning of words or utterances consists in their use. From this it might seem to follow that we simply substitute 'use' for the objects to which words were held to correspond in previous theories of meaning. But what is at issue is not 'use', but the process of *using* words and phrases in contexts of social conduct. Meaning is not constructed by the play of signifiers, but by the intersection of the production of signifiers with objects and events in the world, focused and organized via the acting individual. If this view is basically correct, as I hold it to be, the priority which Derrida gives to writing over speech has to be questioned. For speech — or rather talk — recovers a priority over other media of signification. Talk, carried on in day-to-day contexts of activity, is the fundamental 'carrier' of signification, because it operates in saturated behavioural and conceptual contexts. Writing (in its more narrow conventional sense) has certain distinctive properties that can be explicated precisely only by contrasting them with the character of day-to-day talk. The constitution of meaning in such talk is the condition, moreover, of the signifying properties of writing and texts.

Derrida's emphasis upon writing informs a whole philosophy. But there are three other, more modest, senses in which a preoccupation with writing tends to be generated by structuralist and post-structuralist traditions. One concerns the connection of writing with power. In both Lévi-Strauss and Foucault, this theme is explored via the relation between orality and writing. Lévi-Strauss's structuralist method is supposed to apply only to oral cultures. Societies without writing are 'cold cultures' because they exist within a framework of reiterated tradition, passed on by example and by word of mouth. Civilizations presume the existence of writing, which is first and foremost a medium of administrative power, not simply a novel way of expressing what was previously formulated in speech. Writing not only generates 'history', it demands new modes of adjustment to both the social and material worlds. Society and nature become seen in terms of dynamism and transformation, no longer in terms of the saturation of the present by the past. In Lévi-Strauss's work, this theme is never developed in any detail, since he does not offer an analysis of civilizations. Rather, societies with writing form a backdrop against which the distinctive characteristics of oral cultures can more easily be pin-pointed.

In Foucault, a concern with the connections between writing, orality and power is more direct and more extensively spelled out. Foucault shows that the discourse of the social sciences and psychiatry does not simply form a set of theories and findings about a 'given' subject matter. On the contrary, the concepts and generalizations developed in these disciplines come to constitute new fields for the operation of power. Such fields of power are codified through and dependent upon writing. The keeping of written records — as for example, in the recording of the proceedings of law courts or of psychiatric case histories — is integral to the forms of disciplinary organization which Foucault seeks to analyse.

At the same time as, through the recording of events, writing 'makes history', those whose activities do not come to the attention of the record-keepers are excluded from 'history'. That is to say, while of course their activities comprise 'history' in the sense of the elapsing of events, neither their actions nor their ideas form part of that reflexive appropriation of the past that is written history. Thus as Foucault points out in *I, Pierre Rivière*, the case record of the criminal or the vagrant is one of the few modes of entry that those not ordinarily written into history have of figuring in its field of discourse.[29]

A second sense in which the theme of writing constantly recurs in structuralism and post-structuralism is simply in the guise of a fascination with texts generally. In formulating the outlines of a programme for semiology, Saussure initiated the possibility of a study of sign systems that goes well beyond textual materials. The call for the development of semiology was not ignored, and in many subsequent works we find developed the idea that any cultural difference can provide a means of signification. Yet although the idea of a unified discipline of semiology, or semiotics, has its advocates, on the whole it has to be said that the study of cultural signs remains a rather stunted enterprise. Those influenced by structuralism and post-structuralism continue to return to the text as their main preoccupation. It is surely not by chance that these traditions of thought have had more influence upon students of literature than in any other domain.

The absorption with texts symbolizes some of the greatest strengths, and at the same time the most consistent weaknesses, of structuralist and post-structuralist traditions. On the one hand, it has allowed authors within these traditions to develop analyses that have no rivals in Anglo-Saxon philosophy. The theory of the text is both made central to certain elementary philosophical issues and is elucidated through consideration of those issues. Apart from those within the relatively specialized field of literary criticism, English-speaking philosophers and social theorists have made very little contribution to such discussion. On the other hand, the overriding concern with texts reflects limitations in accounts of the nature of signification that can be traced from Saussure onwards. The thesis of the arbitrary character of the sign, as Saussure developed it, tends to elide the difference between texts which claim to deliver some veridical description of the world and those that are fictional. The positive value of such an elision is readily demonstrated, for example, in the subtle treatments which it makes possible of the use of figurative mechanisms in scientific texts. Its weaknesses are apparent in respect of the basic issue that has haunted these traditions: how to relate the text back to

[29] Michel Foucault: *I, Pierre Rivière . . . .: a case of parricide in the 19th century.* Harmondsworth: Penguin, 1978.

an exterior world. Not only have structuralist and post-structuralist traditions failed to generate satisfactory accounts of reference that would make sense of scientific achievements, they have become more or less completely cut off from the study of ordinary talk. Ordinary talk is precisely that 'medium of living in the world' in which reference and meaning interlace. I believe such to be the case, at least, and I think that pursuing this issue allows us to come to terms with some of the most deep-seated deficiencies of structuralism and post-structuralism.

A third sense in which these traditions of thought tend to produce a concern with writing is in respect of writing as an active process. The term 'writing' is ambiguous, since it can refer to what actually is recorded in a given medium, or to the actual process of bringing about that recording. In respect of the second of these meanings, writing has also come to take on a particular significance as the penning of books of imagination or invention. The 'writer', or literary author, tends to be accorded a special esteem in modern culture. In fastening upon the theme of the 'author', structuralists and post-structuralists have been able to make major contributions to our understanding of cultural production. Here obviously there is a major overlap with the more general theme of the decentring of the subject. The source of the 'creativity' displayed in texts is not to be discovered in the individual or individuals who wrote them. The text generates its own free play of signifiers, constantly open to appropriation and reappropriation by different generations of readers. Here there are interesting connections between structuralism, post-structuralism and the latter-day development of hermeneutics. In the work of Gadamer and others, as I have mentioned previously, we also find affirmed the autonomy of the text from its author and we find emphasized the multiplicity of readings that texts can generate. The processes of writing and reading become closely intertwined, with reading being the temporary stabilizing of the indefinite range of meanings generated by processes of writing. But again we find characteristic weaknesses here. Writing is sometimes portrayed as though texts wrote themselves; the relegation of the author to the role of a shadowy adjunct to writing is manifestly unsatisfactory. We might accept the significance of the theme of the decentring of the subject, and therefore the need to construct what an 'author' is. But we shall have no proper grasp of the process of writing unless we manage to recombine satisfactorily the elements that have been decentred. Structuralism and post-structuralism have in my view been unable to generate satisfactory accounts of human agency, in large part because of shortcomings already noted; and this weakness reappears in the shape of the tendency to equate the production of texts with their inner 'productivity'.

History and temporality

In Saussure's writings, it might seem as though the theme of temporality is thoroughly repressed. For after all Saussure's greatest innovation was to treat *langue* as existing out of time. Whereas previous forms of linguistics had concentrated upon tracing changes in the usage of linguistic items, Saussure placed language as a system at the forefront of linguistic analysis. *Langue* does not exist in a time-space context; it is built up inferentially from the actual practices of language users. Of course, Saussure did recognize a differentiation between the synchronic study involved in the analysis of *langue* and the diachronic analysis involved in tracing out actual changes in linguistic usage. Whether or not Saussure himself intended to give priority to synchrony over diachrony, it is certainly true that much of the subsequent attraction of his writings has concerned the diagnosis of properties of *langue*. Paradoxically, however, it is just this emphasis which has tended to stimulate a recurrent concern with temporality within structuralist and post-structuralist thought.

Some of the issues involved here are brought out rather clearly in the work of Lévi-Strauss. The methodological repression of time involved in Saussure's conception of *langue* is translated by Lévi-Strauss, as it were, into the substantive repression of time involved in the codes organized through myth. Myths do not so much take temporality out of social life as provide for a particular mobilization of time separating it from what is later understood as 'history'. Lévi-Strauss's notion of reversible time is deliberately contrasted to the movement of time in history, where 'history' is understood as the linear charting of social change.[30] As Lévi-Strauss has effectively emphasized in his debate with Sartre, a preoccupation with history is not at all necessarily the same thing as a concern with time. The Marxian adage that 'human beings make history' actually expresses the dynamism of a particular culture rather than representing a portrayal of the past existence of humanity as a whole. Hot cultures

[30] Claude Lévi-Strauss: *The Savage Mind*. Chicago: University of Chicago Press, 1966.

exist in dynamic interchange with their environment, and mobilize themselves internally in the pursuit of social transformation. Modern culture very substantially accelerates this dynamism. History for us therefore becomes the linear unfolding of dates, within which certain forms of change are mapped out. Oral cultures are genuinely 'prehistoric' when contrasted to such dynamism. For them, time is not mobilized as history. The writing of history is thus associated with that very historicity which separates hot cultures from their oral forerunners.

While Lévi-Strauss's conception of the structures of the human mind has often been criticized for being unhistorical, it might be more accurate to see him as seeking to provide a subtle and nuanced account of what history is in relation to temporality. Lévi-Strauss has sometimes even been said to be 'anti-historical', but this surely fails to discern the subtlety with which his discussion contrasts time and history. Structuralism, in its Lévi-Straussian form, has certainly not proved to be refractory to history, as some have claimed. Lévi-Strauss is effectively carrying out what Foucault was later to call an 'archaeology', digging below the historical consciousness of hot cultures to unearth the ground of temporality characterizing those forms of culture dominating human 'history'.

In Derrida, temporality of course appears as fundamental to the critique of the metaphysics of presence. To differ is also to defer, and time is regarded as inseparable from the nature of signification. The sliding of presence into absence becomes the very medium of understanding temporality. Here the concern is not so much with 'history', real or written, but with the understanding of being as becoming. Time is for Derrida bound up with the very nature of his appraisals of the limitations of structuralism as practiced by Lévi-Strauss. It is intrinsically part of the process whereby signification generates a play of meanings.[31] In replacing, in Culler's phrase, the 'anguish of infinite regress by the pleasure of infinite creation' Derrida affirms the evanescence of processes of meaning; everything should be understood 'as an active movement, a process of demotivating, rather than the structure given once and for all'.[32] I have already criticized this view, and not a great deal needs to be added to what was said previously. The tendency to reduce time to the spacing of

---

[31] Jonathan Culler: 'Jacques Derrida', in John Sturrock: *Structuralism . . . .*
[32] Jacques Derrida, *Positions*, p. 103.

signification effectively precludes a satisfactory treatment of the time-space relations within which the signifying practices occur.

Foucault writes as an historian, and it is in his work above all that the themes of temporality and structural analysis are explored. Foucault's critique of 'continuous history' is in his view closely related to the necessity of decentring the subject. Not only does history have no overall teleology, it is in an important sense not the result of the action of human subjects. Human beings do not make history, rather history makes human beings. That is to say, the nature of human subjectivity is formed in and through processes of historical development. Continuous history depends upon:

> the certainty that time will dispense nothing without restoring it in a reconstituted unity; the promise that one day the subject — in the form of historical consciousness — will once again be able to appropriate, to bring back under its sway, all those things that are kept at a distance by difference, and find in them what might be called its abode.[33]

Foucault's style of writing history therefore does not flow along with chronological time. Nor does it depend upon the narrative description of a sequence of events. Reading Foucault is an uncomfortable experience for those accustomed to more orthodox modes of writing history. Topics are not discussed in a temporal order and there are breaks in the description when the reader tends to expect continuity. Very little indication is given of whatever causal influences might be at work in the shifts or changes which Foucault analyses. Obscure though his epistemological reflections might often be, Foucault makes it clear enough that this historical style derives from a particular view both of time and of the historical nature of writing about history. The past is not an area of study formed by the secretion of time. If the elapsing of past time has any form at all, it is that of the interweaving of layers of epistemic organization, layers which need to be unearthed by means of 'archaeology'. There is more than an echo of Lévi-Strauss in Foucault's view that history is one form of knowledge among others — and of course, like other forms of knowledge, a mode of mobilizing power.

To have separated time from history, to have shown that there are properties of signification systems that exist outside time-space, and

[33] Michel Foucault: *The Archaeology of Knowledge*. New York: Pantheon, p. 12.

to have connected these with a re-examination of the nature of human subject — these are major achievements of structuralism and post-structuralism. But in these respects, as in the others previously discussed, the results are less than completely satisfying. Foucault's manner of writing history has a definite shock value. But in spite of his elaborate methodological discussions, the mode in which he practices history remains highly idiosyncratic. No real unification is achieved between the diagnosis of epistemes, as existing 'out of time', and the generative processes involved in historical organization and change. Having decentred the subject, Foucault is no more able to develop a cogent account of human agency than is managed by other writers in structuralist and post-structuralist traditions. That 'history has no subject' can readily be accepted. But Foucault's history tends to have no active subjects at all. It is history with the agency removed. The individuals who appear in Foucault's analyses seem impotent to determine their own destinies. Moreover, that reflexive appropriation of history basic to history in modern culture does not appear at the level of the agents themselves. The historian is a reflective being, aware of the influence of the writing of history upon the determination of the present. But this quality of self-understanding is seemingly not extended to historical agents themselves.

Signification, cultural production and writing

A theory of cultural production cannot be properly developed unless we possess an adequate account of the nature of human agents. In demanding a 'theory of the subject', in place of the presumption that subjectivity is the unmediated ground of experience, structuralism and post-structuralism have made a major contribution — albeit one which is not unique to these traditions of thought. But it is essential to insist upon the need for an interpretation of the agent, rather than the subject, and of agency rather than subjectivity alone. 'Subjects' are first and foremost agents. In explicating human agency, two elements which tend either to be lacking or downplayed in structuralist accounts need to be brought to the fore. One is what I have elsewhere called practical consciousness, the other is the contextuality of action. Structuralist thinking tends to operate in terms of a contrast between the conscious and the unconscious. For Lévi-Strauss and Lacan, the unconscious is the 'other face' of language. It is what cannot be said in words, but makes such saying possible. Now, we may agree that a concept of the unconscious is necessary to provide a comprehensive account of why human agents act as they do. We may also accept that the relation between what can and what cannot be put into words is of elementary significance in human activity. However if, unlike structuralism and post-structuralism, we seek to grasp human life within frameworks of practical action, we reach a different view from that characteristic of these schools of thought. What cannot be put into words, as Wittgenstein proposes, is what has to be *done*. Human action does not unfold as the result of programmed impulses. Rather, human beings reflexively monitor what they do as an intrinsic part of what it is that they do. Such monitoring is ordinarily not expressed discursively. It is carried on on the level of practical consciousness. It is nonetheless extraordinarily elaborate, and is a chronic feature of even the most trivial of human activities.

In speaking of the contextuality of action, I mean to rework the differentiation between presence and absence. Human social life may be understood in terms of relations between individuals 'moving' in time-space, linking both action and context, and differing contexts, with one another. Contexts form 'settings' of action, the qualities of which agents routinely draw upon in the course of orienting what they do and what they say to one another.[34] Common awareness of these settings of action forms an anchoring element in the 'mutual knowledge' whereby agents make sense of what others say and do. Context should not be identified with what makes a particular segment of action idiosyncratic. Settings of action and interaction, distributed across time-space and reproduced in the 'reversible time' of day-to-day activities, are integral to the structured form which both social life and language possess.

In this view, signification is presumed to be saturated in the settings of practical action. The meanings engendered within language would not exist were it not for the situated, yet reproduced, nature of social practices. Timing and spacing are basic to the generation and sustaining of meaning, both in respect of the ordering of settings and in the reflexive use of such settings to formulate verbal interchange. Rather than 'speech', which sounds formal, we should refer here to 'talk'. Talk, the casual exchange of conversation in the settings of day-to-day social life, is the grounding of all the more elaborate and formalized aspects of language use — or so I want to argue here. Talk, as Garfinkel has done more than anyone else to show, operates via the

[34] Anthony Giddens, *The Constitution of Society*, chpt. 1 and following.

indexicality of context and via the 'methodological devices' which agents use to produce a 'meaningful' social world.[35] Indexicality should not be identified with context-dependence. Such an identification was one of the main problems facing the early elaboration of ethnomethodological studies. Indexicality refers to the use of setting in order to produce context-freedom just as much as to the use of items specific to a particular time and place in the generation of meaning. The fact that meaning is produced and sustained via the use of methodological devices is fundamental to correcting the lapses of structuralism and post-structuralism. Meaning is not built into the codes or sets of differences associated with *langue*. The use of etcetera clauses, formulating, and other methodological devices, organizes meaning contextually. A competent language user has not merely mastered sets of syntactical and semantic rules, but the gamut of conventions involved in 'going on' in day-to-day contexts of social activity.

Cultural analysis focuses on the relation between discourse and what I shall henceforth call 'cultural objects'. By cultural objects, I mean artifacts which escape from contexts of presence, but which are distinct from objects generally in so far as they incorporate 'extended' forms of signification. Texts are the principal type of cultural object in this definition; however in modern times we have to add media of electronic communication. There are definite ways in which cultural objects contrast with the 'carrying' of language as talk. We can enumerate these characteristics as follows:

1) Cultural objects involve a distanciation of 'producer' from 'consumer'. This quality is shared with all material artifacts. All artifacts, not just cultural objects, involve a process of 'interpretation' in some part distinct from that implied in the monitoring of talk in contexts of co-presence. In ordinary talk, individuals routinely employ a diversity of aspects of setting in order to understand others and to 'gear' what they themselves say to such a process of understanding. The interpretation of cultural objects occurs without certain elements of the mutual knowledge involved in co-presence within a setting, and without the co-ordinated monitoring which co-present individuals carry on as part of ongoing talk.

[35] Harold Garfinkel: *Studies in Ethnomethodology*. Cambridge: Polity Press, 1984.

2) As a consequence of this, the 'consumer' or receiver becomes more important that the producer in the interpretative process. In contexts of co-presence, the production and interpretation of speech acts tend to be closely intertwined, as part of the serial and participatory nature of conversation.

3) Cultural objects, as distinct from artefacts in general, involve the following characteristics:

a) *A durable medium of transmission across contexts.* 'Medium' should be taken to refer both to the physical substance of the cultural object and to the means of its dissemination across different contexts.

b) *A means of storage,* which in the case of cultural objects involves *encoding.* 'Storage' means here the leaving of traces whereby information can be 'rescued' from the evanescence of talk. Information cannot be stored as material resources can be stored. Information is stored — just as structuralist and post-structuralists say — as the specification of differences. 'Encoding' refers to the ordered properties of differences between traces.

c) *A means of retrieval.* To retrieve information is to have a mastery of the forms of encoding it incorporates. Retrieval presumes a human agent who possesses certain skills e.g. literacy. It may also, at least in modern times, involve the use of mechanical devices without which access to the encoded material is unavailable.

The nature of cultural objects can only be understood in relation to talk. It is accepted by everyone that there is a close relation between culture, language and communication. According to the foregoing observations, this relation should be understood in terms of the basic role which talk, in contexts of practical action and co-presence, plays in the generation and sustaining of meaning. Language is a means of communication, but communication is not the 'objective' of talk. Rather talk expresses, and is expressed in, the variegated range of activities which it informs. The significance of cultural or informational objects is that they introduce new mediations between culture, language and communication. In talk, the agent and the setting are the means whereby culture is connected to communication. In contexts of practical action, communication through talk always has to be 'worked upon' by participants, although most of such 'work' is done routinely as part of the process of reflexive monitoring in practical monitoring. Cultural objects break this symmetry. Since language as 'carried' by cultural objects is no longer talk, it loses its saturation in the referential properties which language-use has in the contexts of day-to-day action. As a visible or recoverable trace, separated from the immediacy of contexts of talk, the signifier becomes of peculiar significance. The preoccupation of structuralism and post-structuralism with writing and with the signifier at the expense of the signified can surely be traced to this. The differentiation of the signifier from practical contexts of action at the same time places a new premium upon communication, as a result of the greater effort at interpretation that is necessary. Communication is no longer more or less taken for granted as a result of the methodological processes involved in the sustaining of conversations. More defined and explicit hermeneutic tasks have to be undertaken in order to forge the communicative link between the cultural object and its interpreter. Given that this is so, it is not surprising that as a formal discipline hermeneutics arose from difficulties involved in the interpretation of texts. If a hermeneutic element has never been particularly pronounced in structuralism or post-structuralism, it is because signification has been primarily dealt with in terms of the internal organization of codes, or as the play of signifiers, rather than as the 'recovery of meaning'.

What is writing, and how far does writing itself contribute to the autonomy of texts? What relation if any, do authors' intentions in writing texts have to interpretation subsequently made of them? Should a 'theory of the text' essentially be a theory of reading? These are all questions that have to be confronted in the wake of the impact of structuralism and post-structuralism, which have at a minimum compelled us to look at them in a new way.

We cannot best explicate what language or signification are through writing. In this, Derrida is wrong. We should assert the priority not of speech, but of talk, over writing. But this should not lead us to suppose that writing is simply a 'representation' of talk. For reasons already mentioned, it cannot be so. Just as the invention of writing introduced something new into history, the production of texts involves qualities distinct from those carried within day-to-day talk. The origins of writing are certainly relevant to grasping its generic significance. Writing did not first of all emerge as a means of describing objects or events in the world. Writing was first of all purely a mode of recording — storage in its pure form. In the early agrarian states, writing was an administrative device, making possible the co-ordination of material resources and human action across time and space. Writing was never therefore a 'translation' of the verbal into the visual. It signalled and expressed new modes of the co-ordination of activities in time-space. The earliest texts — lists, collations of items — have no author. That is to say, more important than the persons who produced them is who they were produced *for* and what uses were made of them.[36]

This strongly suggests that writing diverges from talk not just in terms of the intrinsic characteristics of each, but in terms of the broader forms of social organization in which each is involved. Writing in a certain sense gives a primacy to 'spacing' over 'timing' absent in talk. This is surely more important than the simple fact that writing is visual and talk is auditory. Talk (contrary to Saussure's view) is sequential and serial, rather than linear. Writing has no temporal differentiation, although obviously such differentiation is involved in any process of the reading of a text. The spatial order of writing, on the other hand, since it is 'out of time', does not impose upon the reader the same constraints of sequencing which are involved in talk. That is to say, the reader need not follow a text straight through, can look at the end before the beginning and so on.

Once it proceeds beyond simple listing, writing opens itself out to 'art' in ways in which talk does not. Even the most trivial forms of day-to-day talk involve immense skill and presume a great deal of learning. Talk can become art in the sense in which particular forms of convention or contrivance may be employed to secure certain expressive or communicative ends. Story-telling, displays of wit, rhetoric and drama exist in all types of society. The 'success' of these verbal forms, however, is directly involved with their performance in contexts of co-presence. Conceived of as a process of production, rather than as of a given form, writing as art has rather different characteristics. Writing is not a performance to an audience. The skills of a writer do not depend upon his or her capability to employ the qualities available in contexts of co-presence to influence others in desired ways. Talk is necessarily an individualized production, moreover, in a manner in which writing is not. Speech has a serial character, because only one speaker can talk at any particular time in a given context of co-presence. In the case of writing, it is usually irrelevant to any of the terms in which the 'success' of a text might be

[36] Anthony Giddens: *A Contemporary Critique of Historical Materialism.* London: Macmillan, 1981, vol. I.

judged whether one individual or many were involved in its production. Texts of any length have to be produced across periods of time, which may be very prolonged. While 'work' goes into the construction of meaning in even the most casual of conversations, a text therefore tends to be a 'work' in a more protracted sense. It is a 'labour', in which discipline and originality may commingle in the fashioning of the spacing of writing.

Ordinary language is 'open' in an important sense. Most of the words and phrases used in everyday talk do not have precise lexical definitions. As Wittgenstein showed, ordinary language is not thereby necessarily vague or indefinite. What gives ordinary language its precision is its use in context. Settings of talk are used by participants to define the nature of what is said. The openness of writing is rather different — something which may be obscured by the fact that similar linguistic forms, e.g. metaphor and metonymy, may be used in both talk and in writing. The openness of writing derives from the 'suspension' of reference involved in it. We have to be careful to specify what this means. Writing can be, and is more often than not, used to refer to objects and events in the world. This is very obviously the case for example in respect of a list. The referential properties of writing do not depend — although they are always parasitic upon — the referential qualities of talk. Meaning and reference are ordinarily closely combined in talk, not because talk is in any way primarily oriented towards description, but because it is carried on and organized within practical contexts of action. That is to say, meaning is sustained via the constant connecting of talk with the modalities of day-to-day experience. The referential properties of writing cannot be connected with settings in this way. Consequently, even the most bluntly and coldly referential of statements can be read rhetorically or figuratively, and vice versa. As examples of Japanese *haiku* demonstrate, if demonstration is needed, a list may very readily be read as a poem.

All these considerations are relevant to the question of the autonomy of texts. The traditional issue of how far a text can be understood without reference to the intentions of its author is one which can be approached both in the light of these considerations and the account of agency indicated earlier. Agents, as Schutz puts it, have overall projects in terms of which the intentionality of their activities is organized.[37] The writing of a text may involve just such a project or

[37] Alfred Schutz: *The Phenomenology of the Social World*. London: Heinemann, 1972.

projects. That is to say, an author will have a certain range of objectives in mind in producing a given text. However, these are unlikely to be as relevant to the understanding of a text as to the process of reflexive monitoring involved in the labour that goes into the text's construction. A text, to repeat, is a 'work' in the sense in which it involves a chronic process of 'monitored' production. An 'author' is therefore neither an amalgam of intentions, nor a series of deposits or traces left in the text. Rather, the author is a producer working in specific settings of practical action.

This does not resolve the issue that has polarized discussion of the nature of texts, the question of how far there is a 'correct' interpretation of a text which can be fixed in relation to the intentions of its author. As against 'textual relativism', Hirsch and others have argued that the author's intention provides a basis for recovering the original meaning of a text. Now 'intention' here can only be understood as 'project', in Schutz's sense. We can easily see that the projects which lead an author to produce a text are likely to be only marginally relevant to anyone reading that text. Authors may choose to write a given text for a range of particular motives, to gain fame, to make money, for self-satisfaction and so on. Moreover, it does not make much sense to ask what a text as a whole 'means'. We are much more likely to ask what an author meant by a particular sentence or paragraph, or what arguments are threaded through a text, than we are to ask what a text as a whole means; this is entirely consonant with the way in which we deploy the phrase 'what did you mean?' in day-to-day talk. When we examine this type of question, as addressed to texts, it is fairly clear that nothing is being asked about the particular producer. If one were to ask, 'what did Marx mean by such-and-such a section of *Capital*?', Marx's characteristics as an individual are unlikely to be invoked. We could in most cases replace this query with the more anonymous question, 'What did the author mean?'. In ordinary talk, when we ask 'what did x mean by that?', probably we most usually mean 'what did he or she mean to accomplish by saying x?'. That is, we address the issue of the illocutionary force of what is said. But the question might also imply 'what did he or she mean to communicate?'. 'Meaning' in this sense involves, as Grice says, that the speaker 'intended the utterance x to produce an effect upon another or others by means of their recognising this to be his intention'.[38] 'Meaning' here equals

---

[38] H. P. Grice: 'Meaning', *Philosophical Review*, vol. 66, 1957. See also: 'Meaning revisited', in N. V. Smith: *Mutual Knowledge*. London: Academic Press, 1982.

communicative intent and it can be shown that such intent can be discerned only when participants in a given context of interaction share forms of mutual knowledge. In ordinary talk, communicative intent can be checked by direct interrogation and by reformulation on the part of the original speaker. There seems no reason to deny that we can interrogate a text in a parallel manner. That is to say, we can ask what was the communicative intent involved in a given section of a text. Where the author is unavailable, we can seek to answer such a question by investigating the forms of mutual knowledge implied in what the author wrote. This entails in turn that there are criteria for the accuracy of interpretations.

These criteria, and the types of material that must be known to confirm them, are complicated. They involve essentially enquiring into the settings of production of the text as a work. They mean knowing a good deal about the way in which the author set out to produce the text and the intellectual resources drawn upon in its production. But they also involve knowing about the audience to whom the text was primarily addressed. Skinner and others have quite rightly pointed to the significance of this, emphasis upon which does not in any way deny the inherent autonomy of texts.[39] Texts are written within various conventions of form, style and readership. 'How' the reader is to take the text is 'worked upon' by the author in its production.

Structuralist and post-structuralist discussions of the 'disappearance of the author' have been valuable in several respects. We are led to recognize that many texts do not have 'authors' in the sense in which most of the works discussed in modern literary criticism do. This is not just true of texts written in the pre-modern period — biblical texts, sagas, archives and so on. It is also true of the vast majority of texts which circulate in modern societies. Records, files, case histories, bills, and so on — these characteristically do not have authors, in the sense that they are not attributed to one individual, may indeed be the product of several hands, and no one thinks it worthwhile ordinarily to enquire into which specific individuals produced them. It is obvious enough that the conditions of their production as texts have to be grasped both in relation to characteristics shared with artefacts in general and in terms of features of writing previously discussed. All

[39] Quentin Skinner: 'Meaning and understanding in the history of ideas', *History and Theory*, vol. 8, 1969.

artefacts which have a durable character can become more or less completely separated both from the contexts of their initial production and from the projects of those who created them. All artifacts similarly may be put to purposes, or even be 'interpreted', in ways of which their producers may never have dreamed. All texts turn the openness of language away from the modes in which, in talk, closure and fixity are achieved. How open to multiple interpretations a text is probably has little to do with the intrinsic nature of the text itself. Here we have to make the transition to an account of the readings which texts may help engender. Most of the remarks made about understanding the production of texts in relation to the reflexive monitoring of action also apply to reading. No text is read in isolation; all reading occurs within frameworks of 'inter-textuality' as well as in settings involving drawing upon mutual knowledge. Several recent approaches, that only partly if at all derive from structuralism and post-structuralism, are promising in respect of developing accounts of reading. An example is Jauss's 'reception aesthetics'.[40] In this view, a reader approaches a text with a 'horizon of expectations' without which the text would make no sense. According to Jauss, understanding the relation between works and their readers involves answering several questions. We must know what readers understand of the particular genre within which the work is written. We have to know about the reader's knowledge of previous texts similar to the one in question. And we must have a sense of the differentiation between practical talk and poetic language, something likely to shift between different places and different cultural settings. Since all authors are also presumably readers, such discussion has to be closely integrated with explication of the production of texts.

Conclusion

I make no claim in this analysis to have covered all the significant themes raised by the traditions of structuralism and post-structuralism. There are many divergencies between the ideas of the authors to whom I have referred which I have simply ignored or glossed over. I

[40] Hans Robert Jauss: 'Literary history as a challenge to literary theory', in Ralph Cohen: *New Directions in Literary History*. Baltimore: Johns Hopkins University Press, 1974.

have sought to portray the contributions of structuralism and post-structuralism in broad strokes, in order to suggest some general questions which they raise for social theory today. No doubt the assertion that these traditions have proved incapable of handling the very issues they have brought to the fore is contentious. I hope, however, both to have justified this allegation and to have shown how some of those issues might be more satisfactorily analysed.

5

Erving Goffman as a systematic social theorist

No one would question the claim that Erving Goffman was one of the leading sociological writers of the post-war period.[1] His writings have been more or less universally acclaimed for their luminosity, their charm and their insight. Probably no sociologist over this period has been as widely read both by those in neighbouring social science disciplines and by the lay public. Goffman's writings have an intrinsically accessible style that has convinced not a few sceptics that sociology is a rather more interesting subject than they may have thought. But all this having been said, Goffman would not ordinarily be ranked among the major social theorists. His work seems quite different in scope and intent from that of authors such as Parsons or Merton in American sociology, let alone such figures as Foucault, Habermas or Bourdieu elsewhere. For one thing, unlike these authors, Goffman writes for the most part in plain language. His texts do not abound with the strange sounding neologisms favoured by those who are more self-consciously 'theorists'. Moreover, his method seems cavalier. In his writings, observations drawn from social research jostle with illustrations derived from fictional literature and with casual assertions made with very little apparent empirical backing at all.

And yet I propose that Goffman should indeed be ranked as a major social theorist, as a writer who developed a systematic approach to

---

[1] This essay was prepared for a conference discussing Goffman's work held at the University of York in July 1986.

the study of human social life and one whose contributions are in fact as important in this regard as those of any of the other individuals mentioned above. There is a system of social theory to be derived from Goffman's writings, although some effort has to be made to unearth it and we cannot necessarily accept Goffman's own interpretations of his works in elucidating its nature. There are several reasons why Goffman's ideas are not usually approached from this perspective. One is his own perception of what he sought to achieve. He quite deliberately avoided any sort of engagement with issues concerning the large-scale or the long-term — although I shall argue later that his ideas are more relevant to such phenomena than he tended to suppose. Another reason is that Goffman's writings lack a certain cumulative quality. Virtually all of his books are assemblages of essays, rather than integrated works. There is a sense in which it does not matter where one starts to read them: the reader can dip in almost anywhere and pick up the flow of the author's reasoning. Moreover, although Goffman developed and modified certain of his key views over time, his books tend to stand in a similar relation to one another as do the chapters within them. That is, again one can start almost anywhere. Goffman's writings, as it were, mirror that episodic continuity characteristic of the day-to-day forms of social life he seeks to describe and analyse. By this very token his works can appear lightweight, brimming over with acute and delicate insights, yet lacking the overall intellectual power that derives from the endeavour of an author to grapple with general problems of society and history. Goffman might seem to have the brilliant but butterfly mind, like Simmel who was indeed in some degree a source of his inspiration. Simmel wrote over a considerably greater spectrum of issues in history and sociology than Goffman. Nonetheless, as compared with the work of, say, Max Weber, Simmel's writings lack that raw intellectual power generated by the work of his contemporary and friend.

Goffman's writings have been persistently misunderstood. To some degree these misunderstandings are the result of views of his work that Goffman himself tended to foster. But in some part they derive from a disinclination on the part of more 'orthodox' sociologists to grasp the significance of Goffman's writings for their own concerns. Goffman produced his major writings at a time at which sociology tended to be dominated by naturalistic and functionalist models of social activity. His work resisted incorporation within such perspectives. For many of those who thought that the major preoccupations of sociology lay with the then dominant outlook, Goffman's writings tended to be seen as no more than light relief from more serious business. Goffman himself undeniably helped to connive in this. He saw himself as working within a particular field of study having few direct implications for the central areas of sociological interest. Thus in *Frame Analysis*, arguably his most openly systematic work, he comments that his study is not about 'the organisation of society . . . I make no claim whatsoever to be talking about the core matters of sociology — social organisation and social structure. Those matters have been and can continue to be quite nicely studied without reference to frame at all.'[2] It is as if the forces that somehow create the structural characteristics of social systems are quite distant from the activities of individuals in their day-to-day lives. Actors seemingly move in a pre-structured social world, of which they must take account in their actions, but which they play no part in bringing into being or perpetuating. It is no doubt for this reason that Goffman's writings fit quite happily into that division between macro- and micro-studies so characteristic of a good deal of modern sociology. Goffman often labelled his work 'micro-sociological', apparently feeling entirely happy with such a designation. But he was usually careful to avoid the connotation that the micro level is somehow more fundamental than the macro. If he was in some sense a methodological individualist, it was not something he chose openly to defend.

There are four respects, I want to argue, in which Goffman's writings have been commonly misinterpreted. First, it is often asserted that Goffman's work is no more than a series of idiosyncratic observations about trivial features of social life. Brilliant, ironic and mordant as such observations may be, they have no overall intellectual unity. Goffman is thought to be someone overtaken by the tumble of his own ideas, which scatter in all directions and resist any kind of overall consolidation. Familiar though such a view may be, it is surely quite mistaken. From his earliest writings, Goffman has quite clearly been preoccupied with a number of concerns that reappear in all his writings. As he puts it, he has been absorbed by the study of social interaction, which

> can be identified narrowly as that which uniquely transpires in social situations, that is, environments in which two or more individuals are physically in one another's response presence . . . My concern over the years has been to promote acceptance of this face-to-face domain as an

2 Erving Goffman: *Frame Analysis*. New York: Harper, 1974, p. 13.

analytically viable one — a domain which might be titled, for want of any happy name, the *interaction order* — a domain whose preferred method of study is micro analysis.[3]

Second, it is sometimes suggested that Goffman is little more than a cynical observer of white American middle-class mores. However acute Goffman's insights might be, they only apply over a very restricted milieu, to the self-seeking activities of individuals living in a competitive, individualistic cultural environment. Goffman himself seems a little uncertain in this respect. Thus in one of his most well-known works, he remarks: 'my own experience has been mainly with middle-class conduct in a few regions of America, and it is to this that most of my comments apply'.[4] However while this may be an appropriate reserve in respect of some of the generalizations he seeks to make, nothing is more plain than that Goffman's writing is neither perceived by him, nor could be plausibly argued to be, merely a record of certain particular features of American culture. To the contrary, Goffman often makes it clear that he believes the forms of activity and the social mechanisms he describes are of very wide generality indeed. Far from only applying within a particular society, many may actually have relevance to social interaction at all times and places. Whether this be so or not, it is not difficult to see that Goffman's works contain a whole series of generalizing terms. These are not concepts that are incidental to the observations that he generates, but in large part the means of generating them at all.

Closely related to this point is a misunderstanding concerning the nature of the actors portrayed in Goffman's writings. These are sometimes thought of as mere 'performers', concerned to pander to their own vanities by presenting themselves to others in a false or manipulative fashion. Construed in this way, Goffman's works might very well be thought to be a portrayal — and no doubt a slanted portrayal at that — of a culture in which appearance is all and self-seeking individuals predominate. Yet Goffman is neither a disillusioned observer of the modes of activity he analyses, nor are those whose behaviour is examined specifically self-seeking.[5] Gouldner is surely

[3] Erving Goffman: 'The interaction order', *American Sociological Review*, vol. 48, 1983, p. 2.

[4] Erving Goffman: *Behaviour in Public Places*. New York: Free Press, 1963, p. 5.

[5] See Anthony Giddens: *The Constitution of Society*. Cambridge: Polity Press, 1984, chpt. 2.

wrong when he says that Goffman's work is expressive of, not merely particular sectors of American society, but that society at a particular phase of its development — following the decline of the moral discipline provided by the protestant ethic. Goffman's writing, according to him,

> reflects the new world, in which a stratum of the new middle class no longer believes that hard work is useful or that success depends upon diligent application. In this new world there is a keen sense of the irrationality of the relationship between individual achievement and the magnitude of reward, between actual contribution and social regulation. It is the world of the high-price Hollywood star and of the market for stocks, whose prices bear little relation to their earnings.[6]

Goffman is thus held to portray an amoral social universe, in which everyone is busy trying to manipulate everyone else. But this is far removed indeed from the main thrust of his writings, which not only describe a highly moralized world of social relationships, but tend strongly to generalize its moral nature also. Trust and tact are more fundamental and binding features of social interaction than is the cynical manipulation of appearances. Thus people routinely shore up or 'repair' the moral fabric of interaction, by displaying tact in what they say and do, by engaging in 'remedial practices', and helping others to save face. If day-to-day social life is a game which may be on occasion turned to one's own advantage, it is a game into which we are all thrust and in which collaboration is essential.

Finally, Goffman's writings are often mistakenly presented as though they were an ethnography, an anthropology of culture. The reason why is easy enough to see, because Goffman employs none of the sophisticated modes of quantitive research or analysis favoured by many sociologists. If anthropological method be identified with the qualitative study of the small scale, based upon participants' observations, then Goffman's writings do have a definite 'anthropological bias'. Nonetheless, it would be an error to make too much of this. As it is often understood, at any rate, ethnography involves the detailed study of specific communities, analysed over a lengthy period of time. Goffman's work has one of its main points of origin in just such a study, in the shape of the doctoral dissertation which he wrote describing a Shetland Isle community. But most of his subsequent

[6] Alvin Gouldner: *The Coming Crisis of Western Sociology*. London: Heinemann, 1971, p. 381.

studies do not fall into this category at all, or only marginally so. As has been mentioned, Goffman does not undertake any detailed cross-cultural comparisons in respect of the material he discusses and the examples he offers. The presumption is that others might test out the degree of generality of his ideas if they should be moved to do so. Goffman is interested in the alien and the exotic, but not in the sense of comparative ethnology. He seeks to disclose the unfamiliar in the familiar, to produce an intellectual estrangement from what is most common and habitual in our day-to-day activities.

When offering an overall characterization of his writings, Goffman is more prone to invoke the example of ethology rather than ethnography. Social groups of animals interest him because animals lack that capacity so essential to human social organization — which he describes as the outer limits of his studies of interaction — communication with others absent in space and time. In animal groups, almost by definition, all that goes on is the result of the influences of physical co-presence. As Goffman puts this:

> Ethologists are forced to end up being students of face-to-face interaction. So they are a source. More important, they have developed a field discipline that leads them to study animal conduct in very close detail and with a measure of control on preconception. In consequence, they have developed the ability to cut into the flow of apparently haphazard activity at its articulation and to isolate natural patterns. Once these behavioural sequences are pointed out to the observer, his seeing is changed. So ethologists provide an inspiration.[7]

When as he quite often does Goffman refers to his studies as 'naturalistic', this has very little to do with the 'naturalism' involved in the views of those influenced by logical positivism. It denotes both an attitude of the observer and a trait of the interaction that is observed.

Clearing up these misconceptions will allow us quite readily to disclose the systematic content of Goffman's writings. But there is more than one level upon which this can be done. We can first of all attempt to outline the systematic social theory that Goffman himself seeks to advance in his work. Given the rather seamless nature of his writings, this is not quite as easy to achieve as it might be. There is no overall study in which Goffman brings together his main ideas in a fully developed manner. But it is not enough only to set out Goffman's

[7] Erving Goffman: *Relations in Public.* London: Allen Lane, 1971, p. 54.

own understanding of his work. A critical analysis of Goffman's own interpretation of his ideas can help us see how far they might be incorporated into a version of social theory that escapes the brackets he put around his own writings.

Encounters, framing and co-presence

Goffman is above all the theorist of co-presence, not of small groups. His work therefore cross-cuts the distinction between primary and secondary group and other similar distinctions well entrenched in the sociological literature. For one thing, many small groups (for example, the family or kinship groups) endure over time. Goffman is not really interested in the mechanisms of such endurance. Moreover, co-present gatherings can be quite large, as in the case of theatre audiences or crowds. Interaction in circumstances of co-presence tends to oscillate between unfocused and focused exchanges. Unfocused interaction, in Goffman's definition, exists in so far as individuals who are co-present in a particular setting have some kind of mutual awareness. Focused interaction, Goffman's main concern throughout his writings, involves individuals directly attending to what each other are saying and doing for a particular segment of time. While the prototype is conversation, many other activities may claim the attention of parties to a given situation of co-presence. Focused interaction, Goffman points out, shares certain properties with those of small groups.[8] But the differences are at least as important as the similarities. All groups or collectivities, whether large-scale or small, have some general traits of organization. These include a division between roles, provision for socialization, capability for collective action, and sustained modes of connection with the surrounding social environment. Groups exist when their members are not together. Encounters, on the other hand, by definition only exist when the parties to them are physically in each other's presence. From such togetherness a range of characteristics flow. 'Examples of such properties include embarrassment, maintenance of poise, capacity for non-distractive verbal communication, adherence to a code regarding giving up and taking over the speaker role, and allocation of spatial position'.[9] In focused interaction,

[8] Erving Goffman: *Encounters*. Indianapolis: Bobbs-Merrill, 1961, p. 8.
[9] Ibid., p. 11.

the participants must maintain continuous involvement in the mutual focus of activity. This cannot be a property of social groups in general, precisely because of their persistence across different contexts of co-presence. Encounters may be a particular aspect or phase of the existence of collectivities, but to assimilate the two is to miss the distinctive features of encounters upon which Goffman wishes to concentrate attention.

Groups may come together in a regular manner, and their members may even all be frequently present together in particular settings. We might tend to think that these gatherings are 'meetings of the group' and that to study them is to study the group in an immediate fashion. In fact, Goffman says, we should regard such encounters as meetings of the individuals who are the members of a group, and seek to understand what goes on in terms of their participation within a particular form of encounter, not in terms of their membership of the group. Goffman insists on this strongly, because it is a key part of his attempt to mark out a distinctive subject matter concerning the 'interaction order'. The processes which sustain group relations across time and space are not necessarily the same as those underlying such an interaction order. Thus, for example, Goffman proposes that the modes of tension management in each are different. Tensions develop in encounters when the 'official' focus of attention is disturbed or threatened. Modes of managing such tensions may act to inhibit bases of group identity or affiliation. Thus a particular attention focus may be altered or redefined by participants to an encounter in order to cope with perceived threats to the original focus of attention. But this may have the effect of dissolving, at least in the particular context, the group relations in which some co-present individuals are involved.

Goffman's concern is therefore with 'situated activity systems'. He is not interested in, nor does he seek to analyse, for example, the role of a doctor in relation to the wider medical community. He studies the doctor only in terms of his or her activities within the settings of a single social establishment. But even here Goffman chooses to ignore the detailed round of activity which the individual follows. Only some of this round of activities involves the person in situated activity systems — encounters forming focused interaction with others.

> The performance of a surgical operation is an example. Illustrations from other walks of life would be: the playing through of a game; the execution of one run of a small group experiment; the giving and getting of a haircut. Such systems of activity are to be distinguished from a task

performed wholly by a single person, whether alone or in the presence of others, and from a joint endeavour that is 'multi-situated', in that it is executed by subgroups of persons operating from different rooms.[10]

Of course, Goffman does on occasion make an attempt to approach the overall study of social organization directly — most specifically, in his account of 'total institutions'. But even here his prime concern tends to be with how the overall features of the organization influence modes of interaction within specific settings.

A concentration upon co-presence draws attention to the body, its disposition and display — a theme that runs throughout the whole of Goffman's writings. Information conveyed in contexts of co-presence is necessarily embodied and Goffman specifically contrasts this to communications of a disembodied type, such as those involved in a telephone conversation, or an exchange of letters. The body is not simply an 'adjunct' to communication in situations of co-presence; it is the anchor of the communicative skills which can be transferred to disembodied types of messages. There are some circumstances in which embodied messages may be essentially one-way, as for example when one person spies on another through a hole in the wall, or when a psychologist observes subjects in an experiment through a one-way vision screen. Such circumstances, however, are unusual.

Normally any individual who is in a position to receive embodied messages from others also makes himself or herself available for embodied information that is accessible to them.[11] In focused interaction, according to Goffman, this is of basic importance. For it presumes and calls forth a monitoring by each individual of the other's or others' responses in relation to their own. Each individual, in other words, not only has an audience in relation to whom he or she must 'perform,' but knows that others see his or her activities in the same light.

> Ordinarily, then, to use our naked senses is to use them nakedly and to be made naked by their use. We are clearly seen as the agents of our acts, there being very little chance of disavowing having committed them; neither having given nor received messages cannot be easily denied, at least among those immediately involved.[12]

[10] Ibid., p. 96.
[11] Erving Goffman: *Behaviour* . . . , p. 15.
[12] Ibid., p. 16.

The norms or rules that regulate behaviour in circumstances of co-presence thus have a special form, and a variety of nuances, not possessed by other types. In the matter of sustaining face-to-face communication, everyone is in the affair together and can be seen to be so. Certain desired outcomes may be facilitated by this, but there always are attendant risks. In the presence of one another, individuals become open to forms of psychic and physical molestation that cannot be operated at a distance. Given the inherent reciprocity of such interaction, others of course become equally vulnerable. Every instance of interaction thus has an inherently confrontational character, but it is one typically balanced and managed by the resources individuals mutually apply to ensure respect and consideration for one another.

Every individual brings to an encounter a personal biography and a range of personality characteristics. Roles specify generalized expectations to which an individual has more or less closely to conform when in a particular situated context. However all roles can be performed in a manner giving them a particular personal stamp, allowing the individual to utilize particular means of self-expression. In the theatre, the role 'is' the person — even though we may be fully aware that there is an actor playing the part. But in real contexts of social life, neither a single role nor a cluster of roles that an individual plays correspond to the person. The question that is frequently asked of Goffman's work — Is there a self which stands behind the diversity of roles any given individual plays? — has to be answered in the affirmative. Goffman's definition of the acting self, to be sure, is usually rather vague. But he makes it clear enough that 'perduring moral character . . . animal nature, and so forth'[13] has to be distinguished from the multiplicity of roles that are enacted. The person is not some sort of mini-agent, standing behind and directing various role-performances. Such performances are essential to agency and to the demonstration of agency to others. The self consists in an awareness of identity which simultaneously transcends specific roles and provides an integrating means of relating them to personal biography; and furnishes a set of dispositions for managing the transactions between motives and the expectations 'scripted' by particular roles.

All roles involve situated performances. But these are neither exhaustive of the role nor are they necessarily the same as the 'situated roles' that emerge in encounters. Situated roles may consolidate the

---

[13] Erving Goffman: *Frame Analysis*, p. 573.

expectations involved in a more encompassing role, or they may inhibit them. To illustrate this, Goffman gives the example of riders on a merry-go-round.[14] A merry-go-round seems to provide both an objectively prescribed distribution of positions and an 'activity circuit' that is mechanically given. But when individuals are arranged in this fashion, a type of social interaction typically emerges which meshes together the individuals taking the ride. As in other circumstances of co-presence, there is much opportunity for reciprocal communication and the generation of feeling. While the ride goes on, there may be brought into being a mood of collective excitement linking all individuals involved. For children, the modes of expression involved may be consistent with 'expected' behaviour. However for adults, succumbing to the mood of collective intensity can cause problems because this might be seen to diverge from the usual expectations of an adult or parental role; a certain measure of embarrassment might therefore creep in once the ride is over. Those who run the roundabout maintain their distance from such activity systems by casual displays of mastery of the moving vehicle, nonchalantly carrying out manoeuvres which the uninitiated would not dare even to attempt.

Roles may be played at as well as played. Hence the possibilities for children, and stage actors, to mimic what in other circumstances is done with serious intent and with real consequences. The distinction is more blurred than may appear at first sight, however, because all roles demand some sort of authentication of the individual's capability to play them. Hence the significance of the dramaturgical metaphor in Goffman's writings, a metaphor the limitations of which, contrary to what his critics often assert, he is acutely aware. Individuals who act out roles are not and cannot be just like individuals who act at roles. This is exactly why Goffman's analysis of role distance is so interesting and penetrating. Role distance is not available to those who play at roles — unless this is a child mimicking the specifics of a situated role performance of an adult. Role distance depends upon a separation between self and role, but may be the means whereby an identity with the seriousness of that role is maintained. It can be a way of demonstrating supreme confidence in the performance of tasks involved in a particular role. By demonstrating to others that he or she does not fully 'embrace', in Goffman's term, the expectations involved in a role, the individual might actually validate rather than cast doubt upon its authenticity. Thus a surgeon who finds time for small talk,

[14] Erving Goffman: *Encounters*, p. 97.

and even banter, during a course of performing an operation might be able thereby to reassure colleagues about his or her competence, and might do so more effectively than another who adopts a more sober and inflexible demeanour.

In *The Presentation of Self in Everyday Life* Goffman tends to concentrate upon situations in which performances are manipulated in such a way as to conceal the true motives of those who carry them out, and where such performances are deliberately staged. No doubt the view that he portrays a cynical world of self-concerned agents, in which appearance counts above all else, derives from this.[15] It is a perspective that it is corrected in Goffman's subsequent works. Performances do allow individuals to cut a dash; they may be used as a means of concealing feelings of indifference, or even of loathing, towards others with whom role expectations imply some kind of positive relationship. Performances are however just as frequently used to reassure others of genuine motives and commitments as they are to disguise insincerities.

Goffman's preoccupation with co-presence leads him to be constantly alert to the significance of time and space in relation to human activities. As Goffman defines it, social interaction is inherently circumscribed in time-space. The timing and spacing of contexts of encounters gives social life an episodic character. Episodes are 'strung out' in the day-to-day experience of the individual, but also are the occasion of daily collaboration in social settings. The architecture of locales is very significant for encounters, because it focuses specific types of available co-presence and influences the spacing of contacts undertaken. All encounters tend to have 'markers' that establish their beginning and end. All encounters are also limited by the character of the physical setting. Boundary markers, as Goffman puts it, 'occur before and after the activity in time and may be circumscriptive in space; in brief, there are temporal and spatial brackets . . . one may speak, then, of opening and closing temporal brackets and bounding spatial brackets'.[16] The settings of interaction, for Goffman, are not just milieux within which activities happen to occur. Rather, they are routinely monitored, in common with the activities of co-present individuals, in the sustaining of encounters. The time-space zoning of encounters is often fundamental to the performances that are carried

---

[15] Erving Goffman: *The Presentation of Self in Everyday Life*. New York: Doubleday, 1959.

[16] Erving Goffman: *Frame Analysis*, pp. 251—2.

on. The existence of back regions, for example, helps to explain a good deal of what goes on in 'public' settings of activity.

The spacing of individuals within encounters is of vital importance to their form. Goffman's interest lies particularly in settings of interaction which are relatively fluid. In such settings, focused interaction occurs against the background of fluctuating relations of an unfocused kind. This is true, for example, of conversations at parties, of a couple who exchange the time of day against the background of a hurrying street crowd, or individuals who talk to one another in a hospital ward. Of course there are more highly organized and ritual settings of co-presence, in which the timing and spacing of appropriate responses is much more formalized. Goffman in general has much less to say about these than about more informal meetings and gatherings. The logic of this is apparent in the light of his professed concentration upon the interaction order. For there is in his view much more likely to be a direct relation between generalized roles and behaviour in the setting of co-presence in these latter circumstances than in the former. The very formalization of the setting, and of the nature of turn-taking in communication expresses this in, for example, a court of law.

More formalized settings of interaction are those likely to be most closely linked with defined back regions, because in these regions control can to some degree be relaxed. Not just back regions, but a variety of barriers to perception can be used as 'involvement shields', behind which activities that would otherwise be disapproved of can be carried on. All organizations in which formalized role relations are called for have areas, or sometimes only nooks and crannies, which allow such shelter. As Goffman points out, actors may maintain a certain level of presentability in relation to likely responses of others even when alone. For if an individual is inadvertently discovered 'out of play', both that person and the intruder are likely to suffer embarrassment.

In circumstances of co-presence, it is not enough for an individual to be an agent, that is, routinely to monitor reflexively and organize what he or she does; that person must also be seen to 'demonstrate agency' to others. Goffman approaches the analysis of 'action' from three rather different angles. Action means first of all the capability of agents to understand what they do and to use that understanding as part of the doing of it. Action in this sense occurs within primary frameworks, which are the grounding of our experience of ourselves as agents. Goffman's preferred term for this is 'guided doings'. In guided doings we monitor what we do in relation to the natural and to the social worlds. We employ primary frameworks both to direct the course of our own activities and to understand those of others as being different from events of nature. 'When the sun comes up, a natural event; when the blind is pulled down in order to avoid what has come up, a guided doing.'[17] Unlike most of those who have written about agency, however, Goffman suggests that the individual must chronically display agency to others. Actors routinely have to display competence in terms of control of bodily manoeuvring, positioning and the interpretation of communications from others. That this is so, Goffman points out, can be demonstrated by what happens in situations where the individual experiences a lapse of control — either in what is done or in what is said. One category of 'response cries' is bound up with such lapses. A response cry is not a statement, even a highly elliptical one; nor is it apparently directed at another. However, a response cry uttered when one drops something, or otherwise makes a hash of something one can ordinarily accomplish without too much difficulty, has the consequence of demonstrating to others both awareness of the lapse and that it is only a lapse, not a sign of generalized incompetence of bodily management.[18]

There is a third sense of action to which Goffman gives a good deal of attention. This is action in the sense of 'where the action is'. We might see this as a rather inconsequential sense of the term, compared with the two others. Yet its importance in Goffman's eyes is considerable. For discovering 'where the action is' is an exploration and accentuation of those very qualities which define the particular character of experiences and encounters, setting them off from the wider world. 'Where the action is' is where the individual feels a sense of worth and engrossment, 'a plane of being, an engine of meaning, a world in itself, different from all other worlds . . .'.[19]

Focused interaction always involves 'face engagements'. Where two or more individuals are co-present, and not involved in a focused way with one another, they may, in many circumstances at least, gaze quite openly at others. It is equally possible for a person to treat others present on the scene as though they were not there, as not worthy of a glance — although this is something that has to be

17 Ibid., p. 24.

18 Erving Goffman: *Forms of Talk*. Oxford: Basil Blackwell, 1981, pp. 101 — 3.

19 Erving Goffman: *Encounters*, p. 26.

controlled and is very rarely the same as genuinely not noticing something in the environment.

But this kind of behaviour contrasts with what is normal, which Goffman labels 'civil inattention'. The actor shows that he or she is aware that the others are there, while not making those others the object of any special curiosity. Thus the eyes of one person may quickly look over the eyes of someone approaching along a street, but no 'recognition' is typically permitted. Glances of this sort are not sustained as the two individuals actually pass one another, when there is normally a mutual avoidance of gaze. There is, as Goffman expresses it, a kind of 'dimming of lights'. Civil inattention, like all other aspects of the monitoring of the body and its gestures demands chronic attention to detail. Its significance is that each individual implies to others that he or she has no reason to fear them and vice versa. The management of civil inattention demands that the gaze be neither too direct, nor too averted or 'defensively dramatic'; in both cases this might indicate to others the possibility that there is 'something going on'.[20]

The complexities of civil inattention are many. We may ordinarily inspect others in a more prolonged way if we are distant from them and as long as eye contact does not occur. The closer an individual is to another, the more exposed each will be to the other and the greater the obligation they will tend to feel to maintain a clearly demonstrated civil inattention. Mild embarrassment is likely to result if one individual turns suddenly and catches the gaze of another, thereby seeing that person looking too intently at him or her. The person thus caught out might then in a prudent way act as though this was just a coincidental crossing of glances during the course of permissible observation, or perhaps indicate that he or she is in fact trying to catch the attention of someone standing just behind the individual involved. Staring in turn is frequently used as the first mode of sanction when the proprieties of civil inattention are not observed. As Goffman points out, it is often the first and last warning that it is necessary to provide to individuals who transgress in such a manner. Those who bear visible stigmata may feel themselves especially vulnerable to transgressions of the rules of civil inattention; while others might find it particularly difficult both to maintain those rules in a judicious fashion in respect of them and to 'give off' the expression

[20] Erving Goffman: *Frame Analysis*, pp. 84—5.

to the individual that he or she is being treated just the same as any one else.

Focused interaction, requiring continuous face-engagement, always involves the provision of 'openings' demonstrating the abandonment of civil inattention. Where individuals are strangers, the moment of discarding civil inattention is potentially perilous, since a range of misunderstandings can ensue about the nature of the encounter which is being established. Although there are many circumstances in which the nature of the setting allows for a clear-cut definition of the forms of encounter established therein, there are equally many settings in modern societies where such is not the case. Hence even the joining of eye contact may first of all be ambiguous and tentative. An actor who wishes to control the encounters to which he or she is likely to be subject in a particular setting will deliberately avoid certain eye contacts. Thus a customer might unavailingly try to catch the eye of a busy waiter, the latter taking some care to avoid such contact being made. Once a face-engagement has been opened, via the maintenance of mutual gaze and by their spatial positioning individuals tend to maintain a 'huddle', providing the opportunity to monitor each other's contributions and reactions in an intensive fashion — and by the same means to keep others who may be co-present more or less excluded. In situations where, for one reason or another, individuals find themselves in enforced physical proximity, such as in a lift, ordinary conversation may be suspended, or carried on in a limp fashion, being resumed when more normal spacing is possible. Even the most evanescent of encounters tends to establish something of a bond of moral solidarity between participants. The more protracted an encounter is, the more developed such a bond tends to be, and the mutual obligations associated with it to deepen. Once initiated, an encounter brings into being a 'relationship wedge'.[21] As soon as one has extended the consideration to another of attending to what that person says, some sort of moral commitment is established, which each may use as a basis of further claims put upon the other.

> In noting the implicit contract that makes persons present delicately accessible and inaccessible to each other, we can go on to note a basic margin of appetite and distaste to be found in social situations. The reasons why individuals are obliged to restrain themselves from making encounter overtures provide many of the reasons why they might want

[21] Ibid., p. 105.

to do so. And the obligation to be properly accessible often covers a
desire to be selectively quite unavailable.[22]

Naturally, what applies at the beginning of encounters also occurs
when they are broken off, or the individual disengages from focused
interaction. Signals or markers are ordinarily provided of the intention
to close the encounter; in most circumstances these must be
accompanied by the use of tactful devices whereby the moral bond
that has been established between the individual and the other or
others is not placed in question by the termination of the encounter.

Goffman gives a good deal of attention to the timing and spacing of
encounters. When an individual is permitted to move into a particular
region, he or she is usually expected to display some sensitivity to the
boundaries that surround it. Sometimes these boundaries are so
complete that they insulate the situation of interaction entirely. In the
vast majority of circumstances, however, some kind of communication
across the boundary is possible. Physical divisions, such as the walls
between rooms, tend to be treated as though communication were cut
off from the outside regardless of how far in fact this is the case. Walls
are socially respected communication barriers as much as they are
purely material divisions between the enactment of various forms of
encounters. Eavesdropping is a breach of the tact which is expected in
respect of encounters of which one is not a part and hence
embarrassment is the likely consequence if someone stumbles across
the eavesdropper. 'Accessible' face-engagements — those that are
carried on in circumstances where there are others present — involve
special forms of timing and spacing. In addition to the spacing of the
body, this is accomplished also by the sound-level of the voice, and by
what is spoken about at particular phases of the encounter. 'Sensitive'
topics will not be discussed when others to whom they might be
relevant are in the immediate vicinity. This often has to be carefully
managed, even if it is for the most part done quite routinely, or
otherwise a given conversational huddle might look like a furtive knot
of conspirators. However since co-present individuals tend to co-
operate in the maintenance of encounters, those not party to a
particular face-engagement will tacitly collaborate in maintaining
'conventional engagement closure'. Where participants in focused
interaction cast their voices too low, this in fact is likely to be thought

[22] Ibid., p. 106.

impolite, since it tends to discredit the disposition of others to display civil inattention.

Talk is the basic medium of focused encounters and conversation is the prototype of the exchange of utterances involved in talk. Using the word 'talk' rather than 'language' is important for the analyses Goffman seeks to provide. 'Language' suggests a formal system of signs and rules. 'Talk' carries more the flavour of the situated nature of utterances and gestures embedded within the routine enactment of encounters. In speaking of verbal 'conversations', rather than of 'speech', Goffman stresses that the meaning of what is said must be interpreted in terms of a temporal sequence of utterances. Talk is not something which is just 'used' in circumstances of interaction. The meanings deployed through talk are organized and specified by the whole range of subtleties of management of face, voice, gesture and disposition of the body brought into play in circumstances of co-presence generally. In his early work, Goffman both anticipated and helped shape the development of what has subsequently come to be called 'conversational analysis'; in his later writings he has drawn upon it in developing his own discussions of talk and interaction. Only one person can talk at a time in a conversation, so all conversations are organized in terms of turn-taking procedures and mechanisms. The utterances of contributors to a conversation occur at different stages of 'sequence time'. What each individual says is oriented not just to what has been said before, but usually anticipates further contributions to the conversation. 'Sequence time' is most often organized dialogically, even in a conversation where there are several participants. Thus most conversations can be studied as composites of dialogical units, having interjections from other conversational participants. Turn-taking in conversations tends to cut across, and dismember, the units of speech grammarians are prone to call sentences. Sentences are often not completed, or have an 'incorrect' grammatical form, and indeed talk tends to have in general a much more fractured and dislocated surface form than most branches of orthodox linguistics tend to recognize.[23] Neither sentences nor even utterances correspond to the units of talk in a conversation, 'turns at talk'.

However, given that the nature of conversation is dialogical, two or more turns can function as a interactional unit. To analyse this

[23] Erving Goffman: *Forms of Talk*, pp. 22ff.

phenomenon, Goffman speaks of the 'moves' that are made over stretches of talk between conversational participants. A move in a conversation is like a strategy in a game, normally having a ritualized character. Moves include silences as well as actual utterances. Thus a suspension of talk during the turn of a speaker may be very different in its implications from a silence maintained while another talks. While moves may consist of several sentences, they may also be composed solely of short interjections — as when by uttering 'hm', 'gosh', 'gee' etc. listeners indicate sympathetic interest in what a speaker is saying. Speaking without having the floor, or even trying to get it, can be a move in the conversational game. On this basis, Goffman is able to show some of the limitations involved in thinking of talk in terms of statements calling forth replies. Many moves do seem to invoke rejoinders, but there are a variety of ways in which individuals can express intentions, provide approval or disapproval, or otherwise make their views known, without directly committing themselves to turn-taking within the conversation. A key aspect of all talk in situations of interaction is that both speakers and listeners depend upon a saturated physical and social context for making sense of what is said. For most purposes it is therefore not relevant that utterances do not generally consist of the 'well-formed' sentences often given primacy of place in linguistics. 'Well-formed' sentences can in a certain sense stand by themselves: they can for example be interpreted via media other than those of the spoken word. But it is a considerable mistake to assess the nature of talk in terms of models of 'perfect' language. Only in very special circumstances — for example, in the talk of radio or television announcers — is there any requirement that faultless speech should be maintained.

In analysing talk Goffman places a heavy stress upon communicative competence, in the manner in which the concept is developed by Hymes.[24] Many branches of traditional linguistics have approached the study of language as though day-to-day talk were like radio or television announcing. But such an activity depends upon special forms of competence which isolate from the ordinary context of conversation certain capabilities of enunciation. Communicative competence depends upon a mastery of the whole range of proprieties observed in different forms and styles of encounter. Failure at the

[24] D. H. Hymes: 'On communicative competence', in J. B. Pride and Janet Holmes: *Sociolinguistics*. Harmondsworth: Penguin, 1972.

competent execution of an act or communicative move does not in itself compromise the perceived competence of the agent, and is likely to call forth remedial action. 'Remedial interchanges' are both a category of interaction and an aspect of certain forms of interaction. Consider an ephemeral incident on the street. An individual trips over another, says 'sorry', while as the other passes he answers 'okay'.[25] Here, as in lapses in other areas, the offender can be potentially seen as someone not competent to control the movements of his body. He or she might also be potentially perceived as an aggressor. The ritual interchange reassures the victim about the competence and the lack of malevolence of the offender; while the response reassures the first individual that this interpretation is accepted. To show that the interchange is a 'remedial account', rather than merely an 'apology', we can consider the fact that other glosses could have been offered to redeem competence. Thus the offender could pass on through calling out 'have to catch the train' or might replace the apology with a request: 'May I get through?'. As Goffman says:

> The individual does not go about merely going about his business. He goes about constrained to sustain a viable image of himself in the eyes of others. Since local circumstances always will reflect upon him, and since these circumstances will vary unexpectedly and constantly, footwork, or rather self-work, will be continuously necessary. Each lurching of whatever the individual is standing on will have to be off-set, often by his leading into the fall with a self that has been projected as unserious, the real person thereby made free to tacitly take up a counter-balancing position . . . However skittish he might be about behaving properly, he nonetheless takes care to have some behavioural reply ready in any situation where circumstances have suddenly called him into question. He need not honour a rule of conduct that applies to him. He need not even provide virtual accounts, apologies, and excuses for his deviations. But at least he must be at pains to portray an advocable relationship to the negative judgement of him which results.[26]

The highly complicated and more or less constant watchfulness by means of which agents display their overall competence is perhaps most plainly revealed by situations where it is not maintained or comes under pressure. Three main circumstances of such a sort are discussed in Goffman's writings — where individuals have to manage

25 Erving Goffman: *Relations* . . . , pp. 139ff.
26 Ibid., pp. 185—6.

some kind of stigmata which inhibit the maintenance of ordinary proprieties; where the usual conditions of co-presence are systematically constrained, as in total institutions; and where individuals for one reason or another do not display normal competencies, that is, the behaviour of the 'mentally ill'. In modern societies the latter two are obviously often closely combined, because of the incarceration of mental patients. It is no doubt significant that the only type of organization which Goffman discusses in an extensive way is the total institution. Other organizations seem to supply for him only the territories within which interaction is located and encounters occur. But the pressures of total institutions are such that proprieties observed elsewhere come under extraordinary strain.[27]

The maintenance of the competencies and proprieties that the majority of actors display and observe depends upon the time-space separation of some activities from others. Even within small oral cultures, there are a variety of spatial and conventional divisions separating 'inside' from 'outside' in contexts of interaction. Total institutions are physically circumscribed by barriers directed 'at the outside'. It is not just that they enclose individuals, often forcibly, within a restricted and communal milieu; it is that this specifically contrasts with the relative freedom of mobility that exists externally to the institution in the rest of society. By erecting barriers against the rest of the world, total institutions also dissolve the divisions usually separating different spheres of life. All aspects of day-to-day life are subject to a single authority.[28] Much of what is usually carried on in private has to be done in public, and much that is usually within the control of individuals is determined by the administrative authorities. In total institutions, incoming individuals are divested of most of the accoutrements of personal identity in the outside world. They may also be subject to specific forms of material and symbolic degradation. The staff of the organization may often ignore the forms of tact, remedy and respect found in interaction in the outside world. Information that ordinarily can be kept to oneself is available to staff in the form of dossiers or files; just as the spatial preserves that can be maintained between self and role in the external environment tend to vanish. Thus total institutions threaten a whole complex of practices whereby actors are able to demonstrate both to others and to

[27] *Asylums.* Harmondsworth: Penguin, 1961.
[28] Ibid., p. 17.

themselves their competence as agents. This is surely why they are often associated with forms of response that Freud would classify as regressive. A sort of enforced infantilism is the fate of many of those incarcerated within total institutions and may be actively employed by members of staff to facilitate their control.

However in Goffman's portrayal of total institutions individuals do not appear for the most part as broken beings. On the contrary, they find a multiplicity of ways of recovering their integrity, of creating personal territories of their own and of combining together to resist the impositions to which they are subject. There are all sorts of ways in which through their wit or cunning inmates establish counteractive modes of interaction which 'breed and start to infest the establishment'.[29] Many of these might involve conduct which would be regarded as quite unseemly or improper on the outside, but which in essence recapture for the inmate what is provided for by the orthodox proprieties in other settings. Those whom we choose to designate as the 'mentally ill' are perhaps in large part defined as such in terms of their inability, or unwillingness, to observe the standard proprieties on the outside. In the carceral organization, these traits may be accentuated, and thereby seemingly confirmed, by the nature of the settings which such persons experience. What might seem highly bizarre or quite incomprehensible behaviour in the external context of social life might come to appear quite normal even among those who were previously regarded as perfectly sane. In the study of 'mental illness' Goffman is thereby able to provide a particularly acute demonstration of what might be called the 'hermeneutic principle' that guides all his investigations. As he says, referring to the field-work that he carried out in a mental hospital, 'it was then and still is my belief that any group of persons — prisoners, primitives, pilots, or patients — develop a life of their own that becomes meaningful, reasonable, and normal once you get close to it, and that a good way to learn about any of these worlds is to submit oneself in the company of the members to the daily round of petty contingencies they are subject to.'[30]

[29] Ibid., p. 268.
[30] Ibid., p. 7.

Micro contexts and macro-structural properties

Throughout Goffman's career he resolutely refused to enter two terrains that would seem to stretch invitingly open to him. On the one hand, with the exception of his work on total institutions — which in any case is expressed mainly in terms of their effects upon individual activity — he maintained a strict separation between his work and that of sociologists interested in the macro-structural properties of social systems. On the other hand, various comments and allusions throughout his writings notwithstanding, he refused to be drawn into any kind of elaborated account of the psychology of the self. It is quite clear why he chose to work within these self-imposed restrictions. As he saw it, the analysis of situations of co-presence was something of an untrammelled field for social analysis, a field whose contours could only be explored by bracketing out most of the issues with which both sociologists and psychologists traditionally have been concerned. Who could dispute the fruitfulness of Goffman's decision strictly to confine the realm of his investigations? In so doing he brought into view new areas of study, and was able to generate ideas of enduring significance.[31] Rewarding though it may be, I want to argue nonetheless that Goffman's obdurate preoccupation with situations of co-presence led him to underestimate the general importance of his theories for more 'standard' — that is, macro-structural — problems of sociology.

Goffman's own views on the nature of his enterprise were clearly articulated in an article written as his Presidential Address to the American Sociological Association, near the end of his life. (He could not help approaching the occasion reflexively. What was going on in *this* particular situation of co-presence?) In the paper he reaffirms his overriding concern with the interaction order as 'a substantive domain in its own right'.[32] Most of our day-to-day life is passed in the presence of others. Face-to-face interaction is not only bounded in time and space, hence forming a defined subject matter, it is mainly determined by exigencies of the very situation of co-presence itself. There is not a 'latent phase'; the mutual involvement of participants is of critical importance and structures the very same circumstances it is structured

---

[31] See Anthony Giddens: *Central Problems in Social Theory*. London: Macmillan, 1979, chpt. 1 and following.

[32] Erving Goffman: 'The interaction order', p. 2.

by. Goffman here seems much more confident about the universal or near-universal features of interaction in circumstances of co-presence than he does elsewhere. It is plausible to say, he avers, that frequently found characteristics of interaction are 'rooted in certain universal conditions of social life'.[33] But he also goes on to reject an exaggerated 'situationalism'. Most settings of social behaviour extend interaction in time and space well beyond any particular context of co-presence. Moreover each individual within any given situation brings to it a pre-given biography and personality, focused through forms of knowledge shared in common with others. It might be supposed, Goffman points out, that the properties of large-scale collectivities are no more than a composite of what goes on in a variety of circumstances of co-presence. One might think that Goffman might find such an argument congenial, since it would seem to add considerable weight to the sort of work he carries out. However, he will have none of such a view. Such a position, in Goffman's eyes, confuses the situation within which actions occur with the institutional consequences of those actions. We cannot infer from the study of social encounters the institutional shape that those encounters in a certain sense 'support'.

Goffman seemed by this point in his career to reject any suspicion of methodological individualism more strongly than hitherto he had done. Thus he disavows the view that interaction between co-present individuals is any more or less real than relations between social collectivities. 'I claim merely that forms of face-to-face life are worn smooth by constant repetition on the part of participants who are heterogeneous in many ways and yet must quickly reach a working understanding; these forms thus seem more open to systematic analysis than are the internal or external workings of many macroscopic entities'.[34] While continuing to repudiate the idea that there are many direct connections between the interaction order and broader properties of institutions, Goffman does draw Durkheim into service in respect of characterizing the qualities of that order. Relations in circumstances of co-presence tend very frequently to be ceremonial and ritual. These may have connections with broader ritual occasions of a macro-structural kind. But for the most part more pervasive aspects of such ritual are internal to the interaction order. The ritual of social life should not be regarded as an 'expression' of the properties

[33] Ibid., p. 3.
[34] Ibid., p. 9.

of institutions; it is a form of activity established 'in regard' of those institutions. There is only a loose coupling to the qualities of the institutions themselves. Most direct ties that can be discovered are between the interaction order and 'social relationships'. We might tend to think of the frequency of interaction between two related individuals as largely constitutive of what that relationship is. How far there is an 'established' relationship between two individuals who meet in an encounter strongly influences the nature of the interaction entered into, the enquiries made of the other, and the forms of talk conducted. But once more the relationship neither defines nor brings about the range of interactive devices called into play in actual situations of co-presence.

What are we to make of these claims? Probably at no time earlier in his writings has Goffman sketched out his overall position with such clarity and forcefulness. He provides an effective rationale for his work, as a subdivision of sociology having potentially universal implications, yet distinct from other major fields of sociological study and from the psychological analysis of motivation. But it does not need too close scrutiny to see that this stance is not really adequately defended on an empirical level. Goffman has never demonstrated much interest in looking directly at how far the processes he discusses are generalizable. This seems to be because he adopts the attitude of an explorer of uncharted areas, preoccupied with opening up the territory but content to leave its precise mapping to others. But this is not very satisfactory. In the first place, it is one of the main reasons why his writings have seemed to most commentators much less systematic in form and intent than they really are. It also lends latent support to the assertion that the interaction order is a clearly separable domain in its own right. For it is only if the mechanisms influencing conduct in conditions of co-presence *are* generalizable across a wide range of cultural contexts that Goffman's arguments hold much water. Goffman's rather haughty disregard for examining in a concrete way the level of likely generality of his observations potentially compromises the alleged autonomy of the interaction order.

It is striking that most of Goffman's work on interaction has a very 'flat' or homogeneous feel to it, something which is again certainly related to his wish to claim a distinctive order of investigation for his studies. Virtually all of the illustrations Goffman gives of the forms of activity he analyses are on a par in terms of their significance. Goffman's mode of procedure tends to be rather circular here. Since the interaction order is presumed to be a domain in its own right, no

distinction is made between contexts of interaction which are fateful
for the individuals involved or for others and those that are not.
Moreover, Goffman for the most part chooses to analyse situations
in which there is no obvious disparity of power between participants.
His discussion of total institutions is again the major exception to
this. Thus although he often notes that there are formalized settings
in which institutionally sanctioned power is exercised — such as the
court room — he rarely analyses such circumstances in the detail
accorded to other settings of interaction. Nor does he often analyse
the interaction of the powerful — at least, in circumstances in which
that power is being exercised. Decisions and policies having
consequences for very large numbers of people are as often formulated in circumstances of co-presence as are the more mundane
forms of interaction upon which Goffman usually concentrates. No
attempt is made to differentiate these types. What should be actively
established, that the interaction order is more or less everywhere
'the same', is not only taken for granted but tends to be used in a
circular way to justify lack of interest in looking at such issues.

Goffman is surely right to resist characterizing his work as having
any intrinsic relation to methodological individualism as a philosophical
standpoint. The behaviour of individuals in situations of co-presence
is no more or less real than the existence of more overarching social
relationships and social forms. He is also justified in suggesting that
the division he draws between his studies and those concerned with
structural properties of social systems does not recapitulate the
micro/macro distinction as ordinarily formulated. That is to say, it is
a mistake to confuse situations of co-presence with small groups,
contrasting these with larger groups or collectivities. Circumstances
of co-presence may involve large numbers of individuals, as where
several hundred thousand people are present at a mass rally; while
small groups may endure across time and space in a way in which
encounters by definition do not. However, in persistently identifying
his work as 'micro-sociology' Goffman tends to obscure the originality
of his position and at the same time glosses over some of its
shortcomings.[35]

Goffman is quite brilliant at demonstrating that what appear to be
quite trivial and uninteresting aspects of day-to-day behaviour turn

[35] See Anthony Giddens: *The Constitution of Society*, pp. 139—44.

out to be fraught with implications for interaction. Yet many of the traits he identifies have more to do with the reproduction of institutions than he acknowledges. He recognizes several types of circumstance in which there might be, as he puts it, 'situational effects upon social structures'.[36] This is not an appropriate way to express the matter, since the use of the term 'effects' already presumes that situated interaction and more embracing institutions are different orders of phenomena. Such is most assuredly not the case. That this is so can be shown if we grasp the recursive character of the structural qualities of social systems. One of the plainest examples is language itself. Goffman analyses mechanisms of talk whereby communication is established between co-present speakers and their doings 'brought off'. Now talk is not just a situated expression of language, it is the prime means whereby language as an overall form exists at all. The overall structural properties of language, that is, the rules and generalized procedures of language use, are not properties of any individual subject, but of language communities stretching across very long spans of time-space. Knowledge of these properties is the means whereby talk is generated, while the situational elements that are used to 'make talk happen' reproduce what language *is* as a structured form.

We might take as another example Goffman's discussion of the use of tact and other supportive mechanisms as a means of maintaining trust between individuals. Persons who are co-present are inherently vulnerable to one another. Thus even between strangers engaged in a casual and passing encounter, forms of ritual tend to be observed that sustain mutual confidence and respect. Surely, however, it is apparent that the attaining of trust in this sense serves to make possible, or at least facilitate, the existence of contacts and relationships that stretch across contexts of co-presence? As Simmel shows in his essay on 'The Stranger', confidence in meetings with unknown others is not something that is characteristically part of traditional small communities.[37] Studying how such confidence is created and reproduced in modern contexts might thus show a great deal about how large-scale societies are institutionally ordered across time and space.

Social institutions are formed and reformed via the recursiveness of social activity. The techniques, strategies, and modes of behaviour

---

[36] Erving Goffman: 'The interaction order', p. 8.
[37] Georg Simmel: *Sociology*, Glencoe: The Free Press, 1950.

followed by actors in circumstances of co-presence, even in the most seemingly trivial aspects of their day-to-day life, are fundamental to the continuity of institutions across time and space. In his studies of co-presence, Goffman demonstrates that the predictability of much of social life, even on a macro-structural plane, is organized via the practices involved in what he chooses to call the interaction order. But this order is never separate from either the ordering of behaviour across contexts of co-presence, or the ordering of such contexts themselves in relation to one another. Consider again the example of trust. Trust, it might be said, is a device for stabilizing interaction. To be able to trust another person is to be able to rely upon that person to produce a range of anticipated responses. Goffman shows that there is a significant sense in which we tend to trust strangers or chance acquaintances in the settings of modern social life. Of course we also characteristically in a deeper fashion trust certain individuals with whom we are particularly close. Trust in such instances influences and orders what we do in co-present interaction with those individuals, but equally importantly by the very same token it orders our relations with them across a diversity of contexts. Analysing how trust is sustained in settings of interaction in modern societies cannot be meaningfully kept separate from examining other modes of sustaining confidence across separated contexts. Money, for example, may be understood as a token of confidence, allowing transactions between individuals quite ignorant of one another, but who would otherwise be disinclined to have confidence in what the other or others might promise. The pervasiveness of money transactions in modern societies is both relevant to the structuring of contexts of co-presence — influencing, for example, their 'impersonal character' — and intrudes into the very nature of interaction that might be carried on within those contexts.

Money is a vehicle of establishing relations between individuals who may be very widely separated indeed from one another in time and in space. What is interesting and important here is not just the relation between co-presence and 'transcontextual' interaction, but the relation between presence and absence in the structuring of social life. 'Presence' by definition of course exhausts the limits of our direct experience. 'Co-presence' is not really some sort of sub-category of presence in general. It is rather a form of experience, characteristic of large parts of most people's day-to-day lives, in which others are directly 'available', and in which the individual *makes* him or herself 'available', that is, demonstrates agency in Goffman's sense.

Interaction in contexts of co-presence obviously has characteristics not found in 'mediated' interaction — via the telephone, recordings, the mail and so on. But it is a mistake to see these as two opposed forms of social connection. On the contrary, each interlaces with the other in many subtle ways. 'Presence' — what the individual brings to and employs in any situation of conduct, whether there are others in that situation or not — is always mediated by what is absent. Goffman acknowledges, of course, that individuals come to any given situation of co-presence 'carrying an already established biography of prior dealings with other participants — or at least with participants of their kind', and also 'with a vast array of cultural assumptions presumed to be shared'.[38] But the implications of this are considerable. For individuals experience different contexts of co-presence as episodes within the time-space paths they trace out in the course of their day-to-day activities. Mediation between contexts in this sense — that is the 'moving presence' of actors across time-space paths — strongly influences the nature of encounters that are entered into. Once more we are likely to have a misleading, or very partial, account of what goes on in circumstances of co-presence if we do not integrate an analysis of those circumstances with what connects them together in the continuous lives of individuals — and indeed groups.

One might point out that the difference between situations of co-presence and what might be called 'presence availability' is more blurred than Goffman usually seems to assume. In large gatherings, although individuals might be present in the same overall space with one another, they are not continuously within the range of vision or earshot of each other. They are 'available', in the sense that the individual might quite readily seek them out. Yet there may be more effort involved in so doing than in the case of individuals who are in adjoining rooms within a building, or in rooms on the same floor in a building. The study of the mechanisms of ensuring presence availability has to be closely tied to analysing what goes on in situations of immediate co-presence. This means relating sorts of discussion Goffman provides with more extended analyses of the nature of the locales and the modes of regionalization whereby contexts of co-presence are conjoined. For example it seems entirely misleading to separate, as a distinct 'interaction order', the tissue of encounters in contemporary societies from urbanism as a social form.

[38] Erving Goffman: 'The interaction order', p. 4.

Goffman's writings thus contribute much more to an understanding of 'macro-structural' properties than Goffman supposed; and this very insight means seeking to connect in a direct way Goffman's analyses of co-presence with mechanisms of social reproduction across extended spans of time and space. However, Goffman's attempt to distinguish the interaction order as a clearly delimited field also gains plausibility from his disinclination to confront questions of motivation. If Goffman's writings are 'flat', lacking that vertical dimension which an enriched treatment of institutions would provide, they are also in a certain sense 'empty' in respect of the motivation that leads actors to behave as they do in day-to-day life. Perhaps this is another reason why, as portrayed by Goffman, actors might seem often to be shallowly cynical in their manipulation of what goes on in their social environments. Goffman makes it clear enough that there is a unitary person behind the roles that are played in the diversity of social contexts, but his discussion of this self tends to be rudimentary. He offers an analysis of motivation of sorts, established mainly as a critique of interpretations of the interaction order which he rejects. People might be seen to do whatever they do in interaction with one another because they are motivated to form implicit contracts — everyone profits from following certainly mutually agreed conventions in their transactions with others. A rather different interpretation is that such motivation derives from the internalization of some sort of overall normative consensus, which is then applied in the situations of face-to-face interaction. Goffman does not so much show either or both of these interpretations to be false as see each as partial. Conventions of conduct in situations of co-presence do not imply a general belief in the desirability or prudence of observing an implicit contract, nor a commitment to the value of norms that sanction the expectations followed. There are, Goffman says, 'mixed motive games' in interaction, and individuals conform to the relevant conventions 'for a wide variety of reasons'.[39]

We might very well accept that this is so. Since, as Goffman defines them, situations of co-presence cover so much of social life, it is unlikely that conformity to the conventions involved would be reducible to any fairly simple formula. On the other hand, Goffman frequently (although, as I have mentioned, inconsistently) stakes a claim for the very general nature of the practices he analyses. If such

[39] Ibid., p. 5.

should indeed be the case, it would definitely tend to suggest that generic mechanisms of a psychological sort are at work. It is in fact possible to speculate what such mechanisms might be and although I shall not attempt to identify them here, it can be shown that we thereby add substance to the accounts Goffman offers of interaction.

In conclusion let me raise the question of social change. Have Goffman's writings any relevance to processes of profound transformation which social institutions might undergo? What relation, for example, could the study of circumstances of co-presence possibly have to more encompassing issues such as the development of modern capitalism? In approaching such matters it might seem as though we have to decamp from Goffman's world completely. This again would be mistaken. Social changes of a deep-rooted kind, by their very nature, involve alterations in the character of day-to-day social practices. So long as we do not accept Goffman's formulation of the autonomy of the interaction order, but think rather in terms of the intersection of varying contexts of co-presence, connected together by the paths that individuals trace out across locales in which they live their day-to-day lives, it is not far-fetched to see a resemblance between the work of Goffman and that of Braudel. Goffman seemingly concentrates on the highly transient, Braudel on the long-established patterns of life of overall civilizations. But both shed light on the nature of day-to-day social life and more specifically the modes in which everyday social activity is implicated in very broad patterns of institutional reproduction. There are long-term processes of change that are built into and expressed through the very contingencies of such reproduction. There also occur, obviously, more violent and dramatic processes of change. If Goffman's work seems irrelevant to these it is not because there is an interaction order which somehow continues on regardless of them. On the contrary, it is because he does not examine how shifting institutional alignments condition, and are conditioned by, transformations of the settings in which social life is lived. There is no reason why a more embracing approach to social theory should not undertake those tasks while incorporating the key ideas that Goffman has developed.

6

Time and social organization

Time, philosophy, culture[1]

Heidegger says:

> if Being is to be conceived in terms of time, and if, indeed, its various
> modes and derivatives are to become intelligible in their respective
> modifications and derivations by taking time into consideration, then
> Being itself (and not merely entities, let us say, as entities 'in time') is
> thus made visible in its 'temporal' character. But in that case 'temporal'
> can no longer mean simply 'being in time'.[2]

What can Heidegger mean here? Heidegger's statement has to be seen
against the backdrop of his criticisms of Kantian philosophy, and
Kant's categories of time and space. Kant's various discussions of
time and space are not uncomplicated, nor are they always seemingly
mutually consistent. However it probably would be fair to say that in
Kant's view time and space are ordering dimensions of reality. For
Kant, time as well as space are empty categories. In respect of space
such a view probably conforms to conventional canons of common
sense. We can remove an object from one position, and place it in
another, the vacated space then being empty. The same does not seem
to be true of time. For Kant, however, such is the case, since time and
space are connected through intuition, which gives form or shape to
the world. 'Empty time' is time when nothing exists. Time and space

---

[1] 'Time and social organization' was given as a lecture at the University of
Uppsala in February 1984.

[2] Martin Heidegger: *Being and Time*. Oxford: Basil Blackwell, 1978, p. 40.

have an indivisible, or perhaps more accurately, an infinitely divisible continuity. No part of either can be specified, except as enclosed between limits — points or instants — which therefore themselves enclose time or space.

Heidegger seeks to dispute this view. Time is not like space, although it inherently intersects with it. Nor is time either an environment in which objects exist, or an intuition of the mind. Entities do not just exist 'in time'; time expresses the nature of what objects are. It is also a mistake to regard time, as Leibniz did, as a relation between sequences of events. Time is not to be identified with change, since an object only has identity in so far as it has continuity that 'abides in time'. Since it is the horizon of all being, it follows that the 'human being' (*Dasein*) 'finds its meaning in temporality'. Yet the cultural meanings which time has for human beings can not be directly inferred from the intrinsic relation between Being and time. Human existence is characterized by 'historicality', but it is not inherently 'historical'. That is to say, there are different ways in which experience of time may be organized and connected to the framework of human social institutions. Tradition is a mode of capturing time-experience, but one which is refractory to 'history', where this means the explicit study of past development. An era like our own, Heidegger argues, which is radically 'historical', can 'forget' about the historicality of human existence. In this sense, Kant's philosophy of time-space expresses particular features of modern or Western social development, not characteristics generic to time and space themselves. In Heidegger's view, '*Dasein* no longer understands the most elementary conditions which would alone enable it to go back to the past in a positive manner and make it productively its own.'[3]

I neither wish to claim that Heidegger's reflections on the nature of time are limpid in their clarity, nor that he provides a philosophy of time which can somehow be directly imported into social theory. In spite of the very large philosophical literature on time, and on space, I do not think it could be said that there exists a discussion of these topics which could be regarded as in any sense conclusive. Space, but particularly time, retain that ineffable quality which, in his celebrated reflections on the matter, St Augustine so aptly captured. However, those working in the social sciences can certainly profit from an awareness of philosophical discussions of time and space. For it is

[3] Ibid., p. 43.

arguable that the Kantian conception of time-space which Heidegger so effectively criticizes has formed the unthinking backdrop to most traditions of social analysis.

The idea that time and space are 'environments' of social life has helped among other things to reinforce disciplinary divisions. Thus time might appear to be the pre-eminent concern of historians, space that of geographers, with the remainder of the social sciences then effectively ignoring the understanding of these dimensions. I want to propose that problems of time and space are quite fundamental to social theory.[4] Those working in social theory can and must hence pay heed to the works of philosophers on these issues, without supposing that they can extract from such writings a 'finalized' conception of what time and space actually are. We can bracket some of the exceedingly difficult issues concerned with elucidating time and space, while still being sensitized to the puzzles which they present. In modern culture, we tend to think of time as some sort of flow of events, having a direction which runs from past to present. We tend to think of both time and space as mensurable, and as separate from both the existence of objects and the occurrence of our own activities. Reading Heidegger indicates that these assumptions might be themselves restricted by a specific temporal and spatial horizon, limited to Western culture as it has developed over the past two or three centuries.

We can use philosophical reflections about the nature of time and space to wrench ourselves away from such familiar assumptions. It also helps to carry out certain kinds of speculative thought-experiments. For example, we might ask ourselves, what would day-to-day life be like without clocks? As Mumford among others has pointed out, the clock is certainly as much an essential element of the modern order as is the power machine.[5] Clocks do not simply exist in an 'environment of time'. In the modern social order, clocks are co-ordinated through uniform time dimensions, linked globally across space. Without such linkages, which depend essentially upon the formation of standardized social conventions, the modern world simply could not be ordered as it is. To imagine a world without clocks is to imagine a world without

[4] See Anthony Giddens: *The Constitution of Society*. Cambridge: Polity Press, 1985, chpt. 1 and following.

[5] Lewis Mumford: *Interpretations and Forecasts*. London: Secker and Warburg, 1973, pp. 272ff.

the standardization of time and space which is such a familiar part of our day-to-day lives that we tend to take it for granted. But of course, for the vast proportion of human history human beings have not lived in a world of regulated time-space of this sort at all. The early civilizations are associated with the regularizing of time and space, evinced most obviously in the development of calendars. But the tenor of social life from day to day, month to month and year to year always remained firmly bound to the iterative character of tradition.

Or consider a clock that goes backwards. Such clocks are in fact on sale as amusing gadgets. A clock that goes backwards is actually very easy to adjust to, although at the beginning it seems specifically unnatural. The example drives home the fact that clocks have little to do with the 'linear' notion of time which we might imagine dominates in modern culture. The hands on a clock need not move in any particular direction; the important thing is that the clock conforms to the repetition of the day-to-day cycle. Consider one final example, drawn from studies of the experience of time in modern societies. When asked 'where' time comes from, and 'where' it goes, most people in modern societies apparently have no difficulty either in thinking of time in a spatial manner, or in indicating its direction. Time is pictured as running along a line beginning behind the body and extending out in front. It follows an axis represented by an individual standing with the left arm extended out behind, the right arm extended in front, time following the direction from the left hand side behind the body and running towards the front where the right arm is pointing. Such a picturing of time is surely associated with our typical view of history, which sees the past as 'behind' us and the future as 'in front'. We may even understand the body as an action system through which the future is actively organized in the light of experience of the past. Those living in cultures in which tradition is the primary medium of organizing time experience do not seem to portray time in this way. For them, it may be difficult or impossible to think of time in spatial terms, or to give it a direction.

Time and social analysis

Such considerations at least allow us in some part to wriggle free from how we ordinarily think of time and how we usually think of space as well. Rethinking the concepts of time and space in relation to social theory, I want to propose, involves at least four elements:

1) This concerns essentially Heidegger's point. Just as in the case of natural objects, time is not an environment in which the 'elapsing' of social events occurs, it is constitutive of forms of social activity. The temporality of social items or institutions is not given by some kind of intrinsic tendency to change, as is suggested by the usual interpretations of the Marxian theorem that human beings are inherently 'historical'.

2) Those in different cultures experience time differently. This can to some extent be captured by contrasting modes of time-reckoning. But to suppose that comparing forms of time-reckoning exhausts differences between modes of time experience is itself an ethnocentric assumption. Time does not exist merely as something to be measured, but is bound up with contrasts in the very nature of social activities themselves across cultures. Thus a culture saturated in tradition, in which temporality is experienced as the inseparability of past and present, is likely to be quite different from one in which there exist formalized modes of time-reckoning.

3) While leaving aside the question of whether there is any philosophically defensible sense in which time 'goes backwards', we should complement the notion of linear time with what Lévi-Strauss calls 'reversible time'.[6] Reversible time is time as repetition, temporality as reproduction. Reversible time, in a culture with clocks, is as it were symbolized by the clock that goes backwards. For however much a culture might be dominated by modes of strict time-regulation, day-to-day life remains geared to the repetition of events and activities.

4) For many purposes it is useful to analyse the occurrence of social activities in time-space. This again can leave to one side the question of in what sense, if any, time and space inevitably presuppose one another. Space might best be understood, for the purposes of social theory at least, as referring to the *settings* of interaction. Settings involve not just the 'distribution' of activities but their co-ordination with features of the locales within which these activities are carried on. Such co-ordination always involves time as well as space, the connection between these being the means of the repetition which gives social activities definite 'form'.[7]

We may identify three interlacing forms of temporality that enter into all moments of social life. One is the *durée* of day-to-day life,

---

[6] Claude Lévi-Strauss: *Structural Anthropology*. London: Allen Lane, 1968.
[7] Anthony Giddens: *The Constitution of Society*, pp. 118—22.

expressed in reversible time. 'Day-to-day life' should not be confused with the 'everyday' as analysed by phenomenology. The former refers to the ordering of social activities — their structuration — via their repetition from day-to-day. The latter, on the other hand, tends to denote a certain attitude towards the world, the so-called 'natural attitude'. The *durée* of day-to-day life at every instant intersects with the *durée* of the lifespan of the individual — the second aspect of temporality. All human agents are beings who are born and die, and thus live out their lives, as Heidegger says, in consciousness of their finitude. The duration of the lifespan is experienced as irreversible time, time itself having a fixed quantum. This might indeed be the chief basis of our sense that time, sequence and direction are inherently connected. It may, however, itself be in some part an ethnocentric assumption. In a culture where, for example, beliefs in reincarnation are held, finitude may have a different meaning from that which it has in a more secular type of society. The *durée* of day-to-day life, and that of the lifespan of the individual, both in turn interweave with a third form, the *durée* of institutions — the *longue durée* of which Braudel speaks. All societies worthy of the name endure beyond the lives of those individuals whose activities constitute them at any given moment. Patterns of both continuity and change may be discerned which carry on well beyond the lifespans of any particular generation of individuals. It should be clear that none of these aspects of the temporal organization of human social life is more than analytically separable from one another. The encounters of day-to-day life might seem remote from the long stretches of institutional time. But institutions have the form they do only in so far as they are chronically produced and reproduced in the settings of day-to-day life. On the other hand, day-to-day conduct only has continuity through its involvement with institutionalized modes of activity. The existence of the human organism is the condition for the two other aspects of temporality. However they can no more be derived from the *durée* of the lifespan that it can be derived from them.

We may similarly distinguish three aspects of spatiality relevant to the analysis of social life. One is the physical presence of others in settings of interaction: what Goffman calls 'co-presence'.[8] It is easy to imagine that interaction with others in circumstances of co-presence

---

[8] Erving Goffman: *Encounters*. Indianapolis: Bobbs-Merrill, 1961. (See also my discussion of Goffman in this volume.)

is in some sense the most 'basic' spatial organization of social life. But this is no more the case than for day-to-day life in respect of time. There is no social system which does not mingle presence and absence in respect of interaction. That is to say, no particular context of co-presence is entered *de novo*, but exists in conjunction with an indefinite string of other contexts influencing current interaction. Nonetheless, interaction in contexts of co-presence, as face-to-face interaction, has definite properties which distinguish it from interaction with absent others. 'Absent others' include those who are 'absent in time' as well as those 'absent in space'. So far as the second of these is involved, a focus upon contexts of co-presence has to be complemented by an analysis of the regionalization of social activity. 'Regions' should not be thought of simply as delineated areas of space on a map. Rather, the regionalization of social activity refers to the interlacing of contexts of co-presence whereby the spatiality of social systems of differing extension is organized. To these we must add the spatiality of the body. The body of course has a physical form which positions it in relation both to the physical world and to interaction with others. The significance of the face, of differences between the front and the back of the body, permeate all forms of interaction. But the spatiality of the body is in the most general sense expressed in the sensory media which define its 'presence'.[9]

Although for some purposes it may be necessary to treat time and space as separate, there are many occasions where it is more appropriate to speak of time-space. The concept of the 'setting' of interaction presumes time-space relations. A setting is not just a passive backdrop to interaction. Rather, agents organize the setting as their field of conduct, drawing upon its features in order to warrant and regularize what they do. Similarly, we can analyse the routines of day-to-day life in terms of the time-space paths which individuals regularly follow. The concepts and techniques of time-geography can to some degree be used fruitfully to analyse these. In conjunction with the notion of time-space distanciation, we can thereby examine the connections between routines of daily life and extended forms of social system which individuals produce and reproduce in their day-to-day actions. I have discussed these issues in a fairly exhaustive way elsewhere, and so shall not recapitulate them in any detail here.

However it is worth pointing out some of the substantive

[9] Anthony Giddens: *The Constitution of Society*, chpt. 2.

implications of these emphases. The most important concern the significance of time-regulation and its relation to spatial organization in modern social life. To understand these we must go back to the differentiation between the *durée* of day-to-day life and that of institutional time. In all societies these are bound to one another through oral culture. That is to say, day-to-day talk and conversation, which draw upon a framework of institutionalized discourse and conventions of action, are also the basic means whereby such institutionalized forms are reproduced. Although he has indicated the importance of the contrast between oral and literate cultures, the writings of Lévi-Strauss have been rather misleading in this regard. For they have tended to emphasize the importance of formalized types of story telling, in particular the relating of myth, as the principal medium of the continuity of tradition. However tradition is first and foremost embedded in, and the means of reproduction of, the practices that constitute day-to-day activities. There is a certain sense in which no culture is purely oral. Virtually all have some method of making marks or pictorial representations which give a certain material form to the nature of tradition. But in oral cultures the integration of time and space with the settings of interaction, together with time-experience, are necessarily different from cultures which possess writing and other means of information storage. Such cultures are 'prehistoric', or exist 'out of history', not because they do not exist in time, but because there are no records, chronicles or narratives which embed the present in the past. Past and present are intertwined through the hold over custom that tradition provides. It is possible that small oral cultures tend to change considerably more than Lévi-Strauss's characterization of 'cold cultures' would suggest. Tradition itself is not necessarily resistant to change. Nonetheless, those in oral cultures cannot draw the connections between the temporal and the spatial characteristic of cultures which possess means of information storage and writing. With the advent of cultures having writing, there develops the phenomenon of 'location in time', allowing quite different modes of organization from those of oral cultures. It is important to see that the lists — always in large part directed to administrative purposes — which formed the earliest versions of writing were already 'histories'. History is elemental to the existence of writing, just because writing survives the evanescence of the spoken word, bringing present and past into a new conjunction. This should not be understood simply as a mode of time-experience. A society in which there are records, used to systematize social relations across time and space, is inevitably structurally different from a purely oral culture.

Nevertheless there are clearly also differences in respect of the experience of time. If all cultures possess modes of time-reckoning, the existence of writing tends to be associated with modes of measurement and recording of temporal intervals unknown to oral cultures. The invention of calendars does not just permit a more accurate calculation of the phases of the annual cycle, it allows the comparison of divergent experiences from year to year, building up interpretations of social organization quite foreign to oral cultures. Past, present and future become dismembered from one another. It becomes possible to use knowledge of the past to 'bite into' the future, thereby mobilizing the present. This no doubt is the essence of the phenomenon that Lévi-Strauss had in mind in distinguishing hot from cold cultures. Of course, since literacy is confined to the few, access to writing reinforces differential power while also generating a tremendous acceleration in the 'quantity' of power available. Every culture no doubt has its mysteries, that can only be interpreted by individuals or groups having access to special wisdom. But the arcane qualities involved in the minority possession of literary skills certainly effect a more clear-cut closure of 'specialist knowledge' in respect of the mass of the population.

Time-space zoning

All societies, even the smallest, can be analysed as consisting of time-space zones, within which individuals trace out the recurrent paths of their day-to-day lives and which are structured through the very tracing of those paths. The introduction of quantified forms of time-reckoning always has direct implications for spatial organization. Thus calendars make possible the regularized co-ordination of groupings of individuals across space in the context of the yearly cycle of social and economic activities. Although the point has rarely been developed by those who concentrate their attention upon spatial distribution, it is evident that co-ordination across space cannot be achieved without co-ordination in time. A hot culture is not only one which introduces 'history', as the means of interpreting the past so as to shape the future. Hot cultures also involve an accumulation of power, made possible by the 'stretching' of time-space organization. With the advent of modernity, these phenomena are accentuated in the sharpest fashion. What writing was to traditional states, printing — and later electronic media — are to the modern era. Mass literacy, of course, post-dates the arrival of printing by a considerable period. But it was surely not accidental that the combination of printing and widespread literacy was associated with pressures towards political democracy. For while these phenomena greatly swell the amount of power generated by the societal collectivity, the media of storage and retrieval involved with that power are by definition no longer associated with the privileges of a minority. Modern states, i.e. 'modern societies', are inseparable from the collation, storage and retrieval of enormous quantities of information about the characteristics and activities of their subjects.[10] What is true for states, as I shall argue in more detail below, is also true for organizations in general in the modern age. If the modern period is the era *par excellence* of organizations, it is by the same token an era of the maximizing of information, employed in that bracketing of time and space upon which time-space distanciation depends. This is inevitably associated with more precise and pervasive modes of time-reckoning than ever existed before. The monastery, which used precise timing of the activities of day-to-day life to organize its inmates, is the precursor of modern forms of organization in general. There is an important intersection here between time and industrialism on the one hand, and time and capitalism on the other. Control of time is the essence of industrial production, something which explains the close affiliation between industrialism and modern organizational forms — not just within the sphere of industry itself, but over a general terrain. The machine is at the core of industrialism. Mechanized production, depending upon the regular operations of the component parts of machinery, inherently involves regularizing the activities of those who work with the machines, or who organize the distribution of the products thus created.

From at least the late eighteenth century onwards, capitalism and industrialism have been so closely connected that the two have frequently been confused. Marx early on spotted the nature of the relation between capitalism and time. In prior types of production system, Marx points out, labour was organized in relation to the disposal of the fruits of production. There were even then types of

[10] See Anthony Giddens: *The Nation-State and Violence*. Cambridge: Polity Press, 1985, chpt. 1 and following.

production system involving the appropriation of temporally defined quantities of labour on the part of exploiting classes. Thus, for example, a bonded peasant might be compelled to devote two days of the week to working for a local lord. But except where such a system was tied to *corvée* labour, it was not labour-power but produce which the master appropriated. Capitalism involves the commodification of labour, which means its translation into abstract labour power. Labour-power is energy which has no determinate relation to any particular context of production or form of product. It can thus be exchanged against other commodities, and hence brought within the scope of a monetary system. The translation of labour into labour-power, and products into commodified goods, creates a decisive shift in patterns of socio-economic organization. The 'working day' comes to replace the more fluid and continuous mode of labour associated with pre-capitalist production. The ideas that time is money, and that capitalism involves an 'economy of time', are more subtle and interesting than they first appear. Units of time become what labour *is* in respect of the contract which employer and worker enter into with one another. There is a direct tie between the formation of abstract labour-power, thus defined, and the character of money itself. The value of money, according to Marx, is ultimately to be explained in terms of the creation and quantification of value through units of abstract labour.[11]

We need not accept all aspects of Marx's account to see the significance of what might be called the 'commodification of time' in modern society. But we should once again stress that this tends to be closely related to the commodification of space. Space becomes a commodity to be bought and sold like any other, something of major significance in separating the early development of modern urbanism from pre-existing types of city. Use of the terms 'city', 'urban', and so on, to refer both to settlements in pre-modern times and to the modern built environment can be highly misleading. To the degree to which it becomes commodified (for there are always countervailing influences) urbanism in the modern era becomes what could be more accurately called a 'created environment'. In pre-modern cities, there was almost always a close relationship between the built environment and the contours of nature. Such a relationship is almost wholly dissolved in

[11] Karl Marx: *Capital*, vol. I. London: Lawrence and Wishart, 1970, especially pp. 94ff.

much modern urbanism, especially where cities are organized in a geometrically ordered form.[12]

The time-space regionalization associated with modernity thus comes to take on certain very distinctive characteristics. The most mundane and obvious of these — but no less significant for all that — is the separation of the home and workplace. Once more this is not simply a spatial separation, but a matter of the time-space zoning of activities. The separation of home from workplace is in turn only one aspect of broader processes of time-space regionalization involved in modernity. 'Sequestration', expressed above all in what Foucault calls 'carceral institutions', and Goffman 'total institutions', is the most pronounced form of time-space zoning.[13] The effect of sequestration is to alter radically the nature of day-to-day experience. New forms of relationship between public and private come into being; new boundaries between concealment and disclosure come to operate. Most of the experiences critical to the existential bases of human existence — birth, sickness, death, madness — become separated from the core experiences of the majority of the population. As I have argued elsewhere, this has definite implications for the sense of 'ontological security' upon which a relatively stable psychological existence depends.

Adjusting to a world of commodified time demands a considerable process of learning on the part of those accustomed to a different temporal ordering of day-to-day life. In a celebrated discussion of this issue, E. P. Thompson has analysed the lack of conjunction between the habits of agrarian workers and the time discipline of capitalist industrial labour.[14] The variant uses of the metaphor of 'clock-work' demonstrates the pervasiveness of the matter. There are, as it were, natural work rhythms in traditional types of labour. Work from dawn until dusk is more or less an exigency during the harvest months in a farming community. Sheep have to be looked after at lambing time; cows have to be milked at certain periodic intervals; fishermen have to integrate their work with tide and season. Time-reckoning in such

---

[12] Anthony Giddens: *A Contemporary Critique of Historical Materialism*. London: Macmillan, 1981, chpt. 6.

[13] Michel Foucault: *Discipline and Punish*. Harmondsworth: Penguin, 1979.

[14] E. P. Thompson: 'Time, work-discipline and industrial capitalism', *Past and Present*, vol. 38, 1967.

contexts is organized in terms of task orientation. But when labour becomes abstract labour and emptied of content, time does also. 'In all these ways — by the division of labour; the supervision of labour; fines; bells and clocks; money incentives; preachings and schooling; the suppression of fares and sports — new labour habits were formed, and a new time discipline was imposed.'[15]

Adjustment to the temporal demands of modern labour has aspects which are primarily capitalistic and aspects which are more connected to the generic character of industry. The selling of labour as abstract units of time undoubtedly is one of the elements likely to promote feelings of alienation on the part of those involved in the capitalist labour contract. For the 'time' that is sold has no connection with the temporal orderings of which the individual is the author. But in other respects these phenomena belong to more general parameters of modernity. For a world which is co-ordinated in terms of time-space organization globally, as the modern world is, demands the penetration of abstract time-reckoning into virtually all spheres of life. The clock is not, as Thompson tends to suggest, simply the epitome of capitalism. The concept of 'free time', the ability to control the temporal organization of one's day-to-day life, and more generally one's enduring projects and aspirations, undoubtedly is relevant to counter-balancing the commodified nature of time. However time never becomes fully commodified; the de-commodification of large stretches of work-life would not alter the fact that the modern world depends upon precise time-reckoning in the co-ordination of social activities. We have therefore to be wary of employing an unexamined notion of 'clock time'. Clock time is quantified time, separated from and set against the phenomenal experience of individuals. Understood in terms of its significance for modern culture, clock time is above all the synchronization of activities in time-space. People have to 'know' the time, most of the time, for such synchronization to be possible. Yet there must also be a 'universal time' for them to know.[16] And this in turn really involves the precise co-ordination of space. Consider, for example, international time zones. The establishing of such zones was a more recent occurrence than might be imagined. But international time zones are not so much a matter of reckoning time as of ensuring co-ordination across time and space. They are integrally involved in

[15] Ibid., p. 90.

[16] See Eviatar Zerubavel: *Hidden Rhythms: Schedules and Calendars in Social Life*. Chicago: University of Chicago Press, 1981.

the tremendous time-space distanciation characteristic of social relations in the twentieth century.

A theory of social organization

The word 'organization' has cropped up frequently in the foregoing sections. This is not mere happenstance. An account of modern organizations must be firmly based upon a theory of organization. As I would understand it, a theory of organization converges closely with the basic tasks of social science. An essential issue for the social sciences is the resolution of 'problem of order'. By this I do not mean the 'Hobbesian problem', as diagnosed by Parsons — the question of how social cohesion is possible in the face of a multiplicity of conflicting individual interests.[17] Rather, I mean precisely how social systems bracket time and space — how they stretch across greater or lesser spans of time-space. The problem of order is the issue of time-space distanciation. Certain factors relevant to this therefore are characteristic of all societies, no matter how small and no matter how 'primitive'. Not just organization 'in' time-space, but organization of time-space, is elemental to all societal systems. I want to draw a distinction however between organization and organizations. Not all societies either are organizations, or include organizations. The development of organization as organizations is convergent with the rise of agrarian states. The agrarian state was the first and most embracing type of organization prior to the modern era. Traditional states were already differentiated: they involved other organizations, which also in some part cut across their borders. The most important of such organizations were everywhere religious and military. But organizations only really began to proliferate with the advent of modernity and certain key aspects of modern social life have to be identified in seeking to explicate how and why this should be so.

What, then, is an organization? It is a social system which is able to 'bracket time-space', and which does so via the reflexive monitoring of system reproduction and the articulation of discursive 'history'. This definition needs some unpacking, but its nature should be fairly clear in the light of the preceding discussion I have already set out. While

---

[17] Talcott Parsons: *The Structure of Social Action*. Glencoe: Free Press, 1949.

social systems of an enduring sort by definition stretch across tracts of time-space, oral cultures do not monitor the conditions of their own reproduction. Like all forms of social interaction, they are produced and reproduced through the knowledgeable practices of their constituent actors. But tradition, combined with the needs of practical adjustment to the material environment, are the main elements guiding overall system reproduction. Since the past is 'retrieved' via its immersion in current practices, the mobilization of reflexive control of social stability and change is relatively rudimentary. Writing is the condition, as well as in some part the outcome, of the articulation of discourse within which 'history' is created. Reflexively-monitored conditions of social reproduction involve the documentation of such reproduction with a view to its co-ordination and control. The formation of such monitoring processes thereby considerably expands the level of possible time-space distanciation which can be achieved.

All organizations involve the mobilizing of two types of resources, the administrative and the allocative. While in the literature discussing modern organizations the accumulation of allocative resources has often been given primacy of place, more significant is the development of authoritative resources. Authoritative resources in turn presume surveillance. There are two aspects of surveillance, which in all organizations are more or less closely combined. One is surveillance as the accumulation, coding and retrieval of information; the other is surveillance as the direct supervision of the activities of some individuals or groups by others. The collation of information is vital for the generation of administrative power, because of the control over time-space which it generates — particularly control over the timing and spacing of the activities of individuals whose behaviour is then made part of the organization. One of the most important connections between the two forms of surveillance is the relation between the accumulation of 'organizational history' and that of personal histories or personal data. Life histories, personal documents and inventories are part of the core of even the earliest forms of organization. However there can be no organization without at least some level of supervision of the activities of those subject to administrative power. Supervision is in turn impossible without some degree of control of locales — the physical settings of interaction. For an organization to be effective, supervision within a locale does not necessarily involve all those whose conduct is in some way subject to organizational imperatives. What matters is that the upper echelons of the organization are available in co-present settings. The physical layout of the palace, the temple, the barracks, and more generally of the pre-modern city are hence of basic importance to early types of organization. Of course even in traditional organizations modes of supervision have varied quite widely. Moreover, all forms of supervision have been backed by the presence of coercive sanctions of some sort.[18]

The modern world is the world of organizations. Why should that be? At the most general level, the ubiquity of organizations is bound up with the significance of historicity within the culture of modernity. Historicity means using history to make history. The social world is not taken as given, but as intrinsically malleable in respect of the accumulation of knowledge about that world. When this outlook is regularized as a discursively available foundation of system repro-duction, we have the core of an 'organizational culture'. A modern organization is a social system in which information is regularly used, and its discursive articulation carefully coded, so as to maximize control of system reproduction. We can specify the distinctive characteristics of modern organizations in the following manner.

1

Such organizations involve the intensification of surveillance as information collation and retrieval. Modern organizations can only exist against the backdrop of modern states, those states themselves being organizations. Characteristic of the modern state is a tremendous acceleration in processes of information gathering used to co-ordinate the activities of subject populations. The modern state is tied to the spread of printing and mass literacy, with consequences as previously noted. All organizations draw in an extensive way upon documentation provided by states (the reverse of course is also true). Inside organizations, the file is the key to the intensification of surveillance. Whether concerning past events or the behaviour of members of the organization themselves, files are a means whereby the organization inserts itself in the past and is able to secure some measure of control over the future. Max Weber makes this point, writing that 'the management of the modern office is based upon written documents (the files) . . .',[19] but he does not develop it in the same way as I wish

[18] Anthony Giddens: *The Nation-State and Violence*, chpt. 1.
[19] Max Weber: *Economy and Society*. California: University of California Press, 1978, vol. 2.

to, nor does he relate it to his equally important emphasis upon the role of double-entry book-keeping. The latter Weber quite rightly connects to the emergence of modern capitalism, but does not analyse as a quality of modern organizations as a whole. However accounting is a storage and retrieval mechanism *par excellence*. Double-entry accounting procedures regularize the activities of organizations across time and space in large part because they are an anticipation of the modern form of money. Money is essentially credit and as such a mode of 'binding' transactions of individuals removed from one another in time-space. Money is above all an informational medium. The more effectively, therefore, information on inputs and outputs is calculated in reference to transactions, the more organizations can both control time-space in a direct way and at the same time contribute to the external spread of processes of time-space mediation.

As has been mentioned above, files — in the form of dossiers or personal histories — are also a basic means whereby surveillance in the sense of supervision is carried on within organizations. All organizations maintain some kind of biographical inventories of those who are their members. Such data, of course, facilitate fairly concentrated forms of what Foucault calls 'disciplinary power'. That is to say, they allow individuals in principle to be kept under minute and scrupulous observation. Records can be looked at in conjunction with what is directly witnessed of the conduct of employees in such a way as to attempt to focus organizational control of that conduct. However, dossiers also have more subtle applications. As an inventory, which charts a 'history', a dossier may be used to provide the overall direction of the activities of an individual which constitutes an organizational 'career'. It thus becomes a structuring medium, used in various ways to regularize conduct across time-space.

As Foucault remarks, speaking of the development of hospitals in the eighteenth century:

> the keeping of registers, nurse specification, the modes of transcription from one to the other, their circulation during visits, their comparison during regular meetings of doctors and of administrators, the transmission of their data to centralising bodies (either at the hospital or at the central office of the poorhouses), the accountancy of diseases, cures, deaths, at the level of a hospital, a town and even of the nation as a whole formed an integral part of the process by which hospitals were subjected to the disciplinary regime. Among the fundamental conditions of a good medical 'discipline', in both senses of the word, one must

include the procedures of writing that made it possible to integrate individual data into cumulative systems in such a way that they were not lost; so to arrange things that an individual could be located in the general register. . . .[20]

The individual is kept 'under the gaze of a permanent corpus of knowledge'.

2

A feature of modern organizations is their association with specifically designed locales. This is also something to which Foucault has helped particularly direct our attention. Since the very earliest states there has always been an 'architecture of power'. However the tendency has been to interpret this as simply an expression of accumulated power rather than integral to it. Palaces, temples, ceremonial buildings, are often treated as though they were simply the physical glorification of already existing power. No doubt such buildings have had symbolic implications. But it is also fruitful to see them as 'power containers': physical settings which through the interaction of setting and social conduct generate administrative power. The assembling of an administrative staff within a locale allows for the development of a range of supervisory methods, most of which however are connected to patrimonial means of administration. The most developed locale for generating administrative power in such societies has very often been the barracks. Military organization is the closest ancestor to modern organizations in this respect. Pre-modern armies vary widely in terms of how far they secure anything like 'military discipline' in the modern sense. Nonetheless, there are examples of quite intensely developed modes of military organization, based on training inculcated through the use of continuous supervision.

It would be a mistake — a mistake Foucault appears to make — to treat locales and the concentrating of administrative power as coterminous, even in traditional societies. From this regard, the barracks is in fact not the typical case of administrative power, any more than is the prison within more modern forms of society. Rather, the 'architectural concentration of power' permitted by particular sorts of locales typically provides for consolidated administrative

[20] Michel Foucault: *Discipline and Punish*, p. 190.

organization 'at the top'. This of course tends to be closely connected in turn with the access to informational resources that those at the higher levels of an administrative hierarchy tend to have. The capability of an organization to extend beyond the locale or locales where operations are directly carried on depends upon a range of factors. Thus surveillance in the form of supervision may be deployed by agents of the organization 'in the field'. The traditional Chinese imperial state, for example, maintained a complex network of political informers and moral educators who were supposed to ensure that the ideals of the state were properly observed. In general it can be said that the more such individuals are removed from the immediate locales where administrative power is concentrated, the less the degree of overall co-ordination with the policies of the organization which can be achieved. In traditional states in particular, the degree of real control achieved by centre over periphery through the use of such means was very low. Such individuals could not themselves be kept effectively subject to the demands of the centralized political administration, and in practice had their own local supervisory practices, often with results quite divergent from those required by the central administration.

The locales involved in most modern organizations are simultaneously more and less enveloping than traditional forms. There are types of 'total institution' which come into being and which enclose the whole of the lives of their inmates — at least for specified periods. Such organizations include in particular, of course, prisons and asylums. These cannot however be taken to be typical of modern forms of organization in general. Most modern organizations, and the locales in which they are situated, depend upon the 'functional specialization' of activity within modern societies. Work in modern organizations is associated with the division of the day into labour-time and leisure-time, and with the division of the week into the working week and the weekend (or a segment thereof). Organizations like schools may only involve membership for a particular portion of the lifespan. Yet it is surely clear that the architecture of all these types of organizations is relevant to the maintenance of various kinds of supervision. This supervision tends to take two forms. Many organizations contain an undifferentiated group of individuals who are subject to the authority from above — workers, schoolchildren, prisoners, or mental patients. The settings within which such individuals work or live are often open and visible, allowing for more or less continuous supervision. This is one of the emphases that Foucault quite rightly makes, and he may well be justified in taking Bentham's Panopticon as the epitome of it. Such 'open' disciplinary settings clearly involve the close regulation of the timing and spacing of activities. The spacing of machines on a shop floor, or of desks in a schoolroom, are closely integrated with the temporal co-ordination of the tasks carried out. Similarity of 'format' in those subject to authority also tends to reinforce the common situation in which such individuals find themselves.

However, as Weber emphasized, organizations tend to be hierarchical at the higher levels. Hierarchies are arranged as offices. Now offices are also normally physical settings of interaction. A specific difference between the office and settings in which 'administered groups' exist is that offices are usually closed off from direct supervision by superordinates. It is very often the case that offices of the same or similar authority level within an organization will be physically proximate. What this makes possible is 'presence-availability', which can be used by those in supervisory roles to look over in a general way what is going on in the offices at that level. The design of separate offices involves the use of time-space to delineate spheres of autonomy within an overall authority hierarchy. The higher one goes in a hierarchy normally the more this is true. Thus at the lowest level of office hierarchies, the physical setting of the office may very well resemble the shop floor. That is to say, a range of individuals — usually most commonly in modern organizations, women — sit in an open and visible setting, where their work can be subject to direct supervision.

As formed by the architecture of locales, settings therefore shape the trade-off between direct supervision and reliance upon trust characteristic of modern organizations. Those in open and visible settings typically are not accorded the trust which would permit authority figures to rely upon their compliance without the control conferred by immediate supervision. Those in high trust positions, on the other hand, have their autonomy reinforced by the architecture of the setting of offices. Obviously trust and direct supervision are not wholly exclusive and are ordinarily intermingled to some degree. A measure of trust is inevitable wherever organizational authority is maintained at a distance — or at a remove in time-space. Herein reside some of the chronic problems of those in the higher administrative echelons of organizations. For it is often the case that those who are part of the organization, but who operate 'in the field', carry out tasks which are fairly mundane and which would, within the settings of an organizational locale, usually be directly supervised.

3

As a characteristic of modern organizations we should point to the relation between locales and the timing and spacing of activities through the various sectors of organizations. The more complex they are — and the larger they are — the more modern organizations depend upon precise chronology. Such organizations could not exist outside the general cultural triumph of 'clock time'. Within organizations the most distinctive chronological device is the timetable. A timetable may seemingly consist of a description of events or activities given independently of it. But all timetables are essentially *time-space organizing devices*. A timetable does not just describe how events or activities are fixed in relation to one another, it is the medium of their very co-ordination. Timetabling organizes the day of the individual just as it co-ordinates the activities of potentially large numbers of individuals. Timetables can only to some degree be imposed upon locales architecturally refractory to the particular organization of time-space which they invoke. Thus increasingly in modern organizations the design of architecture is informed by 'expected' timetables and the reverse. Zerubavel's study of a hospital in terms of its time-space organization provides ample material indicating the significance of the timetable in organizing large numbers of individuals across complicated tracts of time-space. Hospitals are organizations which run for twenty-four hours and for seven days a week, and involve considerable input and output of individuals as a regular part of their working. Timetables are clearly never purely 'internal'. Since all organizations involve regular transactions with those in external contexts, such transactions themselves must be timetabled also.[21]

In most organizations, offices and individual members also have their own timetables. Office timetables synchronize the activities of those within the office, but more importantly with those of other offices within the organization. Since in many organizations there are

[21] See Eviatar Zerubavel: *Hidden Rhythms*.

series of overlapping cycles of temporality, operating in reversible time, offices ordinarily weave together several temporal threads in their timetables. Thus some routine activities are timetabled by the day, by the week or the month; but many of the more important and consequential activities may be scheduled on an annual cycle. For those at the lower levels of organizations, in positions of low trust, a personal timetable is normally wholly convergent with, and determined by, the timetable of the organization. In high trust positions, personal, office and organizational timetables tend to diverge. That is to say, it is part of the autonomy of actors in high trust positions that there is a personal allocation of time which only at certain points intersects with more generalized timetables. Those in more autonomous positions, therefore, need to have diaries documenting their own movements through time-space, whereas those lower down in the organization do not.

In timetabling of all these sorts there is a mingling of chronological timing and timing influenced by the differentiation of settings relevant to the functioning of the organization. Rather few forms of timing and spacing of activities within organizations are organized wholly in terms of chronological time. Most depend either upon the use of such time to co-ordinate differentiations of other activities, or — more usually — there are varying relationships between chronological time-divisions and divisions within activities. As an example we might take the study by Clark of a sugar-beet factory.[22] The factory processes the beet for some one hundred and twenty days per year, during which period it is working for twenty-four hours each day. Over the remainder of the year the factory is dismantled and reconstructed by the same labour force. Thus for this labour force, and those in authority over it, the time frame of the year contains two very clearly contrasted sets of activities. The temporal divisions, and thereby the time-spacing zoning, of what is done in the factory is heavily influenced by such task differentiation. During the phase of actual processing, management are able to exert much more direct supervisory control over the labour force than in the other period. In the second period the workers are dispersed to relatively self-regulating groups, each having specific types of task. Here we have a relatively unusual instance in which the

[22] P. A. Clark: 'A review of the relevance of theories of time and structure for organisational sociology', University of Aston Management Centre, Working Papers No. 248 (Mimeo).

same individuals move between low trust and reasonably high trust positions over the course of the year. Yet such a movement causes considerable problems both for managers and workers.

Time, space, power

All organizations involve a tendency towards hierarchy and there is no doubt that, as Michels stressed, this tendency is more pronounced the larger and more complex the organization in question. However tendencies towards hierarchy, and to oligarchy, are always accompanied by countervailing tendencies towards the recapture of power by those on the lower levels. According to the theorem of the 'dialectic of control' this is characteristic of all power relationships.[23] No matter how complete the power of one individual or group might be over others, resources are always available whereby subordinates can reciprocally influence power holders. The dialectic of control in modern organizations assumes various forms, but mostly these are associated closely with the modes of time-space zoning of the organization. The settings of interaction, and their relation to timetables, allow various forms of concealment which 'balance off' other forms of exposure. Even in the 'open' settings of direct supervision there are circumstances in which individuals can escape the supervisory gaze. These are sometimes 'back regions' in Goffman's sense, where individuals or groups retreat and adopt patterns of behaviour prohibited or disapproved of in the 'open' setting. Whatever is done outside the direct gaze of supervisors might be important in redressing the balance of authority flowing from supervisor to supervised. Usually, of course, there is some kind of 'effort bargain' made by both sets of parties, which implicitly or otherwise recognizes that supervisory control cannot be complete. Any 'open' setting of supervision offers the possibility of collective withdrawal of co-operation, used as a sanction against either supervisors or those in higher authority. For while a common setting maximizes supervisory power, at the same time it stimulates consciousness of mutual interest pursued via co-operative means.

In hierarchies of offices such collective collaboration is much more difficult to achieve. Here there is the trade-off between authority

[23] Anthony Giddens: *The Constitution of Society*, chpt. 3.

and autonomy previously mentioned.[24] Where offices are separated from one another in time-space, many forms of activities or practices can be more or less completely concealed from those in positions of higher authority (as well as from subordinates). Offices may therefore operate both as front and back regions. They may be used to display particular forms of 'model' behaviour thought to be appropriate to the ideal conduct of official tasks. On the other hand, since any such surveillance is necessarily highly incomplete, the office can form a region where formally discouraged practices are carried on. The activities of those in an office setting are often monitored by the 'results' of their activities rather than by the direct supervision of those activities themselves. However such 'results', even if deemed satisfactory, may be reached by methods actually in some part subversive of formal patterns of authority within the organization.

Forms of concealment available to superordinates, however, are as important to the sustaining of their power as practices which subvert formal relations of authority. For the activities which those in higher positions of authority choose to display to their subordinates may be very discrepant from the actual procedures whereby they reach their decisions or formulate their policies. There undoubtedly tends to be a distinction here between those at the very top levels in organizations and those at more middle levels within authority hierarchies. The former characteristically have to engage in certain types of ceremonial display in relation to the mass of their subordinates. These are, as it were, the ritual occasions upon which their power is symbolically reaffirmed. But the activities of those below them in the hierarchy of offices may be effectively wholly concealed from the mass of subordinates. The idea that bureaucracy equals anonymity of power surely has its origins here.

In this regard we might direct attention to what Weber calls the 'rational-legal' character of legitimation within modern organizations, but bend this in a rather different direction from that of Weber. Weber concentrated his attention upon the transition from personal types of affiliation to impersonal rules in the development of office tasks and duties. He also stressed the connection between rational-legal authority and the construction of codes of law more generically within states as the backdrop to such changes within organizations. These emphases are no doubt necessary and desirable for any student of the formation

[24] See Alan Fox: *Beyond Contract*. London: Faber, 1974.

of modern organizations. But they do have implications other than those upon which Weber concentrates. These again connect with the zoning of time-space. In traditional organizations, the ruler was normally in principle an arbitrary authority. As such, he also usually employed sanctions of force to ensure compliance within the organization. This helped to give traditional organizations their characteristically unstable form. Especially at the higher levels of such organizations, recruitment to and stable occupation of positions was frequently dependent upon personal relations with the ruler. There are no modern organizations where this form survives. The basis of legitimacy is never specified in personal terms, even in business organizations of an entrepreneurial type. Instead, authority is perceived as an impersonal set of claims. Moreover, the sanctions possessed by those in authority in modern organizations only rarely involve the direct control of the means of force. States of course maintain that prerogative, but they insist on it so jealously that other organizations rely on different means of securing compliance. Only in the case of those organizations which are essentially either parts of or adjuncts to the state — most notably the military, police and prison system — does direct use of force figure as a major sanction. Even in these its significance is greatly reduced as compared to the extension of impersonally regulated procedures, specifically divergent from the patrimonial power so distinctive of traditional organizations.

Personalized relations of legitimation are inevitably closely bound up with circumstances of high presence-availability. They ordinarily demand close and continuous relations between the parties involved. As the history of traditional states demonstrates again and again, personalized relations of fealty or allegiance that operate at considerable distance in time-space tend to lead to the assertion of autonomous power on the part of those who are supposedly subordinates. Impersonally defined rules of procedure permit vastly greater time-space distanciation. Traditional organizations cannot be stretched over large tracts of time-space. Modern organizations can be — not only because the impersonal definition of procedures permits movements of individuals in and out of positions, without those positions necessarily changing, but because relations between positions are not dependent on the sustaining of high levels of presence-availability. This of course does not deny that there are many contexts in organizations in which personalized ties become significant.

At first sight it might look as though possession of sanctions of force might be a significant means of building administrative power. That such is not the case however can fairly readily be seen. The existence of coercive sanctions does not facilitate the expansion of administrative power to any considerable extent, because such expansion inherently involves the development of trust relations, even if these are concentrated mainly in the hierarchical system of offices. Trust might seem to be primarily a personalized relation of confidence between individuals and so often it no doubt is. However, if trust means the possibility of relying upon another individual or group of individuals regularly to produce responses which can be relied upon to meet certain criteria, then it is entirely consistent with impersonal rules of procedure.[25] Procedural rules do not normally govern activities closely on the shop floor or corresponding 'open' site of activity. There may exist strict rules of procedure, but these are enforced above all by the supervisory staff. In higher administrative positions, by contrast, such rules tend to be followed more autonomously. One aspect of the operation of trust relationships in organizations, therefore, is reliance upon individuals to adopt standardized procedural rules — however many may be the occasions upon which such rules are either ignored or flouted.

Conclusion

The foregoing observations are not intended to offer more than a series of hints about how to think fruitfully about the nature of modern organizations. Nor does the study of organizations exhaust the range of problems that need to be thought through in relation to time-space analysis. However in the connection between 'organization' as a problem of the bracketing of time-space, and 'organizations' as specific features of modern culture, we find issues of the foremost importance for the social sciences.

[25] See Niklas Luhmann: *Trust and Power*. Chichester: Wiley, 1979.

7

Nation-states and violence

We live in a world for which the traditional sources of social theory have left us unprepared — especially those forms of social theory associated with liberal or socialist politics.[1] The world totters on the edge of nuclear disaster, veering out of control. What Marx called the 'anarchy of the market' appears in our times as an international phenomenon. We live in what Wallerstein calls a 'world capitalist economy', in which capitalist economic relations pertain on a world scale.[2] Even more important, we live in a world nation-state system that has no precedent in history, in which a fragile equality in weaponry of the two major superpowers is the only brake upon the political anarchy of the international order.

This world, I think, is quite different from that which most nineteenth-century European social thinkers anticipated, and the traditions of thought that dominate the social sciences today tend to be heavily indebted to their nineteenth-century origins. Virtually everyone sympathetic to Marxism in contemporary times accepts that Marx failed to develop anything more than the rudiments of a theory of the modern state. There has been a great deal of recent Marxist writing attempting to rectify this omission. Much of such work has

[1] Based on a lecture given at the University of Rome in September 1983, this essay was subsequently published in Walter W. Powell and Richard Robbins: *Conflict and Consensus: a Festschrift in Honour of Lewis A. Coser*. New York: Free Press, 1984. Thanks are due to the publisher for permission to reprint.

[2] Immanuel Wallerstein: *The Modern World System*. New York: Academic Press, 1974.

considerable interest. But it is virtually all preoccupied either with the state's role in economic life or with the state as an agent of 'internal' oppression. As Nairn, Poulantzas (especially in his last book, *State, Power and Socialism*), and others openly admit, contemporary Marxist thought lacks a theory either of the nation-state or of nationalism.[3]

However, much of the same is true of liberal political theory also, although in some respects it has had more to say about these issues than most versions of Marxism. Liberal thinkers, such as T. H. Marshall, or Bendix, have written on nationalism, but in their thinking it occupies a strictly subordinate role to what they call 'citizenship' or 'citizenship rights'. The rise of citizenship, according to their analyses, has accompanied the formation of the nation-state. Yet as we can see both from Marshall's little classic, written some thirty years ago — *Citizenship and Social Class* — and from Bendix's most recent and important work, *Kings or People*, their attention has above all been focused on citizenship, on the rights and the mode of rule it implies.[4] The nation-state appears as the 'political community' within which citizenship rights may be realized, not part of a global nation-state system.

What accounts for this fundamental 'absence' in two of the major traditions of social thought? In at least some part it is due to the legacy of Saint-Simon in political theory and to the influence of classical political economy. There is more than a hint in Marx of the Saint-Simonian doctrine that, in the society of the future, the administration of human beings by others will give way to the administration of human beings over things. Durkheim — like later liberal theorists of the welfare state — was less preoccupied with this theme of Saint-Simon's than by the idea that the state in an industrialized order will have a moral role to play in relation to the societal community. That is, in contrast to Marx, he was more influenced by Saint-Simon's later writings than by his earlier ones. But in neither case does there result an understanding of the state in an industrialized society as integrally associated with military violence or administrative control within definite territorial boundaries as a

[3] Tom Nairn: *The Break-up of Britain*. London: New Left Books, 1977; Nicos Poulantzas: *State, Power and Socialism*. New York: Schocken, 1980.

[4] T. H. Marshall: *Citizenship and Social Class*. Cambridge: Cambridge University Press, 1950; Reinhard Bendix: *Kings or People*. Berkeley: University of California Press, 1980.

significant feature of the state. The industrial state, in short, is not a nation-state; the driving force of nationalism is absent, and the industrial order is portrayed as completely different from the rule of absolutism that preceded it. Both Marxist and liberal conceptions of the state were heavily influenced by their respective critiques of political economy. Whatever their differences — which are in some respects very profound — these schools of thought conceived of industrialism as essentially a *pacific* force, and one which transcends international boundaries. Marx's conception of the state as substantially a malevolent agency actually derives from sources similar to those whereby Durkheim conceived of the state as a benevolent agency of progress. In each case the state is seen primarily as a co-ordinating framework within which economic relations are carried on — in the one case expressing mechanisms of class domination, in the other as injecting morality and justice into the occupational order.

In order to associate the state with violence and territoriality, we have to turn to other sources. It is primarily right-liberal or conservative thinkers who have theorized about the state in these terms. One thinks in the earlier generation, for example, of Hintze and Max Weber or, in current times, of the writings of the 'new philosophers' in France. What demonstrates more dramatically the effects of a fruitless encounter with the state power on the part of those on the Left than the aftermath of the 1968 'events'? The new philosophers have moved from Marx to Nietzsche. In turning their backs upon Marxism, and discovering that Marxism lacks not only an adequate conception of the state but a generic theory of power (as distinct from class power), they have made the state and power *the* fundamental components of social life.

In my estimation this stance is not an advance over Marxist and liberal traditions of social theory. Even as set out by Max Weber — who attempted in a certain sense to merge those two incompatibles, Marx and Nietzsche — we do not find a satisfactory treatment of either the nation-state or nationalism. This is partly because Weber defined the state in such a way that it is difficult to pick up the specific significance of the modern nation-state. The characteristics Weber attributes to 'the state' in general are in my opinion in some degree characteristic only of modern states. In any case, however, Weber did not work out an account of the emergence of the contemporary world state system, although much of what he has to say about the European absolutist state and its differences from empires has a great deal of value.

In my discussion here I want to propose a series of concepts that might fill in the 'absence' in social theory mentioned above. To keep things relatively short, I shall cover some of the phenomena involved in a schematic fashion. I ask for the reader's indulgence in this regard; what I have to say here I have formulated in more detail elsewhere. My analysis depends upon the following themes:

1) The system of European absolutism of the fifteenth and sixteenth centuries is of crucial importance to the form in which Western capitalism emerged and spread across the face of the world.
2) The absolutist state must be clearly distinguished from the modern nation-state, however significant may be the historical connections between them.
3) The internal pacification of states, associated especially with the development of police forces and what Foucault calls 'a new disciplinary apparatus of power', is inherently bound up with the consolidation of control of the means of violence in the hands of the state.[5] The processes involved here, however, I shall argue, can be related more closely to Marxist theory than might be imagined from what I have said previously.
4) While these notions are often used interchangeably in the literature, the concept of 'nation-state' has to be carefully separated from that of 'nationalism'.

European absolutism and the nation-state system

One must distrust the nature of the contrasts drawn by Montesquieu and his contemporaries between Europe and the 'despotic' East. But, as more recent historical and archaeological research has shown, Europe, as a set of sociopolitical formations, differed over the long term from the imperial societies of the Far and Near East and from those of Meso-America. During the sixteen hundred years or so that succeeded the disintegration of its empire — Rome — Europe did not experience the rise of another imperial society in its midst, although it was constantly menaced by others from the outside. Europe was a state system for the whole of this period, which can be divided very crudely into two phases. The first was stamped by the influence of the

[5] Michel Foucault: *Discipline* . . . .

Papacy, the Holy Roman Empire, balanced by the localized powers of regional warlords and independent or semi-autonomous city-states. In neither period could any single state power re-establish the Roman Empire in the West or create a new empire that would dominate the Continent.

We are today so accustomed to the dominant role that European capitalism has played in transforming the world that it is difficult to appreciate that for hundreds of years the independence of Europe was often only tenuously maintained in the face of the threat from outside powers. Medieval Europe, although founded upon a militaristic culture, was militarily weak (on land particularly) when confronted by external intrusions. As Cipolla points out, the Europeans were not numerically strong (probably never numbering more than 100 million people) and were chronically engaged in warfare among one another.[6] The disastrous confrontation with the Mongols in 1241 showed that Europe was militarily unable to block the Mongol advance. If Toynbee is right, the ascendancy of the West over the rest of the world begins only after 1683, the time of the failure of the second Ottoman siege of Vienna and the beginning of a Western counter-offensive.

These broad historical considerations form the backdrop to the development of the European state system. In analysing the European state system, we must make some preliminary conceptual distinctions. We should distinguish the *absolutist state*, which coincided only with the very early formation of capitalism in Europe, from the *nation-state*, which has some of its origins in absolutism but is a later development; and, as I have indicated before, we have also to distinguish the nation-state from *nationalism*. The absolutist state, as Weber emphasized so forcibly, was partly built upon a diffuse inheritance from the lingering influence of Rome, especially the persisting influence of Roman law. The absolutist state was not a nation-state, and although there are some dissenting voices among historians, I think it is generally agreed that sentiments of nationalism were scarcely developed at all. I regard the 'absolutist state,' the 'nation-state,' and 'nationalism' as each, in origin, European phenomena. By the absolutist state, a formation limited to some two centuries or so in Europe, I refer to a political order dominated by a sovereign ruler, monarch or prince, in whose person are vested ultimate

---

[6] C. M. Cipolla: *Guns and Sails in the Early Phases of European Expansion 1400 — 1700*. London: Collins, 1965.

political authority and sanctions, including control of the means of violence.

The configuration of states elaborated in the period of European absolutism was certainly the proximate source of the European system of nation-states, and many observers appear to acknowledge no distinction between the absolutist and the nation-state for this reason. The wars conducted by the absolutist monarchs shaped the map of Europe with lasting effect. We should not forget that the long-enduring European powers, England, France, Italy, and so forth, are the survivors of protracted periods of bitter warfare in which most of the protagonists failed to survive. There were some five hundred more or less autonomous political units in Europe in 1500, a number which by 1900 has shrunk to about twenty-five. The transition from the absolutist state to bourgeois rule has characteristically been thought of in terms of dramatic political revolutions. But a concentration upon immediate processes of revolutionary strife actually hinders a grasp of how closely connected the ascendancy to power of the bourgeoisie was with the more gradual transformation of the absolutist state into the nation-state, which is why the nation-state and capitalism have integral structural connections in eighteenth- and nineteenth-century Europe. We should remember that the creation of a capitalist *society* or *state* is not just a matter of the extension of commodity production writ large. There is indeed an intimate association between modern capitalism and the nation-state. Some historians have claimed that this association was no more than fortuitous. Thus it has been said that some early capitalistic enterprises — like the Hanse — were quite foreign to state formation, while on the other hand strong states that were formed early on, such as Spain or France, were not principal centres of capitalist development. This is true of the period of the absolutist state but not of the period of transition to the nation-state. In the latter, to develop a capitalist-industrial infrastructure became the *sine qua non* of a strong state able to survive or expand within the state system.

In the section that follows I want to pursue this line of reasoning. Let me first offer a general conceptualization of the 'nation-state' and 'nationalism.' The nation-state, which exists in a complex of other nation-states, is a set of institutional forms of governance maintaining an administrative monopoly over a territory with demarcated boundaries, its rule being sanctioned by law and direct control of the means of internal and external violence. Two things are worth noting about this definition, or it risks being confused with a quasi-Weberian conceptualization of the state in general. First, all states seem to have been associated with 'territoriality', but in empires and in most absolutist states, the boundaries were diffuse. What is specifically late European is the fixing of very precise boundaries that actually *do* effectively mark the realm of the administration of the state. Second, control of the means of violence, as a monopoly or near-monopoly in the hands of the state, became possible only with the internal pacification of nation-states. The differentiation between the police and standing army, or armed forces, has remained a fairly clear — although never wholly unambiguous — one in most European countries since the middle of the nineteenth century. This different-iation can be said to express the 'inward' and 'outward' stance of the state in respect of violence and its control.

What makes the 'nation' integral to the nation-state in this definition is not the existence of sentiments of nationalism but the unification of an administrative apparatus over precisely defined territorial bounds (in a complex of other nation-states). Such a unification depends very significantly, as Deutsch and others have indicated, upon advances in transportation and communication.[7] Communication became distinct from transportation only with the invention of the electromagnetic telegraph. When Morse transmitted the message 'What hath God wrought?' between Baltimore and Washington in 1844, he initiated new bases of administrative order (as the invention of writing had done millennia before).

I shall define 'nationalism' as the existence of symbols and beliefs that are either propagated by elite groups or held by many of the members of regional, ethnic, or linguistic categories and that imply a commonality between them. Nationalistic sentiments do not necessarily converge with citizenship of a particular nation-state, but very often they have done so. A definition of nationalism has to be a fairly generalized one, because studies of the phenomenon show that there is no single criterion that forms the focus of commonality. On the basis of the European experience in the nineteenth and twentieth centuries, for example, one might suppose that speaking a common language is a prime feature of nationalism. But looked at in a world context, the factor of common language seems to be the exception rather than the rule.

---

[7] K. W. Deutsch: *Nationalism and its Alternatives*. New York: Knopf, 1969.

The nation-state, capitalism, violence

I have claimed that the connection between the development of capitalism and the nation-state is less contingent than many analysts — such as Tilly — have argued.[8] Justifying this claim has important implications for the 'absence' in Marxist and liberal theories of the state I have alluded to earlier. The association between capitalism and the nation-state, I propose, can be prised open by concentrating upon some specific and distinctive features of the capitalist labour contract. As Marx accentuated, the capitalistic labour contract differs in a basic way from modes of exploitation of surplus production found in pre-capitalist societies. In the latter, the exploiter is in some sense — which varies in different systems — an agent of the state and possesses access to the means of violence, or its threat, as a principal instrument ensuring the compliance of the subordinate class or classes. The capitalistic labour contract, on the other hand, does not involve the exploitation of surplus production or labour; it depends upon the extraction of surplus value, an exploitative relation that is hidden in the overall system of production and distribution. The capitalistic labour contract establishes a purely economic relation of mutual dependency between employer and worker. Capitalist relations of production, which the bourgeoisie fought to extend and which eventually became the dominant economic order, were not brought about through military power or through a direct class monopoly of the means of violence.

These considerations are, to my mind, of quite essential significance to understanding both the workings of capitalist economic enterprise (Marx's overwhelming focus of attention) *and* the co-ordination of the development of capitalism with the nation-state. A historical conjunction of decisive significance was the centralization of power in the hands of the absolutist monarchs in a context of class alliances with rising bourgeois elements. Marx, of course, pointed this out, but he did not pursue its implications for the co-ordination of the means of violence. The monopolization of the means of violence in the hands of the state went along with the extrusion of control of violent sanctions

[8] Charles Tilly: 'Reflections on the history of European state-making', in *The Formation of National States in Europe*. Princeton: Princeton University Press, 1975.

from the class relations involved in emergent capitalism. How this occurred historically, varying according to time and place, is a matter well beyond the scope of this discussion, but the outlines seem clear. Commitment to freedom of contract, which was both part of a broader set of ideological claims to human liberties for which the bourgeoisie fought and an actual reality that they sought to further in economic organization, meant the expulsion of sanctions of violence from the newly expanding labour market. The sphere of 'private' freedoms in regard to both capital and labour, which excluded the forcible plunder of labour products or resources, became institutionally distinguished from 'public' authority bolstered by monopoly of the means of violence.

To develop this analysis further we need a concept that does not appear in a prominent way in either Marxist or liberal accounts of the state: that of what Foucault calls surveillance.[9] Surveillance on two levels is basic to understanding the nature of the processes whereby the spread of the capitalist labour contract was associated with state monopoly of violence:

1) surveillance in the workplace and
2) a massive expansion of the surveillance activities of the state in the eighteenth and nineteenth centuries, closely connected in turn with the internal pacification of emergent nation-states.

'Surveillance' I take to mean two closely related phenomena. One is the collection and organization of information that can be stored by agencies or collectivities and can be used to 'monitor' the activities of an administered population. The second is the direct supervision or control of the activities of subordinates by superiors in a particular organization or range of social settings.

In pre-capitalist societies, even in European absolutism, levels of surveillance exercised by the state and dominant class were necessarily low. This was true both of the administrative apparatus of the state and of control of the worker in the labour process. Terms like 'absolutism' and 'despotism' are potentially misleading in reference to the power of rulers over their subjects in pre-capitalist societies. A despot in a certain sense had extreme power over his subjects — the power of life and death — but he did not have the capability to administer directly the day-to-day lives of his subjects, which were

---

9 Michel Foucault, *Discipline* . . . .

largely ordered by local traditions and practices. Despotism, I should add parenthetically, is thus a very different phenomenon from modern totalitarianism, which depends upon the vast extension of surveillance activities of states that has occurred over the past two centuries. Much the same applies to the labour process, to the process of production. In pre-capitalist agrarian production, exploiting classes generally had little overall control of the labour process, the pace of work and so on. This was true even well into the period of industrial capitalism. In Britain at the midpoint of the nineteenth century, for example, a high proportion of the manufacturing work force still toiled in cottage industries. The expansion of the factory, or the 'capitalistic workplace,' separate from the home, as Pollard and others have shown in the case of Britain, was due more to the perceived needs of employers to secure regularized labour discipline than to the sheer technical effectiveness of the factory.[10]

Surveillance in the capitalistic enterprise is the key to management. Since wage-labour is 'formally free' and moreover is directly integrated into complex production processes, the main negative sanctions possessed by employers are economic — the need of the propertyless workers to earn a livelihood. One of the most important historical sources for analysing the origins of modern labour discipline, in Britain at least, is Pollard's *The Genesis of Modern Management*. Let me include a substantial quotation from this book, for it encapsulates some of the main issues:

> Did not the ancient Egyptians build their huge pyramids, or the Chinese their wall, or, more recently did not Louis XIV inaugurate a magnificent system of main-road building in France? If the control of large masses of men was in question, had not the generals controlled many more, over the ages, than the manager of even the largest industrial country? . . . All these developments, it must be admitted, preceded the industrial revolution, often by several millennia, and it is equally true that the entrepreneurs and managers of the industrial revolution learnt one or other aspect of their work from them. The innovation, and the difficulty, lay in this: that the men who began to operate the large industrial units in the British economy from the middle of the eighteenth century onwards had to combine these different objectives and methods into one. Like the generals of old, they had to control numerous men, but without powers of compulsion: indeed the absence of legal enforcement

---

[10] S. Pollard: *The Genesis of Modern Management*. London: Arnold, 1965.

of unfree work was not only one of marked characteristics of the new capitalism, but one of its most seminal ideas.[11]

However much as a class they may have promulgated ideals of individual liberty, employers were often reluctant to forgo the use of direct sanctions of violence against their workers. The volunteer force raised in England in 1794, consisting mainly of gentry, shopkeepers, and 'employers on horseback', operated partly to discipline recalcitrant workers. Regular troops were in action internally until well beyond the Chartist period. They enforced the daily 'imprisonment' of labour within the workplace.

The emergence of disciplined labour was thus very closely intertwined with the increasingly successful creation of modes of industrial management, operating with a variety of partly novel techniques of surveillance. This was one major dimension of internal pacification and has ever since remained entangled with citizenship rights or what Marx more scathingly called 'bourgeois freedoms'. But the creation of the management of free labour also took place in the broader context of the expansion of disciplinary power in the institutions of the state. Disciplinary power, as Foucault has illuminated so brilliantly, contrasts with the 'exemplary power' of violence characteristic of previous ages. Violence is no longer a display, a spectacle, sanctioning power through its very display. Violence, as controlled by the state authorities, becomes an underlying sanction — a hidden but available threat — while control is sustained primarily through the disciplinary power of surveillance.

Since I have just quoted from Pollard, allow me to mention a short passage from Foucault:

> If the economic take-off of the West began with the technique that made possible the accumulation of capital, it might perhaps be said that the methods for administering the accumulation of men made possible a political take-off in relation to the traditional ritual, costly, violent forms of power, which soon fell into disuse and were superseded by a subtle, calculated technology of subjection.[12]

What Foucault fails to note is of quite essential significance to my argument. The supersession of 'ritual, costly, violent forms of power'

11 Ibid., p. 7.
12 Michel Foucault: *Discipline* . . . , pp. 220—1.

was decisively important to the internal formation of the state. But the maintenance and consolidation of these forms of power became an inherent feature of the nation-state system. The characteristics of the European state system I pointed to earlier then started to become diffused across the world. As Wallerstein says, in pre-capitalist military empires the scope of military sanctions basically determined the boundaries of economic relations within and between those societies. With the development of capitalism, however, this situation is in a sense reversed. The capitalist state maintains a monopoly of political and military power within its own bounds, but the world system it initiates is fundamentally influenced by capitalistic processes operating on a world scale.

Nationalism

Before drawing some of the threads of this discussion together, I have to make some comments upon the relation between the nation-state and nationalism. Liberal accounts of the state, associated with so-called modernization theory, have been particularly prone to assimilate the concepts of nation-state and nationalism. This is the literature of 'nation-building,' closely connected with concepts of citizenship. It has tended to ignore the more noxious aspects of nationalism — its association with fascism and with the waging of wars. Nationalism is treated pre-eminently as a beneficent force, one closely involved with the achievement of citizenship rights in the Third World (socialist nationalism also being largely ignored). Nationalism, like the nation-state, is a phenomenon generated originally from within Europe, and I think it is right to stress that it would not have emerged without the bourgeois idea of popular sovereignty that ushered in the modern phase of European liberalism.

It would be foolish to play down what Deutsch calls the 'dreams and images of savagery' produced by nationalism along with its images of 'self-government, enlightenment, and social justice'.[13] Many commentators on nationalism have acknowledged its Janus-faced character. Just as many writers of the 'nation-building' type have tended to accentuate the positive side of nationalism, others have been much more inclined to the opposite view. Kedourie stands out as

[13] K. W. Deutsch: *Nationalism* . . . , p. 53.

one of the most prominent of these, holding nationalism to be 'an antiquarian irrelevance, a baneful invention of some misguided German philosophers'.[14]

What accounts for the Janus-faced character of nationalism, and what explains its tremendous significance in modern world history? In order to reach even a provisional approach to such questions, we have to recognize that, however frequently nationalistic feelings have been fostered and invoked ideologically by dominant elites, nationalism is not merely a set of symbols and beliefs force-fed to an unwilling or indifferent population. Moreover, if nationalism is not distinguished from the nation-state, a range of phenomena that are rooted in the *Realpolitik* of the interests of the state are easily misunderstood as the direct outcome of a nationalistic spirit. One might almost define the fascist state as comprising a successful linkage between an aggressive and exclusivist nationalism and a generalized commitment to the state as the ultimate arbiter of the interests of the community.

Nationalism is in substantial part a psychological phenomenon, involving felt needs and dispositions, in contrast to the nation-state, which is an institutional phenomenon. To grasp its importance, we must realize the needs it corresponds to. The significance of nationalism in the modern world is quite clearly related to the decline of tradition and to the fragmentary character of the everyday life in which lost traditions are partly refurbished. This applies both to modernized societies and to those suffering cultural strain or conflict. These circumstances render fragile what Laing calls the 'ontological security' upon which day-to-day life is based.[15] Ontological security means the security of taken-for-granted routines, giving a sense of the continuity of being. In traditional cultures the sustaining framework of ontological security is well bolstered by the continuity of practices in the local community. But in large-scale societies, in which routinization has substantially replaced tradition — where moral meaning and self-identity have retreated to the margins of the private and the public — feelings of commonality of language and belongingness in a national community tend to form one strand contributing to the maintenance of ontological security. Nationalistic sentiments both have an affinity with and may directly express cultural similarities within or between groups, and language is a major carrier

14 E. Kedourie: *Nationalism*. London: Hutchinson, 1961, p. 21.
15 R. D. Laing: *The Divided Self*. London: Pelican, 1964.

of such similarities. This is why, in the original setting of the formation of nationalism, Europe, language appears as a major medium of nationalism. The leading nation-states were already — with various important exceptions — fairly settled language communities. The post-European expansion of nationalism is obviously in some ways quite different from its first development in Europe, not least because the criterion of a common language by no means readily converges with the boundaries of newly established nation-states.

If the foundations of nationalist sentiments are perhaps not too difficult to elucidate, how are we to explain their Janus-faced character? I think we have to do so by giving attention to the phenomenon of leadership. The influence of leaders has been very prominent in waves of nationalist sentiment and in nationalist movements, and it is surprising how little attention has been given to this by most of those who have written on the subject. The theory of leadership, or at least its psychological origins, has been well established in the classic writings of Le Bon and Freud.[16] According to their ideas — and this would apply especially in circumstances where ontological security is under threat or strain — emotional affiliation with a leader figure is essentially a regressive phenomenon. Regressive identification with a leader figure, and the symbols represented by that figure and his or her doctrines, carries with it that essential feature of nationalism, whether benign or militant, a strong psychological affiliation with an 'in-group' coupled with a differentiation from 'out-groups.'

If the Le Bon—Freud theory of leadership is valid, regressive object-identification with a leadership figure is connected psychologically with increased 'suggestibility' and emotional volatility. Emotional identification creates a dependency that can be channelled in quite opposite directions. This seems to make sense of the Janus-faced nature of nationalism. For individuals would become vulnerable to identification both with figures who may exemplify 'populist' or 'democratic' virtues, or a range of 'heroic' values inspiring acts of either nobility or savagery. This type of theory, incidentally, seems a possible adjunct to Weber's account of charismatic leadership. For Weber does not explain the source of the emotional identification such leaders are able to inspire.

[16] Gustav Le Bon: *The Crowd.* Dunwoody: Berg, 1900; Sigmund Freud: *Group Psychology and the Analysis of the Ego.* London: Hogarth, 1972.

I shall not attempt to discuss the various typologies of nationalist movements that appear in the literature dealing with the subject. European nationalism, as is very apparent in the various regional nationalisms that today exist within the European countries, is itself not all of a piece. And certainly the history of European nationalism differs very significantly from subsequent developments elsewhere.

The world system

The nation-state system has today become a worldwide one. As a historical problem, the connections between the expansion of the capitalist world economy and the universal transformation of pre-existing societal forms into nation-states still have to be adequately documented. The majority of proponents of world system theory, especially those influenced by the two traditions of state theory I referred to at the beginning of my remarks, the Marxist and the liberal, have continued to place most emphasis upon economic developments. Thus Wallerstein divides the world capitalist economy into three principal zones: the capitalist 'core' (Europe, the United States and, more latterly, Japan); the 'semi-periphery,' which is both exploiter and exploited; and the 'peripheral' regions, dominated by what he calls 'coerced cash-crop labour'.

However, Wallerstein does not adequately relate the emergence of capitalism to the European state system, and hence underplays the role of military power and warfare among states in shaping the contemporary world. In this respect, while breaking with the long-established tendency in the social sciences to treat societies or states as though they were self-contained entities, Wallerstein's discussion continues the subordination of the politico-military to the economic, which I mentioned as deeply embedded in social theory. We live not only in a world capitalist economy but in a world politico-military order of anarchically organized nation-states.

To someone sympathetic to, yet critical of, Marxist theory and of the libertarian aspirations of socialism, it should be clear that my discussion has important implications for normative political thought. In his own day Marx looked forward to the achievement of socialism as the overall transcendence of capitalism; there is no indication he anticipated a world in which the capitalist core would not experience a successful socialist revolution and in which capitalism would coexist with societies governed by groups claiming affiliation to his doctrines.

Marx, I think, genuinely believed that 'the workers have no country'. How distant we seem today from that idea, and from pronouncements such as that of Bakunin, not at all uncharacteristic of the nineteenth century:

> No more wars of conquest, nothing but the last supreme war, the war of the revolution for the emancipation of all peoples. Away with the narrow frontiers forcibly imposed by the congress of despots, in accordance with the so-called historic, geographical, commercial strategic necessities. There should be no other frontiers but those which respond simultaneously to nature and to justice, in accordance with the spirit of democracy — frontiers which the people in their sovereign will shall trace, founded upon their natural sympathies.[17]

Marx anticipated the transcendence of the state in the future society he envisaged. Yet the state, as capitalist or socialist state, has turned out to be a far more formidable phenomenon than many nineteenth-century thinkers, including Marx, envisaged. The theme of the transcendence of the state has perhaps not lost its interest or importance as a key theme of socialist political theory. But the phenomena upon which I have centred my attention in this paper are to my mind of elementary significance in reshaping political theory in our era.

In the contemporary world we are between capitalism and socialism in two senses, and any discussion of normative political theory must be concerned with both. In the shape of the actually existing socialist societies, socialism is a reality, part of the power-bloc system that tenuously controls the anarchy of the world nation-state order. It no longer is plausible, if it ever was, to say that they are not really socialist at all or that their insufficiencies have nothing to do with shortcomings of Marxist thought in general. On the other hand, if socialist ideals retain any validity, we are between capitalism and socialism in the sense that such ideals seem capable of much more profound development than has been achieved in any society to date.

Three aspects of my analysis are especially relevant to any discussion of the political theory of socialism today, on each of these related levels.

[17] M. Bakunin: 'Appeal to the Slavs', in S. Dolgoff: *Bakunin on Anarchy*. London: Allen and Unwin, 1973, p. 278.

1) Surveillance as a medium of the disciplinary power of the state,
    and other aspects of repression, has to be theorized. Lacking such
    a theorization, totalitarian aspects of political control are left
    unanalysed — as they are in orthodox forms of Marxist theory.

2) We cannot just ignore the fact that, to date at least, the nation-
    state has proved as significant an aspect of socialist as of capitalist
    societies. Socialist states are nation-states and have shown
    themselves to be as jealously territorial and aggressive as others.
    This is the era of the gulag, of confrontations of a warlike character
    between socialist states, of Pol Pot, and something close to
    genocide in Kampuchea. Neither socialism more generally, nor
    Marxism in particular, walk innocently in this world.

3) The most fundamental problem facing us today is the seemingly
    implacable expansion of the means of violence in the hands of
    nation-states. There is no matter that presses more heavily upon
    the contemporary world than the actuality of international violence
    and the looming threat of nuclear war. Yet leftist political theory
    has no tradition of theorizing about the world violence of the
    system of power blocs and nation-states. Practical political
    programmes that have relevance to the nation-state as the
    propagator of violence seem of the first priority for socialist
    thinkers as much as anyone else. It is difficult not to feel sombre
    in the face of the anarchy of the nation-state system. Marx
    thought he discerned a real movement of change — the labour
    movement — that would provide history's solution to the anarchy
    of the capitalist market and the degradation of work. But where
    is the dialectic process that will transcend the political anarchy
    that threatens us all with imminent destruction? So far as I can
    see, there is none in view. Every existing form of world
    organization at the moment seems impotent in the face of the
    monopoly of violence in the hands of nation-states. There is no
    sense in not admitting that today we stand at the outer edge of the
    precipice of history. Our existence now is unique in an eerie way.
    After a half a million years of human history, we are the first
    human beings whose individual lifespans might terminate with
    that of the whole of humankind. Has the cunning of reason here
    deserted us?

8

Social theory and problems
of macroeconomics

_____

This discussion needs to be prefaced by some cautionary remarks.[1] I
am not an economist and the ideas set out in what follows cannot be
said to be based upon an exhaustive knowledge of current economic
thought. What I attempt here is limited to seeking to connect some
leading themes in economic theory today to more general trends in
social theory as a whole. Moreover I shall concentrate upon a restricted
number of questions and shall by no means attempt to confront the
whole range of issues potentially raised by such a subject.

Economics is a social science, but one more separated — particularly
in recent years — from its neighbouring disciplines than they are from
one another. There is a conventional view of the relation between
economics and the rest of the social sciences which is well-entrenched
in the literature. According to this view, we can identify a distinct
arena of specifically 'economic' problems — to do with markets, the
production and distribution of goods — which serves reasonably
clearly to distinguish the concerns of economics as a field of study
from the other social sciences. Outside the arena of the economic there
are other institutions whose basic nature is 'non-economic'. The
relationship between economics and the remainder of the social
sciences is therefore one of institutional complementarity. Economics
has a distinct and isolable subject-matter; surrounding this there are
a range of 'institutional' questions which economists may for the most

_____

[1] This chapter had its origins as a lecture given to the Sociology Seminar at
the University of Cambridge.

part put to one side. These are issues with which sociologists, political scientists, anthropologists and others must grapple. The other social sciences, as it were, crowd in around the perimeters of what economists do in economic thinking and analysis. This has long been something of an 'official' view, held by most economists as well as by other social scientists having an interest in economics.

It is not a perspective I wish to reject altogether. But I do want to argue for a new view of the connections between economics and the rest of the social sciences. This view proposes that there are problems of both a substantive and a theoretical kind that concern economics and the other social sciences equally. It is based upon the idea that there is a series of convergent changes taking place throughout the social sciences — occurring in economics just as elsewhere. But because economics, with the exception of some schools of thought, has become so insulated from its sister social science disciplines, these convergences have not been apparent either to those working inside or outside economics. I want to try to indicate that there is a direct tie between developments in economic theory and those occurring in other areas — and demonstrate that each of these may be used to illuminate the other.

There are three themes upon which I shall concentrate. First, I shall analyse changes going on in economics, particularly economic theory, since the early 1970s. These can be shown to resemble changes in sociology and the other social science disciplines. I shall take it that such similarities are not gratuitous and that certain influences are operating across the whole spectrum of the social sciences. Second, I shall propose that within the flurry of novel economic theorizing over the past few years there is one type of endeavour which is particularly interesting and important — that which has come to be called 'rational expectations' theory. Third, I want to trace through connections between rational expectations theories and some broader problems in social theory as a whole. By so doing we can suggest some of the limitations of rational expectations thinking, as claimant to the leading position with macroeconomics — supposedly supplanting Keynesianism — as well as indicating its relevance for other areas of social science.

Parallels and divergencies

Over the course of the post-war period, until roughly the early 1970s, there was something like an 'orthodox consensus' in economic thought. That is to say, in the English-speaking world at least there was a body of theory and method distinguishable as 'mainstream economics'. By no means all economists affiliated themselves with mainstream perspectives — one might instance Joan Robinson and Nicholas Kaldor as prominent dissidents — but these perspectives nevertheless served to orient both defenders and critics. Marxist economics, and the 'evolutionism' of followers of Veblen and Commons, always remained distinct. But these did not, and do not today, command the support of more than a relatively small minority.

In sociology especially, but in no small degree in most of the rest of the social sciences, there was also a definite 'orthodox consensus' during the post-war period. Just as in economics, this had its critics — including in particular those associated with Marxism, which retained a stronger influence than within economics. There were some interesting similarities between the orthodox consensus in economics and that in sociology and elsewhere — and there were some instructive divergencies. The dissolution of the orthodox consensus has probably been more pronounced and complete in sociology than in economics. But the overall pattern in certain key respects has not been very different.

The background to the development of 'mainstream' ideas, in all the social sciences since the Second World War, has to be understood in socio-economic terms. For some quarter of a century there seemed to be stable patterns of growth established in most Western societies. If the fluctuating nature of market economies was recognized to persist, it seemed at least as if the worst of the perturbations could be controlled. This indeed was taken to be the essence of 'Keynesianism' — that through demand management, with government playing an active role, progressive economic development could be achieved. Two other elements were taken to be correlated with this process. One was the successful institutionalization of liberal democracy within the political systems of the Western societies. Modes of democratic organization within many societies prior to the War were partial, leaving quite large segments 'unincorporated'. The successful involvement of the mass of the population within the democratic order, such that the majority of the working class acquired a range of 'citizenship rights', was held to 'complete' the triumph of liberal democratic institutions. The state became a 'welfare state', providing a wide range of benefits for its citizenry.[2]

---

[2] One of the most influential analyses of these issues, which deservedly has achieved something of a classic status, was T. H. Marshall: *Citizenship*

Looking back at this period it is quite extraordinary how confidently, both in economics and the other social sciences, trends were generalized to an indefinite future.[3] Among most mainstream sociologists and political scientists, for example, it was more or less taken for granted that there would be a progressive expansion of welfare institutions, that the higher education system would continue to embrace more and more of the population, and so on. No doubt few economists were sanguine enough to have believed that the problems of 'steering' market economies had been permanently resolved, but nonetheless the mechanisms providing for controlled economic development seemed well enough understood. No one could pretend that, even within the 'developed' world, this was a period without major tensions and conflicts. However it would probably be true to say that for most these seemed of less enduring significance than the 'successes' of the era.

The apparent stabilizing of social and economic development was the source of the security that the orthodox consensus offered. Let me sketch in briefly what that consensus was, and how the dominant views in economics contrasted to those found elsewhere. In economics its main characteristics were as follows. There was a plundering of Keynes which, combined with ideas drawn from pre-existing versions of neo-classical economic theory, created the 'neo-classical synthesis'. Certainly this exegesis largely ignored some of Keynes's most important contributions to economics. What became the neo-classical synthesis might even be plausibly regarded as an aborted Kuhnian revolution in economics. Keynes's writings are far from being internally consistent. But some of the major emphases in Keynes's economics — upon the fundamental influence of time and contingency, upon the habitual and non-rational in human conduct, combined with a disavowal of the 'long run' — broke very substantially with existing orthodoxy. Rather than undermining the pre-existing frameworks of economic thought, however, elements from Keynes were selectively appropriated, discarding or modifying the features just mentioned, and rendered compatible with a defence of marginalism in economic theory.

---

and Social Class. Cambridge: Cambridge University Press, 1950. Marshall's discussion was later expanded and elaborated under the title *Sociology at the Crossroads*.

[3] See Anthony Giddens: 'Class division, class conflict and citizenship rights', in *Profiles and Critiques in Social Theory*. London: Macmillan, 1982.

It seemed to most economists at the time — and still seems to many today — that there is a sort of 'unified field theory' in economics, a theoretical schema that can be made effectively to cover the whole field of the 'economic'. Such a schema — into which Keynes's ideas were absorbed, or reabsorbed — depends essentially upon marginalist assumptions, plus the notion of the theoretical parity of the factors of production, land, capital and labour. What happens at the margins of the use of the factors of production is held to be most instructive for analysing the 'centre', at which supply and demand curves intersect. There is no obvious reason why marginalism should have maintained its hold in this way, and it was a large part of the triumph of the orthodox consensus that alternative ideas — stressing surplus or the basic influence of non-economic institutions — gained virtually no foothold. Nor is it at all obvious that there should or can be a 'unified field theory' able to eliminate all important economic questions. Nevertheless this has been a persistent idea — and one that still survives as a feature of most introductory economics textbooks.

A second characteristic of the orthodox consensus was the idea of economics as a positive science, a view associated perhaps above all with Friedman but widely accepted within the subject as a whole. Of course this standpoint has been developed with greater or lesser degrees of sophistication. Basically the view was that economics is, or should become, a science, where 'science' is understood in terms of a logical empiricist model of natural science. This was the same version of 'social science as science' which influenced most of the other social science disciplines at the period. Like sociologists and others, economists did not perceive logical empiricism as one philosophy of science among others, but as an unquestioned account of the basis of natural science.

In economics there was one aspect of such a position that was particularly important. This concerned predictability. It seemed to Friedman, and the many others who took a similar stance, that the key criterion of the scientificity of a theory concerns its capability to generate accurate predictions. The notion is consonant with the main ideas of logical empiricism, but it has a significance for economics that does not apply in most of the other social sciences. One reason for this is that economists are much more centrally concerned with 'expectations' than are other social scientists. Another is to do with the type of analysis specifically developed by Friedman.[4] According to

[4] Milton Friedman: 'The methodology of positive economics', in *Essays in Positive Economics*. Chicago: Chicago University Press, 1953.

his views, which were worked out in a fairly elaborate fashion, what really matters about an economic theory or hypothesis is how far it is able accurately to predict a given course of events or series of outcomes. It can be inferred from this that it is of little consequence whether a model is 'realistic' or not. What is important is whether it generates good predictions about its subject-matter. Partly on the basis of this argument the most complicated sorts of mathematical models have been constructed, freed from the need to match up to the real world save in respect of their predictive capacities. The issue has been much discussed, and the Friedman argument criticized in various ways. I shall want later to reject it on the basis of a rather different claim from those ordinarily advanced by economists in criticism of it.

A third element of the orthodox consensus in economics — the notion perhaps above all associated with 'Keynesianism' — was the emphasis upon demand management. Keynes held that wage reductions did not necessarily decrease unemployment; they might simply reduce aggregate demand. The implications of this relatively simple observation were far-reaching, for they suggested a role for the state of a developed and necessary kind in economic life. As one observer puts it, it became very generally recognized that it is an obligation of government 'to control the level of total effective demand for goods and services. If demand is insufficient to provide full employment, it is the government's duty to raise it by stimulating the injections (investment, government expenditure, and/or exports) and/or by discouraging the leakages (by reducing the proportions of income saved, paid in taxes, or spent on imports). If demand is excessive, then it is the government's duty to restrain the injections and encourage the leakages.'[5] Of course, these ideas were interpreted in different ways in the detail of their application.

The neo-classical synthesis shared with the orthodox consensus in sociology and political science its affection for 'positive science'. But there are certain respects in which there were considerable contrasts. In contrast with the view taken by the other social sciences rational action, especially as defined in relation to a specified number of goals (profit maximizing and utility), was accorded a prime place. Models of rational action used in economics also remained associated with

    [5] James Meade: 'The Keynesian revolution', in Milo Keynes (ed.): *Essays on John Maynard Keynes*. Cambridge: Cambridge University Press, 1975, pp. 87—8.

'voluntarism'. That is, agents are pictured in neo-classical theory as individuals who have preferences and thereby choose courses of action in pursuit of them — regardless of whether they are producers or consumers.

In the social sciences outside economics such an orientation was uncommon, and widely thought to be incompatible with an emphasis upon 'positive science'. For such an emphasis, it was believed by many, involves identifying invariant laws of social conduct; and the causal relations involved in laws must necessarily operate to constrain action 'externally'. However the differences between economics and the remainder of the social sciences on this point can be exaggerated. For the models used by economists were mostly heavily deterministic. In such models, preferences were assumed to be given, as was complete optimization. With the specifying of 'initial conditions', there was no room for 'choice' where this implies deliberation over possible courses of action in contingent circumstances.

In sociology and the other social sciences the orthodox consensus was never *as* orthodox — never as generally shared — as in economics. And the elements of the 'neo-classical synthesis' remain more of an orthodoxy today in economics than is the case in the other social sciences. Characteristic of views in non-economic social science was what might be referred to as 'institutionalism' — something that differed very substantially from marginalism. It is not what happens 'at the margins' that is significant, but what goes on at the 'central pressure points' of institutions. The concepts of role and status were typical organizing notions in this respect. The notion of role can be made something of a voluntaristic one, as where roles are 'made' rather than just 'taken', but for the most part the idea of role was understood in a deterministic way. Roles are pre-constituted modes of behaviour that shape individuals' actions far more than the reverse. Although logical empiricism made its impact throughout the social sciences, a stress upon predictability as the aim of social analysis, while common, did not become quite as important as in economics. The reason surely was that it was less problematic: those sectors of social activity upon which non-economic social science concentrated were just those in which people tend to behave in regular, predictable ways — enacting institutionalized roles.[6]

[6] See the contrasts between 'sociological' and 'economic' views drawn by Barry. Brian Barry: *Sociologists, Economists and Democracy*. London: Routledge, 1970.

Parallel to the significance of demand management in economics, as mentioned previously, was the thesis that liberal democracy had become stabilized. Particularly important here was the idea of the 'institutionalization of class conflict'. Prior to the Second World War, and stretching back into the nineteenth century, the 'social question' (class conflict and class divisions) was always regarded as of basic importance. With the exception of Marxist critics, most sociologists and political scientists saw working-class radicalism in the post-war period as having become diffused into accepted bargaining between interest groups. Labour or socialist parties represented working-class interests in parliament, while unions did likewise in the workplace. If the disequilibrating tendencies of capitalist economies can be controlled by effective state management, so can the class cleavages which in previous eras had seemed to threaten progressive development.

Unlike in economics, in the other social sciences functionalism was a methodological perspective of major importance to the orthodox consensus. Neither functionalism in general, nor that rather more restricted body of thought that came to be known as 'structural functionalism' ever made any impact in economics. But its influence has been felt persistently in all the other social sciences. Functionalism of course tends to depend upon analogies drawn between social and biological systems. Since the 'whole' (that is, the social system or society) is seen as having properties that impose themselves on the 'parts' (individual agents), functionalism has commonly been linked to the view of social causation mentioned earlier — this was certainly true of the period of the orthodox consensus. Most sociologists at that time sought to discover the subject-matter of their discipline not, as in economics, in the choices we make as acting subjects, but in the choices we do not make. We may think of ourselves as agents who make choices and understand why we act as we do; the role of sociology is to show otherwise. All of us are born into societies whose institutions predate us and mould our actions. The fondness which sociologists had for Durkheim's *Suicide*, as a model for social research in general, is symptomatic of this. For what Durkheim was taken to be claiming was that, while suicide seems to be a voluntary act, undertaken by an individual alone, in fact it expresses general properties of social causation.

In the period from the early 1970s to the present, in economics and elsewhere, key premises of the orthodox consensus have either been widely discarded or placed in question.[7] There are still 'mainstream' ideas in most social science subjects, but they no longer command the level of allegiance they once did. In their place, or around their edges, has sprung up a diversity of competing traditions of thought, particularly on a theoretical level, across which communication is difficult, since their underlying orientations vary so widely. In sociology and the non-economic social sciences these include hermeneutics, Wittgensteinian philosophy, structuralism and post-structuralism, a revival of forms of Marxist thought, phenomenology and critical theory. Within economics we may list post-Keynesianism, neo-Keynesianism, monetarism, neo-Marxism, the neo-Ricardianism of Sraffa and others, together with rational expectations theory. Elements of some of these may be combined with others in various permutations. But I shall concentrate my attention upon rational expectations theories, which not only have become peculiarly influential, but which have certain interesting and important qualities. There are basic objections that have to be made against such theories, but nonetheless they have come to develop ideas directly similar to those emanating from non-economic social theory.

Rational expectations theory

The impact made by rational expectations accounts of economic activity has to be understood in relation both to the pre-existing dominance of 'Keynesianism' and to the writings of Keynes himself. As one commentator has put it, 'Up to the 1970s, the economists who opposed Keynes had to be content with pulling a few fish off their opponents' hooks.' But with rational expectations notions 'they could simply dynamite the lake'.[8] If the metaphor is not an especially appealing one, it at least conveys very well the significance that many see in rational expectations thinking. In Keynes's *General Theory* the expectations that economic agents hold were understood in relation to the 'unsettling' aspects of Keynes's views already mentioned — time, contingency, habit, irrationality. But in the appropriation of Keynes that became 'Keynesianism', expectations often tended to become

---

[7] For useful surveys, see Daniel Bell and Irving Kristol: *The Crisis in Economic Theory*. New York: Basic, 1981; and Lester Thurow: *Dangerous Currents*. Oxford: Oxford University Press, 1983.

[8] Mark H. Willes: '"Rational expectations" as a counterrevolution', in Bell and Kristol, *The Crisis* . . . , p. 81.

translated into systems of theory operating in virtual time, in closed models that abstracted from Keynes's original emphases. Such was the backdrop to the invention of the celebrated IS/LM formula and the Phillips Curve. In cruder versions of these conceptions there is effectively no time-space and no contingency. But this was found by most economists to be uncomfortably limiting and the notion of expectations was hence revamped.

Partly as a result of the increasing importance of econometrics, and the growing socio-political influence of economic forecasting, concepts of 'adaptive expectations' were elaborated in more and more sophisticated ways. In the notion of adaptive expectations there is at least a certain place for time and contingency. Agents will revise their expectations in a given period according to the degree of error in their previous expectations about whatever economic variables are in question. This introduces a certain mobility into expectations, and treats the economy as a 'learning machine', but one of a relatively primitive type since agents only gradually alter their behaviour in the light of experience. A great deal of econometric modelling, however, was and continues to be based upon this type of view.

The original impetus to the shift from notions of adaptive to rational expectations is usually credited to John Muth.[9] Muth's objectives in analysing expectations were quite modest, and it took some while before the full implications of the arguments he developed were recognized. Muth's aim was primarily to model expectations in a fashion similar to the way in which other forms of microeconomic behaviour are ordinarily analysed — by proposing that actors use information optimally in forming the expectations that guide their conduct. Economic expectations are not necessarily stable; agents make informed predictions drawing upon the same notions as economists use when attempting to predict *their* behaviour. Actors do not necessarily merely modify a little what they do this year in the light of their experience of what happened last year. They may change their forecasting schemes in such a way as to undermine the validity of expectations according to which they previously operated. Acknowledging this is potentially highly damaging for many of the usual econometric models.[10]

[9] See John Muth: 'Rational expectations and the theory of price movements', *Econometrica*, vol. 29, 1961.

[10] Robert E. Lucas: 'Econometric policy evaluation: a critique', in Karl

The main claims involved in rational expectations theories can be fairly readily summarized. There is an extension of the rationality of action traditionally ascribed to 'economic man'. The traditional view saw economic agents as maximizing their returns in an optimal fashion. In rational expectations accounts, agents rationally understand, and direct their behaviour in terms of, the whole economic environment in which that behaviour takes place. Informational activities are the same as any other actions economic agents undertake, being used with perfect efficiency. Agents know whatever they need to know about the overall organization of the economy in order to foresee correctly the consequences of monetary or fiscal actions that might be taken by the relevant authorities. A rational expectations equilibrium is 'a situation in which people do not make systematic mistakes in forecasting',[11] and the tendency for this to come about is based on the supposition that 'in the absence of rational expectations agents must be systematically making mistakes and should therefore modify their behaviour until they have obtained rational expectations.'[12]

The information available to governments when they pursue particular monetary or fiscal policies is the same as that available to private economic agents. This includes relevant concepts and information generated by economists themselves. Economists make predictions and thereby project expectations; on the basis of these they develop theories. But the same theories are available to agents and allow them to make optimal use of information. All share an 'environment of information' which helps define in fact what that 'environment' becomes. According to the proponents of rational expectations notions, Keynesian macroeconomics has to presume that governments control privileged information, not fully accessible to those who might be affected by policies based on it. In rational expectations theories, the subjective probabilities attached to courses of action are presumed to be real probabilities. According to Muth, Lucas and others, agents assess the expected values of key variables on the basis of the true probability distributions for the system. This

Brunner and Allan H. Meltzer (eds): *The Phillips Curve and Labour Markets.* Amsterdam: North Holland, 1976.

[11] Margaret Bray: 'Rational expectations, information and asset markets', *Oxford Economic Papers*, vol. 37, 1985, p. 164.

[12] L. E. Blume, M. M. Bray and D. Easley: 'Introduction to the stability of rational expectations equilibrium', *Journal of Economic Theory*, vol. 26, 1982.

means denying the view of probability according to which probability beliefs are simply 'wagers' an individual is willing to undertake about a course of events.[13]

Although within this finite universe of probabilities it is presumed that agents know all there is to know about relevant economic outcomes, there is a set of consequences which they cannot know — which are defined as 'unknowable' because they are stochastic. This range of outcomes is not empirically identifiable, because otherwise rational expectations would come into play; they are defined as random events for the purposes of modelling. These are hence quite different from the unintended consequences of action as usually conceptualized. For such consequences introduce a 'mobile zone' of unanticipated events, intersecting with those that are anticipated. Rational expectations models presume an absolute boundary between that which is perfectly known, and hence correctly anticipated, and that which is perfectly unknown, and therefore wholly unpredictable.

A major feature of rational expectations theories — the main reason why they are sometimes known collectively as the 'new classical macroeconomics' — is that they make strong market-clearing assumptions. Not only financial markets, but labour and other types of markets are presumed to clear completely. As Tobin observes, 'contemporary classical theorists are bolder than their predecessors in assuming that the economic world can be described in terms of continuous clearing in competitive markets of supplies and demands derived from utility and profit maximisation.' This 'surge of confidence', he goes on to add, 'is not based, so far as I can see, on new empirical evidence for the assumption. It is based rather on the feeling that this model is the "only game in town".'[14] The 'new classicism' should probably be seen as part of the generalized critical rejection of Keynesianism. Disavowing both some of Keynes's intellectual assumptions and their policy implications tends to be associated with a reversion to the clear-cut world of omnipotent markets.[15]

[13] See Steven M. Sheffrin: *Rational Expectations*. Cambridge: Cambridge University Press, 1983, pp. 144ff. See also, of course, John Maynard Keynes: *Treatise on Probability*. London: Macmillan, 1936.

[14] James Tobin: *Asset Accumulation and Economic Activity*. Oxford: Basil Blackwell, 1980, p. 33.

[15] See W. H. Buiter: 'The macroeconomics of Dr. Pangloss: a critical

One of the most important shafts directed against Keynesianism by the advocates of rational expectations theories has been the idea of policy neutrality.[16] The thesis of policy neutrality effectively declares that the whole of Keynesianism was a sham, at least in terms of the practical effects that were believed to follow from its policies. Governments might have believed that they were intervening effectively in economic life by using fiscal policies to influence demand. In fact they were not doing so because this cannot be done. Since all economic agents have access to the same knowledge, any fiscal policies introduced by governments, other than those involving constraint, can be negated by action taken by those agents to counteract them. Although various qualifications about policy neutrality have been made by proponents of rational expectations notions, this is surely one of the primary sources of appeal of these notions. 'Rational expectations', it has been remarked, 'came along when it did because of the demonstrated failure of the pre-existing theory to explain the dismal economic performance of the period.' For many who had perhaps all along suspected that government should not be permitted to play too significant role in economic life it was a welcome happening within economics that 'not only do national economies seem to be out of control but a theory has emerged to tell us there is little we can do about it' — by means of state intervention at least.[17]

Rational expectations hypotheses have been criticized by economists on a variety of grounds. It has been said that the degree of foreknowledge and rationality attributed to agents is quite improbably sophisticated. If professional economists themselves cannot agree upon the nature of the economic environment, to which their predictions are supposed to relate, what use is there to attribute complete understanding of all relevant variables to lay agents? Moreover, even in the light of whatever reliable information may be available, surely it cannot be supposed that all economic agents are capable and willing to act on it in an efficient manner? Answers of various sorts to these questions are forthcoming from the advocates of

survey of the new classical macroeconomics', *Economic Journal*, vol. 90, 1980.

[16] See Stanley Fischer: *Rational Expectations and Economic Policy*. Chicago: University of Chicago Press, 1980.

[17] Michael Carter and Rodney Maddox: *Rational Expectations. Macroeconomics for the 1990s?*. London: Macmillan, 1984, p. xii, and p. 1.

rational expectations theories. It can be pointed out that rational expectations hypotheses are models, which while they might deviate from reality, approximate to it closely enough so as to derive worthwhile results. It is not necessary for all agents to 'take the lead' in forming accurate expectations of probable outcomes for the model to have sufficient application to make sense of actual conduct.

Many economists hold that some markets clear much more efficiently than others. The rational expectations hypothesis has been used to analyse financial markets, with some degree of success, for a considerable time. In the form of the 'random walk' notion this has even filtered down into quite elementary introductions to economic analysis. Even here there are major difficulties. Does it follow that investment brokers are worthless? Why are share prices often apparently so volatile? How could one explain a stock-market crash?[18] Perhaps after all Keynes's view that share markets are high-flown betting shops is nearer to the mark? When it comes to other markets, particularly the labour market, to propose a strong version of market-clearing seems quite unconvincing. 'Because of the widespread and obvious prevalence of contracts, explicit and implicit, and the prevalence of quantity rather than price adjustments in markets, the assumption of continuous market clearing embodied in the rational expectations models is clearly unsuitable.'[19]

Observations and implications

I do not want to deny the limitations of rational expectations theories. What is interesting about them, I think, does not concern the features that make them attractive to most of their adherents in any case — particularly their recovery of 'classical' views by their emphasis upon universal market-clearing. But in some respects rational expectations accounts make a novel departure from most pre-existing modes of economic theorizing, and it is their very distinction from classical thought upon which I wish to concentrate. Their innovatory character shares a good deal with developments in social theory elsewhere, but this is obscured by the very insistence of their progenitors that they are producing a 'new classical' view.

[18] Steven M. Sheffrin: *Rational Expectations*, pp. 112ff.
[19] Michael Carter and Rodney Maddox: *Rational Expectations . . .* , p. 114.

Among other questions, recent debates in social theory have concerned the relation between the theories, concepts and 'findings' of social scientific observers and the environments of action these are produced to explain or describe. Centrally involved here is the notion of the double hermeneutic.[20] There is, as Winch says, a 'logical tie' between the concepts employed by lay agents — whether discursively or not — in organizing their day-to-day conduct and the concepts of observing social scientists.[21] But there is also another side to this relation, left unanalysed by Winch and most others who have written on the issue. This is that theories, concepts and findings of social science, or versions of them, are routinely drawn back into the social environments they analyse. The ideas of social sciences cannot be kept 'detached' from their milieux of analysis in the manner of the natural sciences. In both economics and the other social sciences, the orthodox consensus tended to involve the supposition that there could be a steady accumulation of knowledge about economy and society taking the form of 'positive science'. We can now see that this was a mistake. The more interesting, significant or 'explanatory' a set of ideas in social science is, the more likely it is to be taken over by lay agents and to enter constitutively into their conduct. It does not follow that such a phenomenon has transformative consequences for that conduct, but ordinarily it does do so. Social science hence 'circles in and out' of what it is about. While the social scientist can usually manage to keep one, or even several, jumps ahead of lay agents in their own interpretations of what they do, there is no way in which there can be developed a wholly 'sealed off' technical discourse of social science. Lay agents, in modern societies above all, theorize about what they do as an intrinsic part of doing it — chronically and routinely.

While social science thus in a certain sense tends to 'disappear' into the environment it is about, at the same time it thereby has a very powerful impact upon the very constitution of that environment.[22] This can take the form of a 'self-fulfilling prophecy', such as Merton has described it.[23] Or it can be a 'self-negating prophecy' of the sort involved in the policy neutrality thesis in rational expectations theory.

---

[20] Anthony Giddens: *The Constitution of Society*, chpt. 6.

[21] Peter Winch: *The Idea of a Social Science*. London: Routledge, 1958.

[22] Anthony Giddens: *The Constitution of Society*, pp. 128ff.

[23] R. K. Merton: *Social Theory & Social Structure*. Glencoe: Free Press, 1951.

Rational expectations accounts therefore focus attention on something of very considerable importance for economic and for social science more generally. It is not a phenomenon of recent provenance, even if the beginnings of a satisfactory understanding of it are. When the discourse of what has come to be 'modern economics' developed in the eighteenth and nineteenth centuries the concepts involved did not merely serve to describe independently-given changes leading to modern industrialized societies; they helped constitute the very nature of those societies. Economics (like all the social sciences) is reflexively tied to what it is about. Theorizing in social science is not about an environment which is indifferent to it, but one whose character is open to change in respect of that theorizing.

The chief contribution of rational expectations theories is to have grasped — however hesitantly and inaccurately — this reflexive relation within the economic field. As a perceptive analyst of rational expectations accounts has commented:

> The idea that expectations about the future behaviour of prices must be important determinants of current market behaviour is an old one, as is the closely related proposition that, only if such expectations are fulfilled, can the economy be said to be in full equilibrium. In extending these notions by arguing, first, that we should think of expectations as being the output of an economic model, knowledge of whose structure is attributed to agents, and second, that for full equilibrium to rule, the model in question must be the 'true' one of the economy under analysis, New-Classical Economics has made a contribution of immense importance to our understanding of these matters. Economic theory has been permanently changed by these insights, and for the better.[24]

These ideas actually have little or nothing to do with classical economics. Rational expectations theories should be seen to have opened up new problems of analysis rather than analysed old problems in a more satisfactory way than pre-existing theories. What is significant in rational expectations hypotheses, it may be argued, can probably only be further developed if some of their chief presumptions are stripped away. There is no logical reason, in the first place, why strong market-clearing premises should be associated with the notion of rational expectations. Tobin is surely right in this regard. An

[24] David Laidler: 'The New-Classical contribution to macroeconomics' p. 21 (Mimeo).

emphasis upon radical market-clearing derived in large part from the juncture at which rational expectations hypotheses came to the fore, and from the impulsion to show Keynesianism to be essentially flawed. The assumption of strong market-clearing helps to allow for the mathematicizing of rational expectations models. But even in economics — where surface technical sophistication counts for much more than it does in any of the other social sciences — we have hopefully not yet reached the stage where logical elegance outweighs all other considerations in the assessment of theories and models. There is no reason why the logical structure of rational expectations should not be incorporated into models that recognize that not all markets clear and that different markets clear in varying degrees (and ways).

We may discard the idea that there is an absolute, and impermeable, boundary between outcomes that can be completely known and stochastic processes. The separation between these, which of course is a purely logical formula, has again been of considerable appeal because it aids formal model-building. It is one factor which helps to make rational expectations hypotheses 'classical' because the theorist can abandon problems of real time and enter the timeless world of virtual time-space. Placing economic theories in real time is important not only because of the implication of contingency — uncertainty in Keynes's sense — but because it makes possible analysis of the complex relations between foreseen and unintended consequences of action. In rational expectations hypotheses this differentiation is foreclosed, because anything that is not stochastic can be discovered, understood, and incorporated within expectations. But this is a legitimate assumption only in an artificial world of virtual time-space. In the real world unintended consequences constantly impinge back on rationally 'understood' courses of action — thus leading to a changed 'understanding', this again producing consequences of an unintended kind. There are logical reasons why this can never become a closed system of the sort modelled in rational expectations; although I shall not attempt to detail those reasons here.

We should recognize that the notion of rationality involved in rational expectations theories is more divergent from that of classical 'economic man' than the proponents of these theories are apt to acknowledge — here they underestimate their own originality. For agents are attributed with a more complex understanding of themselves and their environments of action than is presumed in traditional utility and profit-maximizing behaviour. This is a point at which there seems to be a major line of connection with developments in social theory elsewhere. What is at issue here is a characterization of the 'knowledgeable human agent' — an agent who knows a good deal both about why he or she acts in a particular fashion and about the settings of such action.[25] Rational expectations hypotheses are concerned with how agents rationally understand their environments of action, using that understanding to constitute what those environments are. Now economists are fond of rational models and there is no doubt that the positing of rational conduct — carefully defined — can be a very useful analytical device. But for many purposes it might be more effective to posit 'knowledgeability' rather than 'rationality' *tout court*. In common with social theory, economic theory can no longer proceed without incorporating an understanding of the modes in which its own conceptions shape the environments it seeks to describe. Economic actors may draw upon the same fund of theories and concepts in orienting what they do as professional economic observers. The agent revises his or her activities in the light of what they get to 'know' — but also what they believe, suspect, fear or feel optimistic about — in the environment of action which their behaviour constitutes. The equating of subjective and objective probability is likely to be plausible only in a considerably more restricted range of situations than the advocates of rational expectations theories tend to suppose. In other situations, agents may be supposed to act knowledgeably, but not 'rationally' in the rather strong sense of that term which rational expectations theories presume.

There are issues relating knowledgeability to predictability here that must be clearly spelled out. Rational expectations theories have highlighted these without developing their discussion of them adequately, because of the simplified universe of assumptions they have adopted. The Friedman-type view of predictability is wrong, and not just because it was associated with conceptions drawn from logical empiricism that are now widely regarded as discredited. The justification given for 'unrealistic' models is that the accurate prediction of action or outcomes is the main criterion of their value. However this would only be so if the predictability of the 'economic world' were like that of the world of nature. But it is not. The predictability of economic phenomena, like other social phenomena more generally, is in substantial part 'made to happen' via the

[25] See Anthony Giddens: *The Constitution of Society*, chpt. 1.

knowledgeability of its constituent actors. It is essential, for most purposes other than 'one-off' predictions, to know how far a model implicitly invokes concepts actors use in generating the very predictability it claims to analyse, and how far it comprises variables which lead to regular outcomes of an unintended type. Without such knowledge, the 'predictions' derived from a model may be wholly unenlightening — roundabout ways of stating what agents knew anyway in order to bring about the outcomes they did. The predictive capability of a theory or hypothesis in the social sciences is not a criterion of its 'scientificity'; and its usefulness cannot be assessed without an awareness of the particular 'mix' of intended (foreseen) and unintended outcomes the conduct in question involves.

The value of the type of models developed thus far by rational expectations theorists, if the preceding comments are correct, is hence much more restricted than their more enthusiastic advocates believe. At the same time, such models have served to bring to the fore in economics issues currently being widely discussed in social theory more generally. Paradoxically, the most profitable insights stimulated by rational expectations hypotheses might draw economics well away from those views of the subject that have spawned them. The direction in which macroeconomics will tend to move will surely not be back to what has conventionally come to be known as 'Keynesianism'. The thesis of policy neutrality holds that Keynesianism never worked, or could have worked. But we can at least entertain the possibility that Keynesianism can only be effective in circumstances in which the majority of the population, or certain key sets of business actors, do not know what Keynesianism is. If the policies associated with a Keynesian outlook have become ineffective, it might be because their premises have become widely enough known no longer to apply in the way in which they once did. In my view this is a very real possibility.

The dissolution of Keynesianism might send us back to Keynes for clues about the likely future development of macroeconomics. Rather than turning to the formal and still relatively closed models favoured by rational expectations theories, we might anticipate the occurrence of the 'aborted revolution' in economics which Keynes's writings signalled. If this were to happen, economics would necessarily develop a renewed relationship with the other social sciences, from which all might benefit. There is unlikely ever to be a 'unified field theory' in economics. There is enormous disparity among the phenomena with which economics deals. Even within the sphere of 'markets' there is a chasm between the nature of, say, financial as compared with labour markets. What is and what is not an 'economic' issue is by no means always easy to define, and there is surely no justification for keeping economics as insulated from the other social sciences as many economists seem to presume both possible and desirable.

9

Out of the Orrery: E. P. Thompson on consciousness and history

E. P. Thompson could be described as the sociologists' historian. There are few historians whom sociologists are more fond of quoting, and it is possibly true that Thompson's work is more highly esteemed in sociology than it is among at least certain segments of the historical profession. The affinity which sociologists feel for Thompson's work can be explained on a superficial level by reference to Thompson's concern with problems of class formation and class consciousness, topics which have always been regarded as of primary importance in sociological analysis.

But there is more to the matter than this. There is something in the style of history which Thompson practises that has a definite appeal for those coming from a sociological background. On the face of things this seems quite eccentric. For Thompson has been savagely·critical of the sorts of concepts and approaches which sociologists tend to favour when analysing, not just problems of class structure, but more general aspects of institutions. It is not only structuralist Marxists whose writings resemble the clockwork model that the Earl of Orrery devised; something similar is generic to sociological writing as a whole, in Thompson's view. Why should sociologists find attractive the writings of an author whose comments about their efforts are, for the most part, less than complimentary? The answer, I think, is that those educated within the framework of orthodox sociological thought — whether they be Marxist or non-Marxist — discover in Thompson's work something which they recognize to be absent in much sociological writing. This something we could loosely call a sense of agency. In several of the leading perspectives in sociology, human beings do not appear as the makers of their own history, but rather as the hapless playthings of social forces which they neither control nor understand. Even while they employ such a standpoint, sociological authors must perforce in some part recognize its inauthenticity. For as human beings we do know a good deal about why we act as we do, and that knowledge in some substantial part shapes what we do. In so far as sociological concepts and theories fail to capture the 'active' components of human conduct, they must surely be judged as seriously deficient.

The problem of agency is a philosophical issue of considerable complexity, one unlikely to be resolved with any degree of finality by either sociologists or historians. Thompson's writings nevertheless provide an excellent focus for examining some of its implications, since he places such a strong emphasis upon the capability of the human agents actively to shape and reshape the conditions of their existence. If there is a single Marxian theorem which dominates Thompson's historical studies, it is surely the aphorism that human beings 'make their own history'. This phraseology plainly informs both title and substance of his massive study of the development of the English working class, and indeed the whole range of his historical and political writings. Since some of the problems to do with questions of agency and history have been brought into clear relief by the critical interchanges between Thompson and Perry Anderson, I shall use Anderson's critique of Thompson as a basis for much of what I wish to say in what follows.[1]

The Anderson-Thompson debate

Thompson's remarks about agency and history are characteristically of a threefold character. From one aspect, in writing history 'from the bottom up', he is concerned to rescue the vast anonymous mass of the common people from the condescension of the historian who would see them only as inert and reactive. Second, in a more general sense, he persistently stresses the contextual character of human activity, in terms of which agency should be understood. Those who rule need to be understood in their full individuality just as those over whom they

---

[1] Perry Anderson: *Arguments Within English Marxism*. London: Verso, 1980.

rule. Bishop Trelawny, his stewards, Richard Norton and the others who populate the pages of *Whigs and Hunters* are as alive to the reader as any of the Army of Redressers described in Thompson's study of the origins of the working class.[2] Third, there is Thompson's consistent reserve about concepts that seem to him not to encompass the plasticity of human action. Immediately after the celebrated statement that the working class did not come into being as a process of mechanical change, but 'was present at its own making' there follows a discussion of the concept of class. Strong qualifications are entered about the circumstances in which it may justifiably be employed. Class, Thompson says, is not 'a structure', nor a 'category', but 'something which in fact happens . . . in human relationships'. 'The notion of class', Thompson continues, 'entails the notion of historical relationship. Like any other relationship, it has a fluency which evades analysis if we attempt to stop it dead at any given moment and anatomize its structure. The finest-meshed sociological net cannot give us a pure specimen of class, any more than it can give us one of deference or of love. The relationship must always be embodied in real people and in a real context.'[3] It is not just the imagery of class-as-structure to which Thompson objects. He is equally critical of 'anthropomorphic' conceptions of class. Only human agents have qualities of will, consciousness and morality; classes do not.

How are these views linked to the historical argument of *The Making of the English Working Class*? The book has a diffuse, almost flabby feel to it. It is rich in detail and like all Thompson's writings compelling in style. But it is a work in which historical observations and vignettes predominate over the elaboration of a developed analytical standpoint. Thompson himself refers to the work as 'a group of studies' linked by a common theme, rather than either a chronological history or the concerted marshalling of historical data to support a particular theory. He self-consciously pits his analysis against what he sees (or saw at the time) as prevailing orthodoxies in labour history. In what he regards as Fabian historical writing, the members of the working class are depicted as lacking in collective energy until co-ordinated by prescient leaders and organizers. In the writings of economic historians of a strictly empirical bent, working

[2] E. P. Thompson: *Whigs and Hunters*. Harmondsworth: Penguin, 1977.
[3] E. P. Thompson: *The Making of the English Working Class*. London: Gollancz, 1965.

people appear as merely the numerical items in a migrant labour force, objects of statistical analysis. Finally there is an historicist orthodoxy, in which the early development of the working class is scanned for precursors of the subsequent evolution of forms of labour organization.

Neither of the first two orthodoxies gives sufficient place to the active struggles of working people in forming the conditions of their own lives; while the third blocks off ideas and modes of activity that were not enduring, leaving unexplored those by-ways of historical experimentation which did not leave a lasting trace. The protests of those whose ways of life were destroyed by the advent of modern industry may have been largely ineffectual and very rapidly forgotten. But they are essential to understanding the activities of working people in the period, and they may of course have longer-term lessons to teach us today, since historical defeat can obviously not be equated with lack of significance in respect of any given set of ideas and practices.

In describing the framework of *The Making of the English Working Class*, Thompson outlines a sequence of discussion that proceeds from the subjective to the objective and back again. The book opens with a description of an encounter between Thomas Hardy, John Thelwall and other members of the London Corresponding Society, interrogated by The Privy Council in the year 1794. The personal nature of the exchanges between the progenitors of parliamentary reform and the highest powers in the land, Thompson points out, contrasts oddly with the impersonal clashes which were to characterize a rather later period. Some writers have claimed the London Corresponding Society to be the first specifically working-class political association in Britain. But as Thompson is at some pains to show, the Society was more of a legatee of 'popular Radicalism' than an embodiment of working-class protest. It essentially formed a bridge between the older forms of rebellion and the new. The importance and originality of Thompson's discussion lies in his analysis of beliefs of the members of the Society that served in the end to redirect pre-existing Radicalism towards new endeavours. It is exactly in such discussion that Thompson seeks to redeem the claim that the working class made itself as much as it was made. For example, the rule of the Society that membership be unlimited may seem trite from today's perspective; in fact it was vital to forging a definition of politics freed from the notion that only a minority have the right or capability to govern. With this prescription the Society moved away from the older traditions of Radicalism in which the 'political' remained identified with rights of property. New notions of democratic participation were thereby nurtured — notions which helped develop the momentum subsequently achieved within working-class movements as a whole. Here there is more than an echo, as in many other places in Thompson's writings, of the Weberian challenge to the more mechanical conceptions of Marxism. There is no evidence, so far as I know, that Thompson has been in any direct fashion significantly influenced by Weber, save as refracted through Tawney. But one of the main underlying issues in Thompson's study — the origins of a distinct sphere of 'economic relations' in capitalist development — has a clear affinity with problems Weber helped to bring to the fore. Weber was principally concerned with an earlier period and concentrated his attention upon the formation of an entrepreneurial spirit. Thompson's work is focused upon a different phase of development and upon wage-labourers. Yet in rather variant ways both emphasize that the 'economic' is a cultural category and that religious ideals and practices influenced the ways in which it became shaped. The point is not just that ideas are mobilizing influences, but that notions which in some contexts may be profoundly reactionary in character in others can be twisted to progressive ends.

Thus the world-views of the dissenting sects incorporated ideas that could in some circumstances produce political quiescence, while in others stimulating a radical challenge to the existing order of things. In one context there might be found a fatalism towards the injustices and miseries of this world, bolstered by the expectation of better things to come in the next; in another these self-same ideas might fuel an intense secular reforming zeal. The very clash of interpretations which religious dogma so frequently serves to produce provides a powerful momentum for social transformation. The leading inspiration of the evangelical revival in the eighteenth century, John Wesley, derived his views from a background of the Established Church. Wesley did not seek to establish a distinct 'methodist' organization, but rather to reform the eighteenth-century Church. Methodism was, as Thompson puts it, 'a religion for *the poor*', but at the same time it was distinctively marked by the features of its context of origin. The intermingling of Methodism and traditions of old Dissent was both a stabilizing and a corrosive influence in respect of traditional patterns of behaviour. It may very well be that the spread of Methodism helped block revolution in England at the turn of the nineteenth century. But this was by no means wholly because it constrained the impulse to protestation. Rather, Methodism helped promote the self-confidence and organizational capacity of working people.

The regressive and progressive elements here are indeed hard to disentangle. Nor should the influence of religion be seen in separation from its 'other face': the unenlightened, the indigent and the criminal. The tradition of the riot and the mob stands in no less a paradoxical connection to the subsequent development of the labour movement than does the sway of religious ethics. A distaste for most aspects of the law, riot and popular insurrection — these are not in and of themselves phenomena which can be neatly categorized as the forerunners of a democratically inspired labour movement. If in some part they became so, it is because they generalized opposition to the privileges of property and power. Freedom in respect of the intrusion of the State into day-to-day life: this was perhaps the single thread which unified the respectable and the less salubrious influences upon the active formation of the English working class.

The transition from discussion of subjective to objective influences on the formation of the working class, in Thompson's discussion, tends also to be an historical sequence. Prior to the first decade or so of the nineteenth century, Thompson's narrative concerns mainly the concepts and ideas which informed social protest. His treatment of the subsequent period, however, emphasizes much more a series of impersonally-given social changes. Or perhaps this is not so much a matter of periodization as the intrusion of something like a 'structural' account into Thompson's narrative style. If so, it probably reflects rather basic difficulties that he faces in relating what people 'make happen' to what 'happens to them' — exactly the issue with which I am mainly concerned in this discussion. Thompson writes: 'the changing productive relations and working conditions of the Industrial Revolution were imposed, not upon raw material, but upon the free-born Englishman . . .'.[4] It is as if the 'changing productive relations' and 'working conditions' of the Industrial Revolution did not involve human agency, whereas the reactions to them did. There is a lengthy discussion of the time-honoured problem of how far the material conditions of life of the majority improved or declined over the first few decades of the nineteenth century. One of Thompson's themes is that this has been misconstrued, because the real issue is that of a

[4] E. P. Thompson: *Making . . .*, p. 194.

transition in the totality of a way of life, rather than one of gradations of material income. But here it has to be said that the flavour of the analysis is subtly reversed from that of the opening chapters of the volume. Thompson makes it clear that the class consciousness of the working people in the early and middle 1800s drew upon the traditions of dissent previously established. But there is a curious lack of historical content to Thompson's judgement that in 1831—2 England was in a situation of potential revolutionary crisis. It would seem as though it should be just at this point that the intertwining of subjective and objective influences could be most fruitfully explored. But such an exploration is not developed in any detail at all.

The general orientation of *The Making of the English Working Class* is consistent with views on subjectivity and objectivity which Thompson offers elsewhere — for instance, when commenting on the weakness of Marxist concepts. On several occasions, at widely different times, Thompson has expressed his dissatisfaction with the Marxian model of base and superstructure. What is important in this notion, he stresses, is not that material circumstances produce specific outcomes in terms of culture or consciousness. Rather, appropriately interpreted, it represents a dialectic between social being and social consciousness.[5] It is the dialectical aspect which counts, not the mechanical causation frequently associated with the notion. Once more sociologists come in for some flak here. For many of them, Thompson says, are too fond of 'boxes and building terms' to describe processes that in fact are in continual historical flux. 'We can only describe the social process . . . by writing history.' Any other view of the base/superstructure distinction is either an unrealistic metaphor, or expresses a form of illegitimate reductionism. We must, Thompson asserts, discover a mode of understanding social process that accepts the autonomy of human consciousness, while acknowledging the influence of 'social being'.[6]

Let me now move to Anderson's critique. Anderson has discussed Thompson's writings in more than one place. I shall concentrate only on the more sympathetic and detailed of his assessments. The problem

[5] See E. P. Thompson: 'The moral economy of the English crowd in the eighteenth century', *Past and Present*, February 1971.

[6] E. P. Thompson: 'The peculiarities of the English', in *The Poverty of Theory*. London: Merlin, 1978, pp. 77—81. See also E. P. Thompson: 'Folklore, anthropology and social history', *Indian Historical Review*, vol. 3, 1978.

of agency, Anderson points out, 'is the key organising theme of Thompson's entire work'. His strictures against sociologists, his devastatingly detailed — could one say over-determined? — criticisms of Althusser, his distrust of analytical models in general, all derive from his unremitting emphasis upon choice and meaning in the forging of history. Anderson is able to show rather easily that, while an emphasis on agency is so important in Thompson's writings, the concept is in fact little explicated. A richly suggestive style will not compensate for inadequacies of analysis. Let us construe agency, Anderson says, as 'conscious, goal-directed activity'.[7] When the notion is understood in this way it is evident enough that all of us engage in such activity more or less all of the time. Posed in such a general fashion the notion of agency might remain philosophically difficult, but is uninteresting in its implications for historical study or theoretical debate. We can get some way further, however, by separating three sorts of 'goal' which individuals may pursue.

Over the course of by far the greater bulk of human history, most actors most of the time have followed quite narrowly confined aims in the contexts of day-to-day life. Such projects, as Anderson puts it, 'are inscribed within existing social relations, and typically reproduce them'. This is the 'milieu of . . . universal agency'.[8] The mundane and individualized projects pursued in day-to-day social activities can be distinguished from more public ambitions and endeavours — for example, the formation of political associations, religious movements, military adventures etc. For the most part neither of these types of goal-directed activity transform social organization in a consciously-directed fashion. There is however a third type of purposive collective action which seeks actively to alter existing social relationships. Agency in this sense is more or less specifically associated with modernity, with the idea that understanding history is the basis of controlling it. Secular political revolution is one of the first and most pervasive forms of agency in this sense. However, in Anderson's view the bourgeois revolutions of the eighteenth and nineteenth centuries only vaguely prefigured agency in this guise. He makes the somewhat remarkable claim that it is the labour movement which has been the true founder of this novel mobilization of history and the Russian Revolution which gives it most acute expression.

[7] Perry Anderson: *Arguments* . . . .
[8] Ibid., p. 19.

According to Anderson, Thompson tends to merge the first and second senses of agency with the third, and upon this the cogency of his remarks often depends. One cannot move from the fact that agents purposefully pursue goals in their everyday lives to the assertion that history is organized through collective projects of social transformation. Activities which at an individual level are carried out in purposive fashion may have consequences that are wholly unwilled. We cannot put within the same category the decision of an individual to marry and the distribution of rates of marriage in a given community or over a particular period. When Thompson speaks of history in terms of phrases like 'unmastered human practice', or as produced by 'ever-baffled, ever-resurgent human agents', he ignores the historically shifting nature of purposive action. He tends to make axiomatic what actually should itself be the objective of historical study. In Anderson's eyes, Thompson thereby tends curiously to recapitulate the limitations of the Althusserian structuralism which he seeks to attack. In neither case is the increasing intrusion of historical purposefulness properly illuminated.

One reason given by Anderson for the limitations of Thompson's standpoint is that Thompson tends to identify agency with willing rather than reasoning, with volition rather than knowledge. In some part this is traceable to the role which an unexplicated concept of human 'experience' plays in Thompson's work. Experience is for Thompson the mediator between subjectivity and objectivity, the means whereby 'structure is transmuted into process'. Anderson has little trouble in showing that 'experience' appears in Thompson's writings in a shifting and ambiguous fashion. As Gadamer points out in commenting on Dilthey's use of *Erlebnis*, 'experience' can be taken in at least two senses.[9] It may refer to the subjective outlook of an individual participating in a given range of activities; or it may refer to what that individual actively learns from such participation. The first does not necessarily imply the second, although Thompson's appeals to the significance of agency in history tend to assimilate them. Experience in history is not the same as learning from history, and anyone who seeks to specify the significance of the second of these must somehow distinguish what is valid or useful experience from what is not.

Perhaps, however, we should look to those contexts in which

---

[9] Hans-Georg Gadamer: *Truth and Method*. London: Sheed & Ward, 1975.

Thompson connects experience with 'social being' for a more persuasive treatment of agency. Thompson here seems to speak of the existence of definite forms of 'social being' which are, so to speak, processed by individual actors in the generation of the attitudes, ideas and modes of behaviour they adopt. This seems to be the sense which Thompson himself wishes to extract from the propaedeutic statements that are offered at the opening of *The Making of the English Working Class*. That the working class 'made itself as much as it was made' invokes that dialectic of experience and 'social being' which Thompson regards as the essence of a materialist approach to history. But it is dubious whether the analyses contained in the book actually validate this claim. As I have pointed out, the narrative shifts from subjective to rather more objective changes, but can hardly be said to bring them together in a systematic way. Some of the main institutional processes of transformation involved in the development of industrial capitalism in England are barely mentioned in what is after all a very large work. As Anderson observes: 'the jagged temporal rhythms and breaks, and the uneven spatial distributions and displacements, of capital accumulation between 1790 and 1830 inevitably marked the composition and character of the nascent English proletariat. Yet they find no place in this account of its formation.'[10] The stylistic brilliance of the work tends to conceal the fact that the complex meshing of objective determinants and subjective experience are in fact mostly unanalysed. The spectrum of conditions which actually led to the formation of the English working class are collapsed into an opposition between protest and resistance largely internal to the ideas and behaviour of the members of the working class themselves.

These limitations both make themselves felt in, and are expressive of, Thompson's suspicion of concepts that seem to him 'unusable metaphors'. For Thompson class exists when individuals feel common identity in opposition to others. Class is not a mechanical compartment of the Orrery.

> When we speak of a *class* we are thinking of a very loosely defined body of people who share the same categories of interests, social experiences, traditions and value system, who have a *disposition* to *behave* as a class, to define themselves in their actions and in their consciousness in relation to other groups of people in class ways. But class itself is not a thing, it is a happening.[11]

10 Perry Anderson: *Arguments* . . . , pp. 33—4.
11 E. P. Thompson: 'Peculiarities' . . . , p. 85.

Once again this position opens itself rather easily to criticism. Anderson points out that were it the case that class has only existed where individuals are aware of common interests in a process of struggle, it would be a relatively marginal phenomenon. Particularly in pre-capitalist societies, classes have only very rarely generated significant forms of collective identity. The class consciousness of workers during the early period of the emergence of industrial capitalism in England was specifically different from anything which had gone before. Only if class is defined in an objective fashion, such that it does not necessarily correspond to consciousness of class membership, can we plausibly analyse such phenomena. We must have a means of examining the intersection of the objective and subjective.

The objections that can be levelled against Thompson's analysis of the 'making of classes' can be complemented, Anderson adds, by criticisms of the manner in which Thompson interprets the making of history *by* classes. In criticizing Althusser, Thompson directs attention at one point in his discussion to the scheme which Engels offers for the understanding of historical change. History, Engels says, derives from the conflicts of different individual motivations, whereby events occur that are neither intended nor foreseen by the individuals whose activity produces them. Thompson accepts that this provides something of an overall formula for the grasp of history as 'unmastered practice', but at the same time it leaves something to be desired because agency is, as it were, 'cancelled out' by the non-directive friction of individual intentions. However, if we accept, Thompson continues, that individual motivations are in some essential degree influenced by class, we can improve upon Engels's view. History becomes shaped, in class societies at any rate, by the conditioning of outlooks and activities in class terms.

As Anderson points out, however, such a position does not make much sense in the light of Thompson's own conception of the nature of class. For Thompson tends to accentuate strongly that classes only come into being when individuals share a similar outlook and identity anyway. 'The intractable question', according to Anderson, posed by Thompson's standpoint is: if overall historical processes are the unsought outcome of a large number of individual motivations and actions, what explains their ordered character? Such a problem, he suggests, has occupied both Parsons and Sartre. Parsons's own resolution of what he called the 'Hobbesian problem of order' is entirely unsatisfactory, depending as it does upon the stabilizing influence of common values and norms supposedly discovered in any enduring type of social system. Sartre's response is somewhat more interesting. Sartre seeks to investigate how the diversity of different individual projects followed by human agents coalesce to create their obverse: the 'practico-inert' or the 'dead' sectors of social institutions. How is it that overall trends of history emerge from circumstances not only that no one desires but that resist attempts at conscious direction? Sartre's conclusion contrasts with that of Parsons, expressing a persistent dichotomy in the social sciences between what have often been called consensus theories on the one side and coercion theories on the other. For Sartre, it is essentially power, and particularly the coercive power of the state, that produces the co-ordination of the societal totality.

Anderson finds neither of these solutions satisfactory, for both are incompatible with a Marxist emphasis upon the pre-eminence of economic influences in history. According to Anderson, when Marx criticized the views of Hegel and Dühring he effectively transcended just those standpoints that Parsons and Sartre represent in more recent social thought. The problem of order cannot be illuminated if we begin conceptually with purposive actors and seek to analyse how their endeavours lead to outcomes distant from their intentions. 'It is, and must be, the dominant *mode of production* that confers fundamental unity on a social formation, allocating their objective positions to the classes within it, and distributing the agents within each class.'[12] This results in processes of class struggle, but these are not prior to the derivation of social order, because modes of production produce classes, not the other way around. Of course, Anderson goes on to add, we cannot be interested solely in how order is arrived at, because disorder equally must be analysed. Here again he looks to the established apparatus of historical materialism — contradictions between forces and relations of production, intersecting with conflicts between classes. In the end, therefore, Anderson opts for something closer to a classical interpretation of historical materialism than he believes either Thompson or Althusser to have adopted. He concludes:

Althusser's unilateral and remorseless stress on the overpowering weight of structural necessity in history corresponds more faithfully to the central tenets of historical materialism, and to the actual lessons of the scientific study of the past — but at the price of obscuring the novelty of the modern labour movement and attenuating the vocation of

12 Perry Anderson: *Arguments* . . . , p. 55.

revolutionary socialism. Thompson's passionate sense of the potential of human agency to shape collective conditions of life, on the other hand, is much closer to the political temper of Marx and Engels themselves in their own time — but tends to be projected backwards as a uniform weft of the past, in defiance of the millennial negations of self-determination in the kingdom of necessity. Strangely, of two unbalanced sets of generalizations, Althusser's inclines better towards history, Thompson's towards politics. The classical equipoise of the founders of historical materialism is some distance from both.[13]

Interpretation and evaluation

The debate between Thompson and Anderson carried echoes of long-standing controversies in the social sciences and history as a whole. Schools of social thought tend to divide around the question of agency.[14] Those who, like Thompson, are prone to assert the primacy of agency typically have had considerable difficulty in coming to grips both conceptually and substantively with what might be termed the 'structural constraints' over human action. On the other hand, those traditions of thought that have tended to stress the significance of pre-given social institutions have for the most part generated seriously deficient accounts of action — Althusser's being among the most implausible of all.

That such a dualism in traditions of social thought should have been so persistent is indicative of the difficulties involved in developing a standpoint able adequately to encompass both action and structural constraint. But partly as a result of the sort of interchange developed between Thompson and Anderson, as well as general developments in the philosophy of the social sciences, we can probably be much clearer about these matters today than ever before. Agency, as Anderson stresses, poses philosophical problems of some difficulty. It is therefore a little odd that he skirts such problems almost as completely in his discussion as does Thompson in the various contexts in which he confronts the issue. Anderson confidently equates agency with 'conscious, goal-directed activity', finding only in the notion of 'goals' anything which merits serious analytical reflection. Such is surely not

[13] Ibid., p. 58.
[14] Anthony Giddens: *The Constitution of Society*. Cambridge: Polity Press, 1984, chpt. 1.

the case, and while he goes on to formulate a number of worthwhile correctives to Thompson's viewpoint, he closes off certain important considerations that it is a mistake to ignore.

As a philosophical enquiry, investigation of the character of human agency presumes an answer to at least two main queries. What is it about agents which differentiates them from objects or the operation of impersonal forces in the world of nature? What distinguishes human agents from other beings to whom agency might reasonably be attributed — that is to non-human animals? With due recognition of the complexity of the issues involved, the following answers might be given briefly. Agency is a manifestation of an organism, which therefore possesses a body, that body being capable of intervening causally in the stream of events that constitutes its environment of behaviour. Agency hence presumes a 'motor of events', that is the *agent*. But it also entails that such a 'motor' is a concept-bearing being, whose concepts are employed to organize activities that modify the stream of events in the world. Agency, to put it another way, presumes the capability of 'acting otherwise'. We can suppose that the higher animals are concept-bearing beings, and are thus agents in this sense. Human beings differ from the animals since they possess syntactically differentiated languages. The range of conceptual operations they are able to carry on — whether embedded in the practical content of what they do, or formulated discursively — is immensely larger than that available to non-human animals. Human beings have an understanding of themselves as agents, thus allowing for a reflexive appropriation of knowledge denied to non-human animals. They are also able conceptually to 'bracket' time and space, connecting future and past in a manner not open to the remainder of the animal kingdom. There is no reason to doubt that the behaviour of animal agents is purposive. But in the case of human agents purposiveness is integrated with a continuous reflexive monitoring of what the actor does, intrinsic to what that 'doing' is.

The analytical issues connected with human agency, as these are raised in the Thompson/Anderson debate, concern the significance of the 'could have done otherwise' of human action and the nature of its reflexive monitoring. In particular, of course, there is the question of how these features of human activity relate to the incorporation of individual action within larger social totalities.

Before pursuing these further, it would be useful to attempt a clarification of the appeals to agency and to the nature of 'history' Thompson tends to make in the course of his writings. For the moment I shall simply register how 'history' might be understood, reverting to the implications of this later, concentrating first of all upon the character of agency. It is a banality to say that 'history' has two connotations, meaning both the chronicling of events and the actual occurrence of those events in time. The distinction nevertheless does have some relevance to the claims Thompson makes about the nature of his enterprise, since when he asserts the irreducible character of the 'historical' — for instance, in contradistinction to the conceptual abstractions favoured by sociologists — he sometimes seems to have in mind a distinctive style of writing about human activity. Thus human conduct can only be satisfactorily described, and therefore interpreted, if it is understood in the richness of its historical context. In so far as this is what Thompson means, it is not a point that should detain us for long. Description which is developed in contextual content has nothing much to do with whatever may specifically distinguish 'history' as a specific enterprise. How far 'thick description' is relevant to any particular area or type of study of human behaviour depends entirely on the scope of the investigation in question and its interpretative or explanatory objectives. More interesting is the question raised by Anderson's comments on purposiveness and social change. In what sense 'history' prior to modern times has been guided by its own reflexive appropriation — the use of a generalized understanding of conditions of action in order to transform those conditions — is certainly an issue of some significance. It is something which bears directly upon the reflexive monitoring intrinsic to human activity and I shall return to it after considering more directly the notion of agency as a whole.

The prime importance that Thompson attributes to agency in his writings could be said to involve a number of themes, and it is important to distinguish between these. They include the following:

1) Human beings actively 'make their own history' as much as they are made by it. Thompson is fond of alluding to both Vico and Marx in developing this idea. As has been mentioned, Thompson takes the distinction between base and superstructure in Marxian theory to be defensible only in so far as it is a mode of referring to the dialectic of the subjective and objective in human social life.

2) Historical study should not ignore the underprivileged, even if their activities are much less obviously visible than those of the grand or the powerful. The mass of working people is not just a passive category that can be written out of history. History

should not be just written 'from the top', but from 'the bottom up'. This theme of course unites Thompson's work with some of the most distinguished contributions in British traditions of labour history.[15]

3) Day-to-day events have a significance in and of themselves, which cannot be ignored by the historian. The study of the mundane is as much a part of history as is that of the drama of major events or happenings. This is again in a sense an emphasis upon history 'from the bottom up', but emphasizing the importance of everyday activities rather than the less privileged strata or classes in particular.

4) History is always a contingent affair. There is no overall teleology in history, apart from the purposes of individual agents; and these often eventuate in consequences which they could not have foreseen or intended.

All these issues are important in their own way and no doubt each enters into the effective writing of history. However, it should be clear that (2), (3) and (4) have no direct bearing upon whatever answers might be offered to (1), and therefore have to be kept apart from examination of the problem of agency as such in history. It is probably right to suggest, for example, that the contingent nature of history is most effectively understood in terms of implied counterfactuals of historical analysis. That is, either a direct scenario of 'what might have happened if X had not existed', or if 'Y had happened instead of X', or the unstated implication of these, are routinely involved in the writing of history. Thus Thompson invokes the possible state of affairs that might have ensued in English history if the Puritan Revolution of the seventeenth century had not occurred in the way in which it did. It is also apparent enough that, behind the detailed texture of *The Making of the English Working Class*, there lies the proposition that things could have happened otherwise — as Thompson says, the popular agitation among working people, if certain circumstances had been different, might have culminated in much more dramatic political change than actually took place. However, the 'could have happened otherwise' of history is not in and of itself the avenue to understanding the 'could have done otherwise' of agency.

[15] See Harvey Kaye: *The British Marxist Historians*. Cambridge: Polity Press, 1985.

For although agency is by definition implied in the 'could have happened otherwise' of human history, in other respects the same phenomenon applies to the history of objects and events in nature.

The writing of history 'from the bottom up' is fairly evidently a major corrective to certain traditional styles of both economic and political writing in history. In rescuing the poor and the humble from the 'condescension of posterity' and in emphasizing that failed projects are just as important to the historian attempting to understand a particular milieu as are successful ones, Thompson undeniably makes an important contribution to illuminating the development of classes and of class consciousness. There is a sense in which he attempts to rescue working people as agents, as compared with various other schools of thought in economic history that have discussed the labouring poor. For some of these, as Thompson points out, have concentrated upon an objective style of analysis, in which if they appear at all, individual agents are portrayed as swept along by irresistible tides of change. However, such a 'rescuing' of the underprivileged quite patently does not help resolve questions of agency; rather, it presumes that these questions have been in some sense resolved for such a process to be possible at all.

It is therefore sense (1) of agency which really counts. But the issues involved still need further consideration if they are to be satisfactorily elucidated. We should first of all insist that the question of agency has no intrinsic connection with the 'problem of order', either as designated by Anderson, or by Parsons and Sartre. Anderson sees that an understanding of what agency is, and its relation to history, cannot begin on the level of the intentional actor. He does not seem to notice that this compromises the idea that how 'order' is achieved is the fundamental problem for social analysis. The 'problem of order' has its origins precisely in a Hobbesian notion of a state of nature. But such a state of nature already presumes formed individual wills, which then are portrayed as being mutually incompatible. Nor should we suppose that a ritual appeal to concepts of historical materialism is of any help either. To state that modes of production somehow pre-exist individual purposes, or class conflicts, is simply either mistaken, or takes for granted matters that have to be resolved.

The nature of agency in relation to historical understanding can only be grasped if we have a conceptual hold over concepts of 'structure' and 'structural constraint' as well as that of agency itself. Thompson's wariness of such notions is so acute that he nowhere analyses in any detail how they might best be understood. Even though Anderson has been strongly influenced by Althusser, in whose writings of course notions of 'structure' brook large, he has little to offer on this point. The basic shortcoming of most discussions of agency and structure, including those of Thompson and Anderson, is to suppose that either the individual has a primacy over society (modes of production/social formation) or the reverse. Thompson's inclination is to plump for the reality of individuals, or at least of individual experience. He does not avoid statements involving larger totalities, but he makes it plain enough that he is uncomfortable with them. Anderson's view is closer to the orthodox sociological canon: societies, or social formations, are prior to the existence of individuals and shape their characteristic attitudes and modes of conduct.

We should resist this dualism and instead understand it as a duality — the 'duality of structure'. Except for the constraints of the material world, a phenomenon of course of importance in its own right, there is a basic sense in which agency is 'all there is' in human history. Agency *is* history, where 'history' is the temporal continuity of human activities. The 'could have done otherwise' of human agency, in other words, must not be juxtaposed to constraints on behaviour which derive from the structural properties of collectivities. It is this fundamental error which vitiates both the 'subjectivist' and the 'objectivist' starting points. In the one case, the entirely valid understanding that to be a human agent is to be able to 'act otherwise', and also to know this to be the case, leads to the idea that collectivities cannot have properties of their own, for these would somehow seem to deny such characteristics. Objectivist accounts of social institutions, on the other hand, promote just such a denial. Authors who adopt this second type of standpoint, that is to say, ordinarily imply that agents are not 'free' in the manner implied by the 'could have done otherwise' claim.

Human agency and structure, as again I have tried to show in an extensive way in other publications, are logically implicated with one another.[16] How and why this should be so is not difficult to understand once we have overcome the hurdle of counterposing the 'could have done otherwise' of action to structural constraint. Understood as rules and resources implicated in the 'form' of collectivities of social systems, reproduced across space and time, structure is the very medium of the

---

[16] Anthony Giddens: *Central Problems in Social Theory*. London: Macmillan, 1979; Anthony Giddens: *The Constitution of Society*, chpt. 1.

'human' element of human agency. At the same time, agency is the medium of structure, which individuals routinely reproduce in the course of their activities. All social life has a recursive quality to it, derived from the fact that actors reproduce the conditions of their social existence by means of the very activities that — in contexts of time-space — constitute that existence. Human beings normally know not only what they are doing at any moment, but why they are doing it. That is to say, it is characteristic of human agents that they routinely appraise what they do as a means of doing it, and that they are able discursively to give both an account of what they do and of their reasons for what they do. They can produce such character-izations under some description. But it does not follow that they know all there is to know about the consequences of what they do, for the activities of others or for their own activities in the future. Nor do they know all there is to know about the conditions of their action, that is, the circumstances that are causally involved with its production.

All constraints on human action apart from those involved in the physical world derive from 'bounded rationality' and 'bounded power'. Constraints of action are always contextually located, a point which is obvious once one understands that the relation between agency and constraint has nothing to do with the 'could have done otherwise' of action. Constraint here comprises the following range of phenomena:

1) The time-space 'stretch' of social institutions. All activities, even those of the most powerful individuals, occur within contexts of broader institutionalized settings. These are by no means sheerly constraining, because they always provide possibilities for the mobilization of human capabilities as well as their limitation. But the interlacing of constraint and mobilization is certainly part of the fine tissue of all human social life.

2) What I would refer to as the 'embeddedness' of institutions. Institutions tend to be the more firmly embedded — i.e., durable and persistent — the more they are grounded in the routines of day-to-day life.

3) The use of sanctions, whereby some individuals or groups seek actively to constrain the range of options open to others. It is important in social analysis not to confuse (3) with (1) and (2), or otherwise the door is open to wrongly construed conspiracy theories of power.

4) The truncating or blocking of modes of understanding the conditions of social reproduction, and therefore of potential

transformation, on the part of either individuals, groups of individuals, or the total population of a given societal collectivity. Where this connects to the unequal distribution of power, we are on the terrain of ideology.

We can revert at this point to the question of what 'history' is. When Thompson (and Marx) speak of 'making history', what exactly is it that is made? The phrase is largely devoid of any meaning or interest for the writing of history, as Anderson points out, if it simply refers to the facts that all human activities occur in time and are examples of agency in the sense elucidated previously. What is hinted at in the phrase is really the intrusion of human intentionality or purposefulness into processes of historical change. Anderson draws attention to this, but has not satisfactorily elucidated its implications. All social reproduction is an accomplishment of human beings, reflexively organized by them in terms of their monitoring of what they do. But the attempt to control conditions of reproduction consciously to mobilize social change is not a phenomenon evenly distributed throughout history. In non-literary cultures — even if Lévi-Strauss's characterization of these as 'cold' cultures is less than wholly satisfactory — social change is not brought about in such a fashion. Societies that are based on tradition are not necessarily societies which do not change; but change in such cultures is not for the most part mobilized as part of the generalized conditions of their social reproduction. When 'tradition' becomes known as such, which is more or less convergent with the emergence of states and civilizations, we can speak of the invention of 'history' in a double sense. The advent of writing, almost universally the medium of the organization of administrative power in such states, provides for a chronicling of present and past used to generate resources for the future. Moreover, the elapsing of time — 'history' in its most elemental sense — becomes understood in some part against a background of *social change*.

These issues have been well aired in the celebrated debate between Sartre and Lévi-Strauss.[17] The Marxian standpoint, which sees history as a progressive use of historical understanding in order to make history, only really becomes relevant with the advent of states and civilizations. This is the first phase of human social development at

---

[17] See Claude Lévi-Strauss: *The Savage Mind*. London: Weidenfeld, 1966.

which one can speak of the existence of *organizations*, of which the agrarian state is the prime form. Organizations I take to be forms of human collectivity in which the reflexive monitoring of social activity is extended to cover considerable tracts of social reproduction. However, it is only in relatively modern times that what we might call historicity has become developed with great intensity. It is surely right to see as one of the main features of modernity an increasing purposiveness in endeavours to control the conditions of social reproduction. Modern society is a fertile environment for the development of organizations, and for the formation of social movements, the latter as well as the former involved with the deepened historicity of the modern period. To associate this primarily with the labour movement is, however, more than faintly absurd. Rather than being the prime vehicle of such a process, the labour movement is only one example of the near universalization in the modern era of the principle that 'history may be used to make history'.

It does not follow from this, as Anderson seems to presume, and as Marx may indeed have also supposed, that increasing historicity provides human beings with ever greater control of the whole of their activities. For even in environments in which large tracts of social life are subject to the direct monitoring of social reproduction, there may be a constant drift of unforeseen or unintended consequences away from whatever states of affairs are sought by those involved. Both Thompson and Anderson, in somewhat varying ways, raise the question of the significance of unintended consequences in history. What neither seems satisfactorily to see is that unintended consequences of action may reproduce the familiar at the same time as they may bring about the unfamiliar or the unexpected. The fact that unintended consequences of purposive action may be routinely involved in system reproduction was the origin of some of the main emphases of functionalism, and more generally of those schools of sociology to which Thompson seems to take greatest objection. He is undoubtedly justified in doing so in so far as such approaches seek to understand human social life in terms not appropriate to agents at all — that is, in terms of mechanical models which truly belong with the Orreries of this world. But he is wrong to do so in so far as this leads him to neglect conditions of social reproduction which do not form part of the intentions or reasons for anyone's action, but which nevertheless are fundamental to the occurrence of large-scale or long-term historical change.

Several conclusions might be drawn from these observations as regards the practice of writing history and the concepts that might legitimately inform it. In my view, there are no distinctions between the methods of investigation open to historians and sociologists, or the forms of concepts which they can and should employ. If there is a differentiation between history and sociology, it cannot be anything to do with time, unless we make of it the uninteresting thesis that sociologists deal with the present-day, historians with the past. It cannot be anything to do with agency, or with how social institutions should best be conceptualized. One cannot even say that such a distinction could rest upon an eye to detail in the observation and description of human behaviour, which the historian needs but the sociologist can afford to neglect. As I have indicated earlier, how much detail is needed in a particular study, and what kind of detail, is dependent upon the objectives of the research in question, not something that can support a distinction between two types of discipline, or two types of conceptualization.

Outstandingly original and influential though it may have been, *The Making of the English Working Class* would have been a better book if Thompson had been able to include within its scope phenomena that Anderson rightly censures him for neglecting. The antimony between history and sociology at which Thompson repeatedly hints, I have tried to show, has no more defensible basis to it than has his mistrust of 'structural' concepts. He is no doubt justified in objecting to certain types of sociological writing, particularly those in which human beings appear as the voiceless playthings of social forces. The appeal of his writings to those accustomed to such styles of work derives from just this emphasis. But when subjected to scrutiny, this appeal is defended by an uneasy emphasis upon the particular and upon contingency, together with writing history 'from the bottom up'. When questions of agency as such are addressed, Thompson characteristically expresses a somewhat vague proclivity towards nominalism and voluntarism, a stance as flawed as the standpoint Anderson proposes in combatting it. The strong impress which Thompson's historical writings make upon the reader derives as much from their flair and gusto as from the cogency of the analyses of agency they contain. But an historian could have a worse epitaph than this.

10

Reason without revolution? Habermas's *Theory of Communicative Action.*

Appropriately enough for an author concerned with the expansion of the public sphere and the fostering of debate, Habermas's writings have from the beginnings of his career attracted widespread attention.[1] Habermas has been a public figure in German life since his early association with — and disassociation from — the student movement of the late 1960s. His work has drawn sharp, even bitter, criticism from both Right and Left. For Habermas's writings are not easy to place, intellectually or politically. Self-professedly working within Marxist traditions, Habermas's work is far too revisionist to appeal to most others who would call themselves 'Marxists'. Yet his connections with the Frankfurt School have made him an object of deep suspicion to those affiliated with conservative perspectives. Habermas's thinking has been shaped in considerable degree by the controversies in which he has been involved. The accusation which Habermas directed against certain sections of the student movement — 'Left fascism' — has reverberated through his subsequent intellectual career. His preoccupation with isolating the conditions of rational decision-making

[1] This essay was first published in *Praxis International*, vol. 4, 1982. My thanks to the publishers for allowing it to be reprinted here. Jürgen Habermas: *Theorie des kommunikativen Handelns* (2 vols). Frankfurt: Suhrkamp, 1981, vol. 1, pp. 534, vol. 2, pp. 632; *The Theory of Communicative Action*. Cambridge: Polity Press, 1985—6.

and of specifying the conditions under which a consensus, governed purely by the 'force of the better argument', can be brought about, evidently in some part represent a protracted attempt to come to terms with the implications of this notorious remark. Successive confrontations with Popper, Gadamer, Luhmann and others have also left a deep imprint on his thought.

But it would clearly be wrong to regard Habermas as primarily a polemicist. He is a systematic thinker, who has consistently sought to come to terms with a number of basic issues in philosophy and social theory. Habermas's writings range over an extraordinary variety of topics, and it would be easy to see in this a diffuse eclecticism. Certainly he does incorporate into his own theories ideas taken from a diversity of apparently incompatible approaches. Anyone who has the least bit of sympathy with Habermas's overall project, however, must recognize that he employs such ideas in a highly innovative and disciplined fashion.

Habermas's work can be divided, broadly speaking, into two main phases. The first culminated in the publication of *Erkenntnis und Interesse* (*Knowledge and Human Interests*) in 1968. Although the views Habermas expressed therein have been influential in the social sciences and philosophy, the book also received a barrage of critical attacks. This critical onslaught undoubtedly did indicate some serious shortcomings in the work, and in Habermas's standpoint more generally. Habermas sought to advance a novel conception of critical theory, on the basis of the constitution of knowledge through interests. But the 'interest in emancipation' seemed to exist only as a moment in the conjunction of the other two knowledge-constitutive interests. Habermas's later work can be seen as an attempt to give flesh to the emancipatory potential of social analysis. This endeavour has led Habermas away — just how far, he has yet to specify — from the framework adopted in *Erkenntnis und Interesse*. It seems apparent that Habermas would now regard the attempt to found critical theory upon epistemology as misleading if not actually mistaken. Epistemology, he insisted in *Erkenntnis und Interesse*, is possible only as social theory: social theory which examines the conditions under which, in Habermas's words, 'reason that becomes transparent to itself' is disclosed. However, if the traditional search for a transcendental basis of knowledge — a 'first philosophy' — is to be abandoned, why approach critical theory through the theory of knowledge at all? Habermas seems today to hold that his excursion into epistemology was something of a detour in his endeavour to ground critical theory:

the more direct route is through the embedding of reason in *language* in general, and in *communication* in particular.

Habermas's newest publication, *Theory of Communicative Action*, is a synthetic statement and an elaboration of the ideas developed in this second phase of his writings. Consisting of two large volumes, each of somewhere near six hundred pages, it is a sprawling, uneven work. It is, I would say, quite unnecessarily long. Purposes of communication would surely have been better served, and the main theses of the book would have stood out in greater relief, if Habermas had taken a razor to some of his material. The work is like a bumper edition of Habermas's *Zur Logik der Sozialwissenschaften*, which appeared fifteen years ago, and in which he offered an analysis of a variety of leading contributions to social theory. His new book contains reassessments of most of the traditions of thought he discussed before. The differences are that these traditions are now considered in much more detail; Max Weber occupies a considerably more prominent position; and the exegetical material is more directly focused upon the conceptual schema of Habermas's own thought. I don't think confirmed Habermas-watchers will learn a great deal from this massive work, for nearly all of the main theorems it advances have been introduced in more minor contexts over recent years. But it does bring these together in a central source, and provides a useful opportunity to appraise the current trend of Habermas's thinking.

The theory of communicative action, Habermas asserts in the opening section of the book, is neither a metatheory, nor a continuation of the theory of knowledge by other means. The analysis of communicative action allows us to connect three levels of rationality relevant to social analysis (Habermas is fond of talking in threes; the tables and classifications with which the book abounds are often based on three-fold distinctions). One concerns 'rationality' as debated in hermeneutics and Anglo-American analytical philosophy, related particularly to issues of relativism. If divergent cultures or forms of life have their own inner criteria of rationality, in what sense is it possible to make comparisons of them — and subject them to critique — in terms of universal standards? Another concerns the rationality of action: how are we to grasp the distinctively meaningful character of human conduct? This touches upon questions of the significance of *Verstehen*, and of the role of the social sciences in claiming superior explanations to those which actors themselves already are able to provide as 'reasons' for their behaviour. Finally — and large segments of the book are given over to this — Habermas is concerned with the social expansion of rationality as the rationalization of society characteristic of the modern West. Here is where he makes particular appeal to the writings of Max Weber, seeking to reformulate the conception of reification that links Weber to the early Lukács and to the Frankfurt School.

In defending an overall conception of rationality in each of these domains, Habermas evidently has a strong sense of swimming against the tide. He proposes universal criteria of reason at a time when relativistic styles of thought have become fashionable in various areas of intellectual discourse — as, for example, in 'post-structuralism'. He wants to offer a vindication of enlightenment and modernity when for many these have become effectively discredited. The rise of neo-conservatism is particularly important here. *The Theory of Communicative Action* is written at a characteristically Habermasian level of high abstraction; but there is also a directly political *motif* that runs through the book. Both neo-conservatives, who place primacy upon the achievement of economic growth through the revival of market forces, and the ecological critics of growth, turn against the heritage of Western rationalism. Habermas wants to criticize both standpoints, while seeking to understand why they have come to the fore in the current era. In an interview,[2] he says that his 'real motive' in writing the book was to make clear how 'the critique of reification', of rationalization, can be reformulated to offer a theoretical explanation for the decay of the 'welfare-state compromise' on the one hand, and on the other the critical potential embodied in new movements — without discarding the project of modernity or relapsing into post- or anti-modernism.

Philosophy, Habermas argues, has always had as its main task reflection upon reason. But contemporary philosophy has become a diverse array of specialisms, no longer seeking to provide a unified world-view. This situation is partly a result of the collapse of attempts to found a 'first philosophy': all attempts to provide indubitable foundations for philosophical reason have broken down. Habermas accepts some of the implications of this. Philosophy can no longer hope to develop the sort of grand metaphysical schemes such as were sought after by Kant and Hegel. A new relation therefore has to be established, and is already becoming established, between philosophy and both the natural and social sciences. The procedure of 'rational

---

[2] Jürgen Habermas: interview in *Aesthetik und Kommunikation*, No. 45/6, 1981.

reconstruction' Habermas takes as a key element in this: the process of reconstructing what can be regarded, after the event, as the rational content of a field of research or subject-area. He takes Piaget's developmental psychology as a type case. Piaget reconstructs psychological development not just as a sequence of stages, but as so many steps in the expansion of the rational competence of the individual.

How should we use the term 'rational'? Rationality has less to do with knowledge as such, Habermas asserts, than with the manner in which knowledge is used. If we consider the circumstances in which we speak of something as 'rational', we see it refers either to persons or to symbolic expressions which embody knowledge. To say that someone acts rationally, or that a statement is rational, is to say that the action or statement can be criticized or defended by the person or persons involved, so that they are able to justify or 'ground' them. We cannot, as empiricism does, limit the grounds of rational acts or expressions to knowledge of the object-world. We must complement 'cognitive-instrumental rationality' with a conception of 'communicative rationality'. Habermas says:

> Dieser Begriff *kommunikativer Rationalität*, führt Konnotationen mit sich, die letzlich zurückgehen auf die zentrale Erfahrung der zwanglos einigenden, konsensstiffenden Kraft argumentativer Rede, in der verschiedene Teilnehmer ihre zunächst nur subjektiven Auffassungen überwinden und sich dank der Gemeinsamkeit verünftig motivierter Überzeugungen gleichzeitig der Einheit der objektiven Welt und der Intersubjektivität ihrer Lebenszusammenhangs vergewissern.[3]

Rationality *presumes* communication, because something is only rational if it meets the conditions necessary to forge an understanding with at least one other person.

For those who know anything about Habermas's writings over the past few years it is easy to see where this line of thought leads him. He has often made the case that human language involves a number of 'validity claims', that are ordinarily implicitly made by speakers, but which can be made explicit. When I say something to someone else, I implicitly make the following claims: that what I say is intelligible; that its propositional content is true; that I am justified in saying it;

[3] Jürgen Habermas: *Theorie des kommunikativen Handelns*, vol. 1, p. 28.

and that I speak sincerely, without intent to deceive. All of these claims are contingent or fallible, and all except the first can be criticized and grounded by the offering of reasons. When validity claims are rendered explicit, and when their grounding is assessed purely in terms of how far good reasons can be offered for them (rather than by constraint or force), there exists what Habermas calls a process of 'argumentation'. Argumentation, as he puts it, is a 'court of appeal' of the rationality inherent in everyday communication: it makes possible the continuation of communicative action when disputes arise, without recourse to duress. It follows that the notion of communicative rationality can best be explicated through an examination of the general properties of argumentation. There is more than an echo of Popper in this — a mark, perhaps, of what Habermas has learned through argumentation. Reason, for Habermas like Popper, becomes primarily a phenomenon of methodical criticism: 'by identifying our mistakes', Habermas proposes, 'we can correct our failed attempts'.

The idea of communicative rationality is the basis upon which Habermas counters the tendencies towards relativism characteristic of much recent philosophical literature. In this context he discusses the nature of myths in traditional cultures and the relation between myth and science, in conjunction with the controversies to which Peter Winch's writings have given rise. Myths, Habermas argues, are concretized modes of thought, which integrate many different aspects of life within a single intellectual domain. They express the organization of societies which have not generated separate intellectual domains, or arenas of discourse, within which argumentation may be carried on. Here we reach one of Habermas's main — and, one might add, most questionable — proposals. The development of arenas of discourse, which he tries to trace through the emergence of the 'world religions', and the subsequent differentiation of science, morality and art in modern culture signifies a general evolution towards an expansion of rationality. The more we are able rationally to ground the conduct of our lives in the three main spheres of existence — relations with the material world, with others, and in the expressive realm of aesthetics — the more advanced our form of society can be said to be.

Enlightenment, obviously, is no joke. The modern world for Habermas *is* more enlightened than the primitive. In his evolutionary theory, Habermas tries to demonstrate that this still has some connection with Marx's materialist conception of history. Since in the more traditional cultures the productive forces are undeveloped, social life tends to be dominated by the hazards of nature. The need arises to check the 'flood of contingencies'. These cannot be checked in fact, so they are interpreted away, in myth. Myths merge the worlds of nature and culture, and attribute to elements in nature powers superior to those of human beings. Myths are anthropomorphic since they draw into the network of human relations features of nature; and they reify culture by treating it as the operation of autonomous forces. They suffer, Habermas avows, from a 'double illusion'. He says this 'is certainly not well analysed', referring presumably to pre-existing discussions. But the same judgement could be made of his own treatment of myth, which is cursory in the extreme given the length of the book as a whole.

He does, however, give some considerable attention to Winch's philosophical analysis of traditional cultures, which of course rests primarily upon Evans-Pritchard's celebrated portrayal of Zande sorcery. Habermas argues that the latter's own interpretation of the activities of the Zande is superior to that offered by Winch. For Evans-Pritchard shows that a hermeneutic sensitivity is necessary if Zande beliefs and practices are to be adequately understood. But this does not lead him towards relativism; on the contrary, he is at pains to point out that Zande thought is deficient as compared to the canons of the testing of validity claims embodied in Western science. We can compare different cultures, or world-views, in respect of their 'cognitive adequacy' — which is to say, in terms of the defensible validity claims that they incorporate. Here Habermas leans rather heavily upon the views of Robin Horton. Traditional cultures, he accepts with Horton, usually involve closed world-views, refractory to change; modern culture, by contrast, is more open to modification in the light of learning experiences.

Piaget's conception of learning as stages of cognitive development can help us illuminate what such openness to learning consists in. The three main phases of social evolution — the mythical, religious-metaphysical and modern (shades of Comte!) — correspond to the differentiation of cognitive capacities which Piaget identifies. Habermas is careful at this point to re-emphasize the significance of the procedure of rational reconstruction. The point, I take it, is not that each individual, in a modern culture, recapitulates the development of human societies as a whole. It is that there are several, increasingly extensive and intensive, modalities of the organization of rational thought and action. Cognitive development for Piaget is associated with a 'decentring' process. The decentring of cognition leads the child away from primitive egocentrism, towards the differentiation of the capacity for coping with the external world, the social world, and the world of 'inner subjectivity' — the three dimensions to which Habermas's types of validity claims correspond.

At this point, Habermas introduces the concept of the life-world (*Lebenswelt*). The life-world, as is suggested in phenomenology, is the taken-for-granted universe of daily social activity. It is the saturation of communicative action by tradition and established ways of doing things. The life-world is a pre-interpreted set of forms of life, within which everyday conduct unfolds. It 'stores up the interpretative work of many preceding generations'. The weight of tradition in the life-world acts as a counterbalance to the intrinsic possibilities of disagreement which communication raises. The process of social evolution, involving the decentring of world-views and the consolidation of the three dimensions of discourse, alters the character of the life-world. The more advanced the decentring process, the less the achievement of consensus is guaranteed by pre-established beliefs or codes of behaviour. The expansion of rationality thus presumes a diminution of the hold of the life-world. Looking to one of the sources of Piaget's own thought — the work of Durkheim — Habermas reinterprets the transition from mechanical to organic solidarity in these terms. The writings of Durkheim and G. H. Mead he sees as complementing one another in helping to distinguish the mechanisms of co-ordination of the life-world from the integration of social systems:

> Ob man mit Mead von Grundbegriffen der sozialen Interaktion oder mit Durkheim von Grundbegriffen der Kollektiven Repräsentation ausgeht, in beiden Fällen wird die Gesellschaft aus der Teilnehmerperspektive handelnder Subjekte als *Lebenswelt einer sozialen Gruppe* konzipiert. Demgegenüber kann die Gesellschaft aus der Beobachterperspektive eines Unbeteiligten nur als ein *System von Handlungen* begriffen werden, wobei diesen Handlungen, je nach ihrem Beitrag zur Erhaltung des Systembestandes, ein funktionaler Stellenwert zukommt.[4]

Habermas also seeks to forge here a direct connection with the writings of Max Weber. The formation of differentiated world-views, as these become separate from the life-world, consolidates the rational conduct of life in so far as these meet certain conditions. They must

---

[4] Jürgen Habermas: *Theorie des kommunikativen Handelns*, vol. 2, p. 179.

make concepts available for formulating validity claims for the three dimensions of reality (which Habermas also explicitly connects with Popper's 'three worlds'). Cultural traditions must allow reflective criticism which makes it possible to subject belief-claims embodied in customary ways of life to disruptive evaluation. There have to be institutional mechanisms which co-ordinate learning processes over time, and feed back new knowledge into the life-world. This implies the differentiation of science, law and art, as the primary spheres relating to the 'three worlds'. Such a differentiation in turn presupposes the institutionalization of purposive-rational action, i.e., action which is oriented towards the achievement of specific goals, and which can hence be assessed in terms of its technical effectiveness. Max Weber, Habermas says, has helped us understand how important the differentiation of cultural spheres, and the formation of institutional forms geared to purposive-rational action, are to modernization. The two main spheres in which purposive-rational action becomes institutionalized, and the basis of system integration, are the economy and the state. Money is the dominant 'circulating medium' (Parsons) in the former; power in the latter.

I shall pass over here the complicated typologies of action and modes of discourse which Habermas offers, as well as his attempt to connect these with speech-act theory. His typologies are as difficult to disentangle as ever, but I do not think they add much to what he has written before. More novel is his extensive critical analysis of Weber; his discussion of the relation between Weber's concept of rationalization and the notion of reification as employed by Lukács and others; plus the attempt to relate all this to features of Parsons's social theory.

Weber helped to popularize the idea of *Verstehen* in the social sciences as well as connecting the rationality of action with the rationalization of culture. The notion of purposive-rational action plays a major role in Weber's characterization of the understanding of human conduct. Purposive-rational action can be assessed in terms of how far, given the goals an actor has, it meets criteria that are strategically 'adequate'. Although Weber used this form of assessment as the pre-eminent standard of rationality against which elements of irrationality of action can be discerned, for Habermas of course it is only one aspect of rational conduct. Normatively regulated action (corresponding to the social world) and expressive, or what Habermas also calls, following Goffman, 'dramaturgical action' (corresponding to the 'inner' world of subjectivity) also have standards of rationality.

The notion of *Verstehen* as utilized by Weber needs to be modified in a two-fold sense. Grasping these additional dimensions of the rationality of action is especially relevant to elucidating why people act as they do. But the 'meaning' of action cannot be reduced to actors' intentions and reasons for their action. Here modern hermeneutics, and the philosophy of the later Wittgenstein, are much more important than the schools of thought from which Weber drew. To understand the meaning of action involves being able in principle to participate in the form of life in which that action is incorporated. However, Habermas emphasizes again, this cannot be done without, at least implicitly, assessing the validity claims raised within that form of life. Thus understanding cannot be severed from the rational evaluation of action.

Discussion of metatheoretical and methodological problems of rationality, Habermas asserts, helps drive home that a concern with rationality is intrinsic to the practice of the social sciences; it is not something imposed by philosophers from the outside. Since world-views *already* embody validity-claims and, in differential degree, modes of their discursive redemption, these first two aspects of rationality are inherently bound up with the third: the rationalization of culture. In examining modes of approach to rationalization, Habermas attempts 'a reconstruction of the history of theory' from Weber to Parsons, seeking to disclose how the social sciences have developed conceptual strategies for analysing the nature of modernity. He acknowledges that this is at best an eliptical approach to the questions at issue, but seems to regard it as an important first step.

According to Habermas, Weber is particularly significant for the problems he wishes to analyse because, unlike the other classical social theorists, Weber broke both with the philosophy of history and with evolutionism in its orthodox, quasi-Darwinian, sense — while at the same time conceiving of Western modernization 'as a result of a universal-historical process of rationalisation'. As in his conception of *Verstehen*, Weber allocated to the expansion of purposive-rationality the key part in the historical process of the rationalization of Western culture. He therefore did not capture other aspects in which learning processes have taken place; but his writings do nevertheless contain useful categories for describing them.

Weber mentions many phenomena as involved in the rationalization of Western culture, including science, law, political and economic administration, art, literature and music. What gives a unity to the trends affecting this diverse array? Weber's own use of the term 'rationalization' was rather confused. The main element underlying Weber's various discussions of rationalization, according to Habermas, is the emergence of modes of activity based upon universalistic principles. The rationalized ethics associated with modern law, for example, treat norms as conventions — not as binding imperatives of tradition — governed by decisions based upon generalizable principles rather than arbitrary assessments. In Habermas's interpretation of Weber (which is certainly questionable on this and other points) rationalization is also a process of differentiation — the emergence of three 'value spheres', each with its own logic, corresponding once more to Habermas's 'three worlds'. These are the cognitive, moral and expressive elements of cultural rationalization, and can be analysed on an institutional level in terms of the three-fold typology Parsons develops of society, culture and personality.

One of Weber's most distinctive concerns, of course, was to contrast occidental rationalization with the directions of development of other civilizations. As Habermas points out, however, he did not formulate clearly in what ways the development of modernism in the West is more than one possible form of society among others. If 'rationalization' means the ordering of life according to universalizable principles, in what sense are those principles universally valid? Weber's answer is ambiguous. We know Habermas's standpoint: there are indeed universally valid procedural forms of rationality. In so far as the West has moved towards the 'post-conventional' stage of institutionalized learning processes, rationalization of the Western type equals increasing rationality of belief and conduct.

From Weber to Parsons . . . but of course Habermas does not seek to retrace the path of orthodox sociology. In between Weber and Parsons come Lukács and the Frankfurt School; and Habermas approaches his analysis of Parsonian thought via a 'critique of functionalist reason'. The connections between Weber's interpretation of rationalization, Lukács's discussion of reification, and the critique of instrumental reason formulated by Horkheimer and Adorno, are clear. They all agree that an expanding rationalization underlies the overall trend of development of Western society. In spite of placing different emphases upon the character of rationalization, these writers hold, like Weber, that the primacy accorded to purposive-rational action in modern culture produces both a loss of moral meaning in day-to-day life, and a diminution of freedom. Obviously Weber does not counterpose instrumental reason, as 'subjective reason', to 'objective reason' as Horkheimer and Adorno do; and he does not, like

Lukács, equate rationalization with a reified social world which in principle can be radically transformed. But neither Lukács nor the Frankfurt School are able satisfactorily to free themselves from the limitations of Weber's standpoint. Lukács hoped to restore the missing philosophical dimension to Marxism by disclosing that rationalization, as described by Weber, involves an undialectical account of bourgeois culture. But this led him to relapse into an abstract 'objective idealism' which was in fact something of a retrograde step in philosophy rather than an advance. Horkheimer and Adorno only partly avoided this tendency, and tended restlessly to shuffle back and forth between the poles of objective and subjective reason. Neither they, nor Lukács, were able to show how rationalization, or reification, are connected to the deformation of the communicative basis of interpersonal relationships. Thus, while retaining a necessary critical edge to social analysis, they lagged behind the advances already made by G. H. Mead on the other side of the Atlantic. For Mead made the transition from a philosophy of consciousness to a philosophy of language, centred upon symbolic interaction.

In Habermas's eyes there is something of an epistemological break between what he regards as the termination of the philosophy of consciousness — or of 'the subject' — and the emergence of communicative analysis. The theory of communicative rationality does not posit a self-sufficient subject, confronting an object-world, but instead begins from the notion of a symbolically-structural life-world, in which human reflexivity is constituted. To accept this, and to pursue its implications for social theory, demands however departing from some of Mead's emphases. Mead did not investigate the conditions of reproduction of the social world. As Parsons and other functionalist sociologists have consistently asserted, the conditions of societal reproduction involve imperatives over and beyond those directly involved in communicative interaction. The integration of the conduct of the participant members of societies also involves the co-ordination of divergent interest groups in the face of various specifiable system imperatives. This observation is essential for Habermas's reformulation of the concept of reification. The problematic of reification, he says, should not be associated, as it was by Lukács and the Frankfurt School, with the conception of rationalization (or purposive-rational action) as such. Instead, reification should be connected to ways in which the 'functional conditions of system reproduction', in modern societies, impinge upon and undermine the rational foundation of communicative action in the life-world. A critical appropriation of Parsons's work, Habermas claims, allows us to formulate an approach to reification, thus understood, in terms of the mechanisms of social and system integration.

Many Anglo-Saxon readers, who may have spent their formative sociological years struggling free from the influence of Parsonianism, are liable to receive this proposal with something of a sinking feeling. But for better or for worse, partly through the agency of Luhmann, Parsons's writings have today become influential in Germany, and Habermas accords them a sympathetic reading. As he recognizes, there is a certain parallel between the synthesis of classical social theory upon which Parsons built his own work, and his own enterprise. Parsons indeed helped to make Weber and Durkheim two of the most influential figures in the development of sociology. More than this however, he directed attention to issues that have to remain a foremost concern of anyone interested in social theory today.

From his earliest writings, Habermas points out, Parsons was preoccupied with the relation between human action on the one side, and the constitution of social systems on the other. Although many interpreters of Parsons have tended to accentuate one of these at the expense of the other, Habermas insists that they are of equivalent importance. We can express them in terms of the social integration/system integration distinction. In the one instance, in the continuity of the life-world, we are concerned with the co-ordination of action orientations, in the other with functional conditions of system properties ordered along a broader scale of time and space. According to Parsons, norms and values are constitutive of social integration, but not of system integration, which depends upon more 'impersonal' mechanisms. Habermas accepts this general standpoint, while proffering a range of criticisms of Parsons's own formulation of it. Parsons's conceptualization of action, he argues, is too restricted, and particularly in Parsons's later writings tends to be swamped by a concentration upon system functions; and the account of modernity which Parsons developed paints too much of a consensual picture, neglecting the fundamental tensions which have come to exist in contemporary society. While these criticisms are not novel, the mode in which Habermas seeks to draw upon Parsons's ideas is important (if still questionable).

According to Habermas, Parsons's concept of action — or, rather, the mode in which he sought to build such a concept into his theoretical scheme — represses the hermeneutic dimension of social analysis.

Parsons failed to see that the social researcher must be able 'to go on' in the forms of life involved in the everyday world in order to describe and to account for the nature of those forms of life in a satisfactory fashion. Recognizing this implies seeing that the differentiation of social and system integration has a methodological aspect to it. Social integration necessarily has reference to participants' own concepts, whereas system integration can be described in other terms; the 'translation' from one to the other involves a shift in methodological orientation on the part of the social analyst. Of course, this view continues the line of argument Habermas has set out in previous writings in respect of systems theory. Systems analysis is certainly not illegitimate in social theory; but on the other hand it cannot lay claim to provide an overall framework for the explication of social conduct, as functionalists suppose. The integration of a society involves the constant renewal of a compromise between two forms of imperatives. The conditions for the integration of the life-world are bound up with the renewal of the validity claims (*Geltungsbasis*) underlying the structure of a definite world-view. The conditions for the functional integration of society are to do with the modes in which the life-world is related to a surrounding environment which is only partly controlled through the communicative action of human beings. Such a compromise can only be reached through the institutionalization and internalization of value-orientations (as Parsons also holds). If these do not conform to the functional demands of system reproduction, social cohesion is only preserved if such functional demands remain latent. In these circumstances the illusory nature of the validity claims on which the value-orientations are based may remain opaque. The result is systematically distorted communication.

For Parsons, language, together with power and money are represented as the media of societal integration. According to Habermas, however, language has to be excluded from this role, since it is implicated in all social activity; Parsons is only able to represent language as one medium of integration among others because he obscures the linguistic foundation of the hermeneutic properties of the life-world. However, we can make good use of the Parsonian treatment of power and money, as the media of the extension and co-ordination of purposive-rational action. A high degree of rationalization, produced by the evolutionary movement towards modernity, is the necessary basis upon which money (in the economy) and power (in the polity) become differentiated as 'steering media'. Each presupposes the institutionalization of positive law and the separation of the household

— which it is one of Weber's main achievements to have emphasized. As differentiated spheres of system integration, the economy and the polity remain grounded in the life-world, from which they draw normative support and value-commitment. At the same time, they presume the specialized development of processes of the formation of consensus through communicative action. This in turn involves not only institutional differentiation but the development of personality structures capable of participating in post-conventional discursive will formation.

From Parsons . . . back to Weber and to Marx. In the concluding sections of his analysis, Habermas tries to focus these ideas upon a diagnosis of the pathological aspects of modernity. It follows from Habermas's overall view that the rationalization of communicative action must be analytically separated from the formation of the purposive-rational institutional sectors of economy and polity. This in turn means revising key notions in both Weber and Marx, since neither recognizes this distinction in the mode Habermas formulates it. For Habermas, the disentangling of steering mechanisms from the life-world is not as such pathological, but intrinsic to modernization. Such differentiation therefore necessarily has to be distinguished from conditions — that Habermas thinks have come to the fore in recent times — under which the communicative basis of the life-world is drained of the very supports which the economy and polity demand. This can be described as a process of the 'internal colonization' of the life-world, a destruction of tradition which threatens the very continuance of the reproduction of society as a whole.

The tensions and conflicts which dominate in modernized societies today have to be distinguished from those characteristic of earlier phases of development. The disembedding of steering processes from the life-world in post-medieval times provoked various kinds of protest movements, as the peasantry were forced into the towns and as the centralized state came into being. In the nineteenth and early twentieth centuries, the labour movement became the focus of resistance in the face of further economic and political differentiation. Marx showed how the transformation of concrete into abstract labour was the condition of the co-ordination of modern production. This was one of the very mechanisms distinguishing the economy as a separate institutional sphere. Labour movements may be seen as partially successful attempts to correct an imbalance between life-world and steering mechanisms deriving from the harsh dislocations effected by rapid capitalist development. But a parallel process of 'abstraction' also occurs in political life with the further modernization of the state. This is in fact the type case of the colonization of the life-world, since the public sphere comes to be more and more 'technicized' in the contemporary period.

Here we return to the question of reification. In Marx's writings, this notion is tied diffusely to the process of economic abstraction whereby 'living labour' is subordinated to the rule of impersonal economic mechanisms. In some part this is again a necessary element of modernization, and cannot be regarded as pathological. The latter is the case, however, where monetary mechanisms have penetrated too far into the communicatively ordered life-world. The reification of 'communicatively-structured spheres of action' is thus not first and foremost a phenomenon of class divisions. Here Habermas leans very definitely towards Weber and away from Marx. Against the hopes of revolutionary transformation which Marx anticipated would be achieved through class struggle:

> hat Max Webers Prognose, 'dass die Abschaffung des Privatkapitalismus . . . keineswegs ein Zerbrechen des stählernen Gehäuses der modernen gewerblichen Arbeit bedeuten würde', recht behalten. Der Marxsche Irrtum geht letzlich auf jene dialektische Verklammerung von System — und Lebensweltanalyse zurück, die eine hinreichend scharfe Trennung zwischen dem in der Moderne ausgebildeten *Niveau der Systemdifferenzierung* und den *klassenspezifischen Formen seiner Institutionalisierung* nicht zulässt. Marx hat den Versuchungen des Hegelschen Totalitätsdenkens nicht widerstanden und die Einheit von System und Lebenswelt dialektisch als ein 'unwahres Ganzes' konstruiert. Sonst hätte er sich nicht darüber täuschen können, das *jede* moderne Gesellschaft, gleichviel wie ihre Klassenstruktur beschaffen ist, einen hohen Grad an struktureller Differenzierung aufweisen muss . . . Marx fehlen Kriterien, anhand deren er die Zerstörung traditionaler Lebensformen von der Verdinglichung, posttraditionaler Lebenswelten unterscheiden könnte.[5]

Marx's analysis, Habermas says, repeating a theme of his earlier writings, is most relevant to the early phases of the development of capitalist societies. In these phases, the economic mechanisms Marx identified do tend to be important. However, there is not one steering mechanism (the economy) in modern societies, but two; and the

[5] Jürgen Habermas: *Theorie des kommunikativen Handelns*, vol. 2, pp. 500−1.

second, the administrative apparatus of power, was not satisfactorily grasped by Marx. Partly for this reason, orthodox Marxism is not able to illuminate some of the key phenomena of late capitalism, in which state intervention is increasingly extensive, and in which mass democracy and welfare reforms brook large.

The conjunction of these phenomena in late capitalism, Habermas affirms, produces a new type of 'class non-specific reification' — although its effects are distributed unequally within the class system. His analysis of this is complex, and I shall not attempt to summarize it here. Basically, the theme is that the colonization of the life-world has destroyed traditional bases of communicative action, without replacing them with the forms of post-conventional rationality that are required to couple the life-world to the range of activities controlled by expanding economic and political steering mechanisms. The colonization of the life-world has a double implication. Within the life-world itself, reification has the consequence of loss of meaning or anomie, with the range of associated problems which this produces within personality structures. From the perspective of the steering mechanisms, the result is a set of motivational and legitimation deficits. Whereas in his previous work Habermas saw 'motivation crises' as, in a certain sense at least, more deeply embedded than 'legitimation crises', it now appears that these connect directly to each of the steering mechanisms, and are of equivalent potential importance. Lack of motivational input creates problems for the maintenance of economic organization; while a diminution in legitimation threatens the stability of the political order.

The tasks of critical theory today, Habermas concludes, have to be integrated with this appraisal of the institutional form of, and the tensions inherent within, late capitalism. New conflicts, and new social movements, have developed which diverge from the older types of class struggle centred upon production relationships and the welfare state. Such conflicts no longer primarily concern the distribution of material goods, but rather cultural reproduction and socialization, and do not follow the established bargaining mechanisms associated with the unions or political parties. Since they are an expression of the reification of the communicative order of the life-world, it follows that these tensions cannot be alleviated through further economic development, or technical improvements in the administrative apparatus of government. The new conflicts, and associated social movements, derive from problems that can only be resolved through a reconquest of the life-world by communicative reason, and by concomitant transmutations in the normative order of daily life. How far do such tendencies contain an emancipatory promise which might in a significant way transform existing social institutions? Habermas hedges his bets; but he is inclined to see the new social movements as primarily defensive, concerned with protecting the life-world against further colonization. Ecological and anti-nuclear movements are of this kind, since they are characteristically linked with the impetus to defend the natural environment against despoilation, and to recreate communal relationship of various forms. Whatever the potential for specific movements, however, Habermas affirms strongly that the 'stitching' between system and life-world is likely to continue in the near future to be their point of origin. The theory of communicative action, he contends, helps us to understand why this is so, and can be placed in the service of indicating the pressure-points at which real change might be achieved; it replaces the older type of critical theory, founded upon now untenable philosophical positions.

It will take some time to digest the implications of a book such as this, written in the grand manner. As an initial reaction, however, I would say it displays the same mixture of appealing and frustrating features that mark most of Habermas's other writings. However much one might cavil at its length, it is impossible not to be impressed with the encyclopaedic range of Habermas's discussion. Who else could one think of, among those writing on social theory today, who could cover — apparently without effort — such a diversity of classical and current traditions of thought, connecting these with abstract issues of philosophy on the one side, and contemporary political concerns on the other? As a synthesis of Habermas's own thought, this work brings out the unity of the theoretical standpoint which he has worked out over the past decade or so. It contains at the same time a veritable treasure trove of critical commentary on the works of others. Yet it *is* much too long. Habermas's style does not become any more limpid over the years, and the reader has to do a lot of work trying to puzzle out the relation between some of the main arguments. Habermas has a passion for tables and classifications even where these seem to obscure the process of rational argumentation rather than further it. One table contains no fewer than thirty-two categories! A consequence of this taxonomic fervour is that Habermas's writing has something of a puritanical formalism. Often where one would like to see *evidence* presented to support a view that is proposed, a table is offered instead — as if the way to overcome potential objections is to pulverize them into conceptual fragments.

Habermas's writings have been so consistently subjected to scrutiny by friend and foe alike that it is probably hard to explore any aspects of them where the critical ground has not already been well dug over. Rather than attempting to raise any critical points that are especially new, I will indicate where to me some of the main interest of Habermas's ideas lies, and where it seems to be questionable or open to attack. In offering such an appraisal, however, I shall schizophrenically divide myself into two. Since Habermas's work has a systematic character, it invites the reader to be inside or outside: Habermas has many followers, who try to work within his system, offering relatively minor modifications of it; and just as many opponents, who reject much of his enterprise. My inclination, I suppose, is to side more with the second group than with the first, but for the rest of this article I shall try to throw out fodder to both. On the left hand side of the page I will mention the queries/problems/comments that are likely to occur to the sympathetic critic. On the right hand side, I shall list those which — to borrow Marx's term — a 'critical critic' might ask of Habermas. (This tactic allows me both to have a table of my own, and to formalize a kind of discursive argumentation.)

Sympathetic Critic	*Critical Critic*
1) I have followed the course of your writings from your earliest work up to the present time. Early on, I was led to believe that knowledge is grounded in interest, and that three types of knowledge-constitutive interests could be distinguished. This was an attractive notion, which I adopted with some enthusiasm. It seemed to help with the critique of hermeneutics and the critique of ideology. But having read your most recent work, I feel somewhat puzzled and even rather let down. Am I still to believe that knowledge is founded upon interest? And if so, how exactly do the three	1) There seem to me to be some quite radical, and unresolved, discrepancies between your earlier and your later work. The idea that knowledge is grounded in interest was very bold claim, and the main basis upon which the distinctiveness of your views was founded. To give up this idea is surely to undermine some of the major claims you made — about the 'one-sided' character of hermeneutics, for example, in your debate with Gadamer. a) In your new work you seem clearly to admit the 'claim to universality' of hermeneutics for which Gadamer argued. For you accept that there is a necessary

knowledge-constitutive interests relate to the three 'worlds', and three types of validity-claims, which you now distinguish? You say that working through the theory of knowledge was a roundabout way of approaching the problems that most concern you, but what exactly is the implication of this? I can see how two of the knowledge-constitutive interests seem to correspond to two of the 'worlds', but what of the third? This is a plea for enlightenment!

hermeneutic moment in the description of social activity, involving the capability of the observer to 'go on' in the form of life which is to be analysed or accounted for.

b) In your earlier writings you made space for nomological explanation, drawing upon some of the elements of logical empiricism. You made a distinction between various types of sciences: the 'historical-hermeneutic' and the 'empirical-analytical'. What has happened to these sciences now? What role do nomological accounts play in the social sciences? These questions have become very obscure. Perhaps this is simply because you multiply classific-ations so much that it is difficult to see how they relate to one another. But I doubt that this is the only, or even the main, factor involved.

c) If, as you now say, there are three 'worlds', connecting types of validity-claim that can be discursively justified, surely you have moved towards a sort of neo-Kantian view which your earlier work was specifically concerned to avoid . . . or are you even flirting with some version of realism?

2) In treating 'reason' as 'rationality', you explicitly adopt the view that reason is wholly

2) You claim to be defending 'reason' as 'rationality' — while disavowing the idea of a 'first

procedural — it refers to modes of justifying statements, or the belief-propositions that underlie action. I think I can discern the influence of your interchange with Albert and Popper in the formulation of this standpoint. Because for Popper also, rationality (in the shape of scientific rationality) is also purely procedural. What makes something 'scientific' has nothing to do with its content, or its origins, but depends wholly upon the procedures that can be followed to test it. Popper's view, like yours, derives from the acknowledgement that there can no longer be a 'first philosophy' — that all knowledge is built upon shifting foundations. But Popper does insist upon a clear criterion or criteria (falsifiability, and connected attributes) which can be put to use in seeking actually to differentiate among different theories or propositions. He also holds to a version of the correspondence theory of truth, anchored in the notion of verisimilitude. I am not at all convinced by Popperianism, but it does seem to provide what you have not thus far developed, and what Popper does offer — a means of distinguishing among validity claims relevant to the object-world. It is one thing to say that there are modes of argumentation presumed in the use of language. This is an idea I

philosophy'. But I do not find your mode of defence plausible; and even if it could be satisfactorily sustained, it is so empty of content that it seems to leave unresolved all the main problems raised by relativism. a) I do not see why your approach should be free of the self-destructive tendency of rationality. Once we admit the principle of the critical evaluation of beliefs, how can anything be exempt? The tactic followed by the logical empiricists in defence of the Verification Principle, by Popper, and by yourself — of declaring that your conception is procedural rather than substantive — is hardly convincing. Reason which concerns procedures of rational argumentation still needs to be defended by procedures of rational argumentation. Your approach therefore does not seem to cope with issues of relativism any more effectively than those based upon some kind of version of a 'first philosophy'.
b) Truth cannot be identified with the warrantability of assertions. I take it that the aim of your discourse theory of truth is to show that specifying the truth-conditions of an assertion logically involves explaining what it means to justify, in argumentation, the claim that those truth-conditions are met.

find convincing. But how do such modes of argumentation work in respect of real issues? Nearly all the material you present is of a formal nature, categorizing 'levels' of argumentation and so on. In discussing Winch, Evans-Pritchard and poison oracles you show persuasively that relativism cannot be sustained. But you do not indicate — unless I have missed it — what criteria are to be used in assessing specific validity-claims. How exactly would we show that the Zande are wrong to believe in poison oracles?

This sort of problem relates to a feeling of disquiet I have about your theory of truth. Truth for you concerns the way in which statements about the object-world can be warranted. But what counts as the 'evidence' that can warrant assertions? Since you say little about referential problems, we are left largely in the dark about this. There seems to be a definite need for further development of your ideas here.

But the theory actually presumes this, it does not demonstrate it. No amount of warrants I — or an indefinite community of future observers — bring to bear upon a statement prevent the possibility that the statement is nonetheless false. Whatever the difficulties with Popper's position, it does have the merit of admitting this possibility, because Popper does distinguish between the modes of investigation we can develop, as rational enquirers, and 'truth' as correspondence.

c) Suppose your theory of truth were acceptable. It would still leave unresolved virtually all the major questions raised by the post-positivist philosophy of science and by the relativism debates. You distinguish between 'truth', as a concept referring to modes of establishing consensus in argumentation, and statements having referential properties in respect of the object-world. But once 'truth' has been made a procedural notion, a theory of truth no longer copes with questions of *how* one generates 'evidence', *what* counts as 'evidence', and in what *sense* propositions are 'testable'.

d) The same point could be made in regard of what you call 'practical discourse'. After all, whatever problems — and they of course are formidable enough — may exist concerning evidence about the material world, the difficulties involved in justifying normative claims are even harder to resolve. But your discussion of the character of practical discourse appears no less formal than that of theoretical empirical discourse. e) You claim a connection between language, rationality and a counterfactually-posited ideal speech situation. I have never found this convincing. Is it anything other than the last gasp of a critical theory which, dissatisfied with the uncertainties of immanent critique, and suspicious of philosophical anthropology, pins its hopes upon the 'linguistic turn'? Is not language more aptly regarded, with Wittgenstein, as *all* the things that can be done in and through language? 'Our first sentence', you once wrote, 'expresses unequivocally the intention of universal and unconstrained consensus.' Why not say that our first gesture of recognition of another person promises a universal solidarity of human beings? Or perhaps the idea could be extended even further — to Lévi-Strauss's complicitous glance from a cat?

3) The conjunctions you draw between evolutionary theory, the psychology of cognitive development, and the method of

3) I have never understood how you are able to make such confident — and sweeping — use of Piaget and Kohlberg. Despite

rational reconstruction are evidently essential to your thesis that communicative reason is not just Western reason. I accept your contention that history has to be separated from evolutionary theory, just as empirical psychology is not the same as the reconstruction of levels of competence. At the same time, I am a bit worried by how much reliance you place upon Piaget and Kohlberg, both of whose views have after all been subject to serious critical attack. Some of the parallels you discern between the development of reasoning in the cognition of the individual and the social evolution of the species seem almost too neat and tidy. I was somewhat surprised to see that the section of your book concerned with myths in oral cultures amounts to only a few pages. If you are going to demonstrate that oral cultures — and agrarian civilizations also — operate at a lower stage of rationality to Western or modernized culture, surely a more detailed treatment is called for?

its brilliance, the empirical base of Piaget's work has always been weak, especially when generalized out of a Western context; and the studies on the basis of which Kohlberg claims that his stages of competence are universal are at best sketchy. Surely it is at least somewhat suspicious that the highest forms of human reason turn out to duplicate the ideals of the Western Enlightenment! If, again, you began with Lévi-Strauss rather than Piaget, you would surely have been led to very different conclusions. The fact that you discuss Lévi-Strauss only very cursorily reinforces the uncomfortable feeling I have that you tend to choose theories that *prima facie* fit with the general framework of your ideas — as if indicating how they can be fitted together is enough to validate them.

On the whole I think it was a healthy shift when social theory turned against evolutionism. Evolutionary theories have always been difficult to disentangle from ethnocentrism, and especially from Europocentricism. Although you hedge the concept of evolution with numerous qualifications, and you are very careful to consider the connotations of ethnocentrism, I am not at all convinced that you avoid them. Let us follow the proposal I mentioned above, and relate your arguments to Lévi-Strauss rather than Piaget. There are three respects in which you treat oral cultures as inferior to civilizations, and particularly to the modernized West. Oral cultures involve closed worldviews which fail to distinguish the three 'worlds' you see as integral to rationality; and are founded upon pre-conventional norms. A Lévi-Straussian viewpoint might agree, with some reservations, with such a categorization. But it would see these as involving forms of life that are every bit as 'rational' as those introduced by the 'hot' culture of civilization. Oral cultures are not made up of individuals who have not yet undergone the 'learning processes' that bring enlightenment. On the contrary, the introduction of writing and the other paraphernalia of civilization is an unlearning process — a process of cultural destruction. The division we make between nature and culture is one that dissolves the intimacy with nature which is one of the richest forms of human experience. Finally, norms which are founded upon debate and discussion, it might be argued, are not just new forms of tradition. They mark the undermining of tradition — the security of time-honoured practice as such.

4) One of your most important accomplishments, in my opinion, is in respect of the critical reception of systems theory. You have forcefully emphasized that systems theory is caught up in the technicization of politics, and have demonstrated that the seemingly neutral application of means-ends thinking may become ideological. Your analysis of 'technique as ideology' is one of the most brilliant parts of your writings. At the same time, you have made it clear that systems theory, and the function-alist style of thought that tends to be associated with it, cannot be rejected out of hand. Thus you have adopted some systems-theoretical concepts into your own work, and in this book you have further clarified how such concepts relate to phenomena of the life-world. I am particularly impressed by the manner in which you apply the notions of system and life-world to the elucidation of the nature of modernity. Some questions still puzzle me a little. One of these concerns the question of power. You now adopt a position, following Parsons, according to which the polity is the medium of the organization of political power. Since the polity is defined in terms of a specific institutional application of purposive-rational action, this seems to narrow down the concept of power rather

4) I am unhappy with your distinction between system and life-world — as I was with the differentiation between 'labour' and 'interaction' which appeared prominently in your earlier work. If, as you say, the separation between system and life-world is methodological, how can it also operate as a substantive distinction within modernized societies? Moreover, your use of systems theory, of notions such as 'steering mechanisms' and so on, seems to do scant justice to the active struggles of individuals and groups out of which history is made. The sense of contin-gency in history, which is so strong in the writings of Max Weber, seems absent from your own work. You are critical of 'functionalist reason', but not critical enough.

considerably. How then would you connect the critique of ideology to the critique of domination today — since you seemingly previously employed 'power' in a much broader way?

5) You have brought the ideas of Max Weber much more into the centre of your work than was previously the case. I find your adaptation and critique of Weber's concept of rational-ization both intriguing and compelling. You have shown that Weber's work, in at least certain basic respects, is more important in diagnosing the traits of the type of society in which we live today than Marx's writings are. At the same time, by exposing some of the limitations of Weber's own analysis of modernization, you make it clear how the type of critique Marx advocated can be kept alive. Your theory of the colonization of the life-world provides a new basis for analysing the tensions, and the sources of opposition, character-istic of modern societies. All the same, I wonder if your analysis might lead to somewhat paradoxical conclusions. Aspects of the life-world have to be defended against the encroach-ments of political and economic steering-mechanisms. But how can such a defence be achieved

5) Too much Weber! Too little Marx! Anyone who draws as heavily upon Weber as you do is likely to be also drawn into Weberian conclusions — what-ever disclaimers they might make. You criticize Weber for confining rationalization primarily to the expansion of purposive-rationality, but you are forced to agree that this type of rationality does dominate modern culture. Your diagnosis of the origins, and likely future, of current social movements looks remarkably similar to that Weber might have made — except that you want to speak of 'pathologies', and keep to a more optimistic outlook about the possibilities for social change. I cannot see what justifies your optimism. Weber did, after all, expect there to be protest move-ments directed against the prevalence of rationalization and he expected that these would commonly take the form of religious revivalism or what have come to be called 'counter-cultural' movements. But he did not believe that these could be successful in turning back the

without transforming those mechanisms themselves? I am not sure just what sort of transformations you think are possible, and how whatever possibilities you see might bear upon ideals of socialism as they have been conceived of in the past.

tide of rationalization with its oppressive·consequences. In spite of all you have to say about frustrated validity-claims, and about the colonization of the life-world, I cannot see that your analysis leads to a different substantive conclusion.

Let me at this stage put myself back together again. The fact that Habermas's work prompts so many questions — numerous others could of course also be raised — is indicative of its extraordinary intellectual power and scope. There is no doubt that this book represents a formidable achievement, and all of us working in social theory will be using it as a resource years after most of the current literature in the social sciences has been forgotten.

11

Alvin Gouldner
and the intellectuals

Alvin Gouldner died suddenly in 1981, at the height of an extraordinarily productive — and intriguingly heterodox — career.[1] He
received his education in the Sociology Department of Columbia
University, at a time when that department was the dominant influence
within American social science. But the subsequent development of
his writings took him a long way from the emphases of his mentors at
Columbia, Robert K. Merton and Paul Lazarsfeld. During the 1950s
and early 1960s, Gouldner did in fact follow the path established for
the brightest among the students of the Columbia department. He was
a member of the Council of the American Sociological Association
from 1964 to 1967, made a rapid ascent through the professional
gradations of the American university system, and produced a string
of publications which established him as a significant figure in the
fields of social theory, the sociology of industry and the analysis of
bureaucracy. The writings he published in these areas, to be sure,
were already critical of some of the more orthodox sociological
perspectives that reigned at that time. There was an early 'European'
slant to his writings, derived substantially from his interest in the
work of Max Weber. He derided the pretensions of sociologists to
value-freedom and launched a highly effective attack upon functionalist
theories, showing them systematically to underplay the range of
tensions and conflicts which exist in societies of all types. Nonetheless,
his work was clearly oriented to the main body of professional
sociologists, especially in the United States.

[1] This chapter draws substantially upon a long review that first appeared
in *The Times Literary Supplement* of 6 September 1985. Thanks are due for
permission to reprint the relevant paragraphs.

Gouldner was at that date to some degree already a controversial figure, prone to fits of intellectual belligerence, but he operated from within the sociological establishment rather than outside it. All this stands in rather pronounced contrast to the later phases of his career. He never ceased to regard himself as first and foremost a sociologist and to the end of his life defended the centrality of sociology to the understanding of modern culture. Yet he did become increasingly hostile to those perspectives in the discipline which he had once accepted; but unable wholeheartedly to embrace a Marxist standpoint as an alternative. How did this transition come about? What led Gouldner to shift gear apparently so abruptly, explicitly adopting a marginal position between the main competing schools of social science?

The answer to these questions is to be found in the peripatetic nature of Gouldner's professional career, combined with his sense that his original critiques of orthodox sociology were not nearly far-ranging enough to grasp the full measure of its limitations. The period of the late 1960s and early 1970s, of course, was one of social and political turmoil, overshadowed by the Vietnam war. Gouldner was by no means alone in believing that the dominant traditions of sociology had little to offer to interpret the drama of the period, founded as they were in circumstances of the apparently stable expansion of liberal capitalism. But Gouldner's intellectual response to these socio-political crises was in some respects a quite distinctive one, drawing upon an original intellectual framework of his own.

He spent two years in Switzerland, in the mid-1960s, and several years later returned to take up a position as Professor of Sociology at the University of Amsterdam, where he remained until 1976. To his earlier proclivity to look to European social theory in order to criticize orthodox American sociology was added a physical estrangement from American academia. *Enter Plato*, published in 1965, was not only quite different from anything Gouldner had attempted before, but also broke away completely from the usual run of topics with which his sociological colleagues were concerned.[2] The work sought to trace the origins of European social theory in the Classical age and to apply sociological understanding to a key phase in the emergence of Western culture. It was at the same time directed towards elucidating the roots of Enlightenment reason, seen as involving an appropriation

[2] Alvin Gouldner: *Enter Plato*. New York: Basic, 1965.

of classical thought and at the same time a decisive rejection of it. As an inheritance from the Enlightenment, modern social science, in Gouldner's view, had lost a reflexive sense of the conditions of its own production. In Plato one still finds an account of the relation between the knower and known, whereas in the subsequent developments of European social thought, the position of the knower disappeared from view.

Gouldner's most famous work, *The Coming Crisis of Western Sociology*, made a recovery of the reflexive position of the knower central to what he increasingly saw as a necessary reconstruction of social science.[3] The book was from the beginning curiously titled. What it announced was clearly not a 'coming crisis' at all, but one which was already full-blown. Gouldner did not systematically investigate Western sociology as a whole, but concentrated largely on mounting a critical assault upon the most prominent American social theorist at the time — Talcott Parsons. Moreover, Gouldner's aim was not merely to demonstrate the shortcomings of established forms of sociology; he sought also to generate a critical account of the failings of Marxism. In transferring both symbolically and materially from the United States to Europe, Gouldner did not choose to move unequivocally from sociology to Marxism. None the less, from that time up to his death, the problem of sifting through the mixed legacy of Marxist thought, both on an intellectual level and in terms of its practical impact upon the modern world, became his principal preoccupation. What Gouldner called 'reflexive sociology' was supposed to incorporate certain aspects of Marxism, but he argued that this could not be done unless Marxism itself were examined as 'produced knowledge', rather than as a set of objective claims to knowledge about social organization and social development.

Subsequent to *The Coming Crisis*, Gouldner produced a spate of writings concerned to pursue this theme. Although proclaiming itself an expression of the role of the proletariat in making history, Marxism is in fact largely the creation of intellectuals. In this respect it is not distinct from the social sciences as a whole, although it places an accent on the unity of theory and practice absent in more orthodox forms of sociology. 'Reflexive sociology' is thus for Gouldner very much bound up with an interpretation of the role of intellectuals in

[3] Alvin Gouldner: *The Coming Crisis of Western Sociology*. New York: Basic, 1970.

the shaping of modern culture and in the production of ideologies. In some of the most important of his later works he tried to rescue the notion of ideology from the pejorative connotations usually attached to it.[4] Ideology is certainly, as Marx thought it to be, a means whereby dominant groups manage to sustain their power through persuading others of the legitimacy of their rule. However, Gouldner argued, ideology is also the means of social transformation. The development of ideology in its modern form is convergent with the emergence of printing, and with the formation of a new style of political life. Ideologies are essentially public doctrines, containing evidence and reasons — which can be scrutinized — for whatever they assert. Intellectuals specialize in the production of ideologies, and this gives them a prominence in modern social and political life altogether different from anything which existed before. In Gouldner's view, intellectuals form what he calls the 'new class'. Revolutions are made in the name of the masses, but co-ordinated and organized by elite groups of intellectuals. In the Eastern European societies, the new class is coming to acquire the reins of power. These societies declare themselves to be 'Marxist' and culturally egalitarian, but are in practice very hierarchical. The increasing ascendancy of the new class is not diluted by the operation of market forces as it is in Western capitalism.

Gouldner and Marxism

Gouldner's relationship to Marxism was always a complex and tortured one. Attracted to its critical orientation, he felt distant from most of its substantive propositions about the development of modern society and disturbed by its own potential as an ideology of domination. Gouldner was not content to treat Marxism wholly at arm's distance — to regard it simply as a social phenomenon in its own right. We must not only understand how Marxism has so significantly influenced the twentieth-century world; we must apply to Marxism that very reflexive interpretation of history by means of which it proclaims its own historical role. 'If theory helps to make history, it is also totally impossible to understand that theory except

---

[4] See especially Alvin Gouldner: *The Dialectic of Ideology and Technology*. New York: Seabury, 1976.

as itself made historically, by situating it in its proper context.'[5] Gouldner's reflections on Marxism are both intended to be critical of Marxism as a whole, yet also to derive a critical method *from* Marxism. Marxism of course is not a unitary phenomenon. More than this, according to Gouldner, it is internally contradictory as a body of thought. He does not claim to be the first to have noticed this. Marxists themselves tend to divide according to whether they conceive Marxism to be a science or whether they think of it primarily as a form of critical theory. Scientific Marxists conceive of the development of capitalism, and its transcendence by socialism, as dependent upon a series of objectively-founded changes. For them, there are laws of development determining both the transcendence of capitalism and the emergence of a socialist society. Critical Marxists see Marxism above all as a means of understanding history to change history. The contradiction in Marxism is there from the beginning in Marxist texts. Marx rejects idealism, yet invokes the appeal of ideas in order to transform reality. He speaks of the existence of iron laws of history, but treats history as a human project, to be altered in the light of the accumulation of human knowledge. 'Marx was a paradoxically idealistic materialist who suppressed his own idealism, declaring that he was not really pursuing an ideal but (like Socrates) was only a midwife delivering what had been prepared in the womb of history, and calling upon others to do likewise.'[6]

In Gouldner's view these two forms of Marxist thought have their prime expression in divergent notions of *Praxis*. In one view, *Praxis* refers to the material substratum of social life, the labour expended in transforming nature, which is believed to provide a causal motor of social development. In the notion of *Praxis* congenial to Critical Marxism, on the other hand, there is an emphasis upon self-transformation through practical action. In the first view individuals submit to necessity, whereas in the second they overcome it. Only the second can properly recognize the existence of politics. For politics means contingency and goal-directed action; those who have an active engagement in politics cannot suppose that they may wait for events to take their natural course, 'history being on our side'. In Scientific Marxism, politics is reduced to an epiphenomenon of material processes. There is a brake upon activism because the forces governing

[5] Alvin Gouldner: *The Two Marxisms*. London: Macmillan, 1980, p. 8.
[6] Ibid., p. 33.

social life work themselves out in an immutable fashion. Gouldner will have no truck with those views which seek to reconcile the two versions of Marxism — for example those which claim freedom and necessity are 'dialectically related'. The 'two Marxisms' derive from an attempt to reduce or eliminate the tension in Marxist writings, but it remains generic to those writings.

Scientific Marxism and Critical Marxism differ along a range of dimensions. Those who incline to the critical side, of course, tend to emphasize the continuity between the writings of the young and the mature Marx. For them Marxism is rooted in Hegel, and alienation is a persisting concept in Marxist thought as a whole. Scientific Marxists, on the other hand, see the early writings as essentially uninteresting or even ideological; the writings of the mature Marx are the basis of a scientific interpretation of Marxism. These differences are related to epistemological and ontological contrasts. Whereas one group puts a stress upon fluidity and change, in which contextual interpretation is important, the other group looks for solid structures that can be understood in a 'decontextualized' fashion. Critical Marxism tends to be sceptical of the achievements of science, or at least to see that the expansion of technology has potentially worrying consequences. Scientific Marxists, however, are prone to see science as a relatively unproblematic aspect of the solution to humankind's problems. Critical Marxism frequently may be associated with a certain pessimism about the possibilities of social progress, although this is not inevitably the case. The Scientific Marxists almost universally take a more positive and unqualified view of the future. Finally, Critical Marxism is inclined towards populism and to the systematic mistrust of hierarchies of power. Those who profess Scientific Marxism tend to accept the need for bureaucratic social forms and for structured hierarchies of power, even after the occurrence of socialist revolution. Gouldner is at some pains to emphasize that Critical and Scientific Marxism do not develop entirely separately. The limitations of one creates space for the other, such that each tends to develop in response to the other.

However, the 'two Marxisms' do have in some part divergent social origins, which antedate the incorporation of the relevant threads of thought within Marx's own work and continue to influence their subsequent elaboration after Marx.[7] Marxism developed against the

7 Alvin Gouldner: *Against Fragmentation*. Oxford: Oxford University Press, 1985, chpt. 1 and following.

backdrop of the overall secularization of culture. By the turn of the nineteenth century, and accelerating thereafter, there developed clear tensions between science and religion in terms of their respective world-views. Science did not however merely replace religion. Rather, each tended to find its own sphere, with science increasingly dominant in high culture while religion retained a certain influence over the practical activities of day-to-day life. Marxism emerged at a time at which this new balance was first being established, when the traditional foundations of culture were still shell-shocked by the rapid formation of novel orders of commercial life. Marxism, as it were, stepped into the gap left by the waning of theological influence on the one hand and the fragmenting effects of science on the other. If Marx's borrowings from the style of reasoning of natural science are evident enough, he also no less significantly drew upon certain forms of religious ethic. Marxism thus was not just an expression of the secular triumph of science, but from its origins an admixture of the scientific and the sacred. It commingled an appeal to scientific moderation with a chiliastic creed. In some part Marx's writings are built upon the critique of religion from the standpoint of science. But on the other hand those self-same writings buttress a faith in the progressive emancipation of humanity. It is a mistake, Gouldner avers, to suppose that Marxism is itself a form of religion. Matters are more complicated than that. Marxism, even Scientific Marxism, was a reaction to anxieties stimulated by the combined effect of the decline of traditional religion and the occurrence of new, dramatic forms of social change. It had an elective affinity with some of the sources of commitment and security offered by religion, but incorporated these into a framework that was for the most part new. Marxism confronts the problem of human suffering and suggests that the salvation of the lowly will produce the redemption of all. But this is promised to happen through science and through the application of empirical method. Just as in Comte, an appeal to science is infused with the propagation of the certainty that a better life not only can but will be achieved. In this double grounding in science and religion, then, is to be traced the differentiation of Scientific from Critical Marxism. Scientific socialism is basically gradualist, and stands close to evolutionism. Critical Marxism, by contrast, focuses more upon abrupt and violent transformation, the sudden infusion of energy that sheds the limitations of the existing order of things.

Marx and Engels, Gouldner points out, did not come from the class whose interests their writings purported to represent. They both had comfortable bourgeois origins, and although Marx spent much of his life in something close to abject poverty, both he and Engels devoted themselves above all to a career of intellectual production and reflection. Of course, those hostile to Marxism have often pointed ironically to its origins in the very circles which its proponents affected to condemn. However, Gouldner's purpose is not to disparage the creators of Marxism, but to understand them in the same manner as all intellectuals who seek to develop grand theories directed at improving the lot of the majority. This creates very particular difficulties for Marxism, since one of the main claims of Marx and Engels was that social consciousness and ideology are shaped by the material circumstances in which individuals exist. Those who would seek reflexively to understand the origins and nature of Marxism, therefore, must 'decipher this eerie transformation of elites into elite-devouring revolutionaries'.[8] Marx and Engels devoted little concern to understanding how and why intellectuals become radicalized. In Gouldner's view it is extremely important to understand just this process and to apply that understanding to Marxism itself. Because Marx believed that the only revolutionary class in modern society is the proletariat, and that therefore intellectuals should throw in their lot with its fortunes, he failed to see that intellectuals themselves become a class deeply involved in the system of power of modern societies. For Marx, intellectuals had only one choice: to stick with the bourgeoisie or to ally with the true revolutionary class, the proletariat. He ignored the possibility that intellectuals might break away from each of these major classes, and underestimated the potential for rebellion among the educated sector of the bourgeoisie. In addition, he did not see that groups which specialize in the production of 'knowledge' become increasingly important in modern societies, in virtue of the expanding role which such knowledge-production plays in industrial development.

Marx and Engels assumed that the maturation of capitalism would prepare the way for the development of a socialist consciousness on the part of the proletariat, as it fulfils its historical mission. In fact something like the reverse has occurred. The development of capitalism has served to pacify the proletariat, but has created groups of alienated intellectuals who establish themselves as critics of the system, and who have in the socialist countries played a leading role in

[8] Ibid., p. 38.

overthrowing it. Leninism formed the chief means in the subsequent development of Marxism of overcoming its paradoxical relation to intellectuals. In the conception of the Vanguard Party, Lenin both provided a distinctive role for intellectuals and made clear what their relationship to the masses was to be. The Vanguard Party was not just an expression of the inherent consciousness of the proletariat, which Lenin emphasized was confined largely to trade union affairs. The Vanguard served to create the theory which the working class could not produce through its own resources. At the same time it formed a control device, whereby Party members could be disciplined. Intellectuals were thereby extricated from the institutions of bourgeois culture, and their alienation from it given organizational form.

The Vanguard Party, according to Gouldner, can be regarded as a 'collective holding company', which gives concrete substance to the 'political interests of radicalized intellectuals'.[9] This very same process serves to claim the intellectuals for a new regime of conformity — that of the dominance of the new class. Socialism, Gouldner suggests, is a creation of intellectuals, and has little intrinsic connection with the political involvements of the working class. The main currents of socialist thought derive from a critique of early capitalism developed by intellectuals. The intelligentsia hides its own role in history (even from itself) by projecting it on to the agency of the proletariat. The radicalization of intellectuals is a generic possibility in modern societies in virtue of the importance of ideologies within them. Intellectuals are the bearers of what Gouldner calls 'a culture of critical discourse'. This is a form of speech and writing which emphasizes that all assertions — particularly those in the political sphere — are open to challenge. Whereas most other groups in society are prepared to accept the invocation of someone's authority as a basis for evaluating ideas, intellectuals reject any such viewpoint. The culture of critical discourse is thus the ideology peculiar to intellectuals. It is potentially alienating, because it makes possible the subversion of the claims of the rich and the powerful to truth. It asserts the right of the intelligentsia to form independent judgements of all claims, no matter who makes them. Of course how far the alienative potential of the intellectuals is realized depends upon particular social circumstances. Intellectuals may be radicalized, for example, when normal routes to academic careers are blocked. The radical implications of the

[9] Ibid., p. 16.

'culture of critical discourse' may on the other hand be blunted when intellectuals themselves monopolize power.

It is not Gouldner's intention to treat Marxism simply as the ideological instrument which the new class uses in its rise to power. The claim of Marxist thought to represent the interests of the proletariat is not wholly empty; the proletariat is a metaphor for the ambition of the radicalized intelligentsia to create a rational social order. Because of its commitment to reason and to justice, Marxism is intrinsically resistant to becoming merely an ideology of domination. The history of Marx's own writings, and their reception by his contemporaries, can be written in terms of a dialogue between these tendencies. That is to say, Marx's works contain doctrines directly compatible with the claims of the intellectuals to power; but they also contain the elements of a critique of those self-same claims. Gouldner tries to show how the controversies which pitted Marx against Bakunin exemplify this tension. Bakunin predicted that Marxism would culminate in exactly the situation to which, according to Gouldner, it has in fact led: the dominance of a New Class of intellectuals within a bureaucratized socialist order.[10]

Marx sought to defend himself against this type of criticism by emphasizing the scientific character of his ideas, seeing industrial advancement as the key to the success of socialism. However, this very response tended to dampen the critical aspects of his thought. The history of Marxism after Marx can be understood as a continuing encounter between those adopting a vision of scientific socialism and those who have sought to accommodate Bakunin's critique by adopting some of its features as their own. Gouldner's own views of the potentialities of Marxism lean strongly towards the critical side. The critical edge of Marxism can be sustained by means of its emphasis on the unity of theory and practice and the need to understand societies in their totality. The first of these features saves Marxism from degenerating into pure ideology in the pejorative sense. The second gives Marxist thought the potential of overcoming the fragmented character of intellectual work within the modern division of labour — in Gouldner's view, one of the main factors which neutralizes intellectual activities in terms of their critical implications for society.

[10] Ibid., chpt. 7.

The Intellectuals and the New Class

Gouldner attributes a pervasive importance to intellectuals in the twentieth century. They form the core of a New Class due increasingly to replace the old propertied ruling classes. As Gouldner puts it, 'a new contest of classes and a new class system is slowly arising in the Third World of developing nations, in the second world of the USSR and its client states, and in the first world of late capitalism of North America, Western Europe, and Japan.'[11] The development of the New Class is bound up with the same processes involved with the origins of Marxism. The rise of the New Class has its origins in processes of secularization, whereby intelligentsia are no longer trained by the Church. Secularization is the condition of the development of a culture of critical discourse. Traditional authorities no longer define either the nature of questions and problems that can legitimately be debated, or their solutions. In pre-modern societies, the role of intellectuals was constrained by their need for patronage. But in modern times, they become more and more drawn into an anonymous market, in which knowledge and information are produced and exchanged without such control. The formation of a differentiated educational system, separate from the family, is a further condition of this development. Education becomes part of a 'public' domain in which 'cosmopolitan' values prevail over 'local' ones. Here Gouldner makes use of Bernstein's distinction between restricted and elaborated linguistic codes. The school system promotes the expansion of reflexive speech, the capability to converse in elaborated codes. Such forms of communication tend to be relatively context-free, a phenomenon which in modern societies is accentuated by the importance of mass media.

Gouldner distinguishes his view of the New Class from a variety of other competing standpoints. Thus Bell and others see the New Class as a benevolent elite developing and organizing knowledge used for the benefit of all. Another view sees the New Class as an exploitative social formation, but as a class not substantially different from pre-existing classes in history. According to Gouldner, this is essentially the view of Bakunin, Machajski and others. Yet a further view is that

[11] Alvin Gouldner: *The Future of Intellectuals and the Rise of the New Class*. London: Macmillan, 1979.

the New Class is simply a group subordinate to the old propertied class, assisting its members in maintaining their power. For Gouldner the New Class has its own distinct interests and sustains its own independent power. It also tends to foster developments that are of generalized importance. The New Class, Gouldner says, is a 'flawed universal class', a class able to develop policies which transcend its own particular concerns.

The New Class may be, but is by no means always, politically revolutionary. It is however in all contexts a 'revolutionary class' in the sense that it 'constantly revolutionizes the mode of production'.[12] There are two routes which the New Class may take in its progressive ascent to power. One is directly revolutionary, the participation in or forging of processes of political revolution — a phenomenon thus far confined to the less-developed parts of the world. In the Western societies the New Class comes to power in less dramatic fashion. Both in the economy and elsewhere it emerges first of all under the tutelage of the old propertied class. The more education becomes a distinct mode of recruitment to occupational positions, the more access to a culture of critical discourse determines the creation of ideas, and the more the New Class assumes an independent existence. One area of its development is within the industrial sphere itself. The separation of industrial ownership from management is for Gouldner one dimension of the rise of the New Class. The New Class progressively transforms the property owners into a *rentier* class, functionless functionaries living off their investments. But the New Class also finds a vehicle for its advancement in the welfare state. As more and more aspects of social life are brought within the scope of the 'public' arena of state control or influence, so the scope of power of the New Class, which dominates the state apparatus, further expands.

If the New Class in its beginnings is not easy to distinguish from the old, it is because both possess forms of 'capital'. Money capital, Gouldner suggests, should be seen as a 'special case' of capital in general. Capital refers to any produced object or service that can be disposed of on a market in such a way as to endow its possessor with a return on 'investment'. Education is capital just as much as the possession of money, or material means of production. In Gouldner's view, Comte was the originator of the idea of 'cultural capital'. Comte

[12] Ibid., p. 11. cf. George Konrad and Ivan Szelingi: *The Intellectuals on the Road to Class Power*. Brighton: Harvester, 1979.

points to the origins of capital in labour, in the production of artifacts and information that can be recycled to promote further production. According to Gouldner, Comte wrote 'at that early juncture between political economy and sociology, where culture and capital mixed and were interchangeable, and where one might say that either capital *or* culture was the "basis of social development"'.[13] The most obvious form of 'possessions' members of the New Class have are credentials — diplomas, technical qualifications, degrees and certificates of all sorts. However the possession of diffusely defined 'cultural skills', in particular the capacity to sustain participation in the culture of critical discourse, becomes a very generalized commodity available to secure a range of other returns. Although at first the two are tightly correlated, cultural capital is increasingly separated from the control of money capital. To the degree to which, for example, the possession of wealth and property allows for the 'purchase' of educational advantages — as to the existence of elite private schools — money capital still influences cultural capital. These, however, become more and more marginal circumstances; cultural and money capital diverge.

In both West and East the New Class involves two types of intellectuals: the technical intelligentsia and intellectuals of broader cultural interests and concerns. Each type is committed to the culture of critical discourse and therefore opposes the prerogatives of the old propertied class; but there are internal divisions and tensions between them. The technical intelligentsia are primarily managers and administrators. Within Western societies, these differentiate themselves increasingly from the prerogatives conferred by ownership of property. In the East they become more and more differentiated from the bureaucratic officialdom which is the residue of revolutionary socialism. The expansion of the scope of the New Class is thus not the same as progressive bureaucratization. Bureaucrats order their procedures and decisions in terms of organizational rules. The bureaucratic official is the co-ordinator of decisions within a hierarchy, the logic of those decisions being governed by the commands of superiors and by the designated duties of the office. Hence bureaucrats do not participate in the culture of critical discourse; their activities are not grounded in the need to submit what they do to continuous rational assessments and analysis. However, the technical intelligentsia are closer both in their interests and in their style of work to

[13] Alvin Gouldner: *The Future* . . . , p. 25.

bureaucratic officialdom than are other intellectuals. They are less prone to alienation from the existing order of things and may in fact be subject to censorship by sections of the technical intelligentsia.

Neither in the West nor in the East is the New Class yet a ruling class. But it has the capacity to become so, in virtue of its importance in modern societies as a whole. Only the New Class possesses the scientific, technical and critical skills necessary to economic development in the modern world. Gouldner says:

> The United States is the last hope of the old class throughout the world. It is the centre of the worldwide forces of the old class today as Sparta was the anchor of the waning aristocracy of ancient Greece . . . yet it is dying . . . the dying are entitled to a word of consolation; the old class should know, then, that its enemies — or those whom it once thought to be its chief enemies — the 'Communist' societies of Eastern Europe, are also facing the same destiny. They, too, confront a rising new class of intellectuals and intelligentsia.[14]

Conclusion: Evaluation and critique

Probably no one would dispute the importance of Gouldner's earlier writings. His work on industrial bureaucracy and industrial conflict, together with his more theoretical reflections on Weber and on 'reciprocity and autonomy', are surely of enduring importance. For Gouldner, this style of work was not enough and he quite deliberately sought to extend the scope of his endeavours into more ambitious areas. How successful was this transition that Gouldner attempted to make? Do the accomplishments of his writings in the later part of his career match up to the zeal with which he pursued them?

Anyone who analyses Gouldner's later writings at all extensively is likely to come up with a rather negative response to these questions. Gouldner had a knack of hitting upon important issues. Reading Gouldner is never uninteresting since his works abound so freely in suggestive insights and observations. The wit and verve which Gouldner displayed in his earliest writings did not desert him in the subsequent stages of his career. Nonetheless it is difficult to resist the conclusion that his later writings show some very substantial weaknesses. I shall discuss these under three headings: his assessment

---

[14] Alvin Gouldner: *The Future . . .* , pp. 90—1.

of Marxism; his discussion of the culture of critical discourse and of ideology more generally; and his analysis of intellectuals and the New Class.

As regards the first of these topics, although Gouldner wrote extensively on Marxism, it has to be said that his various discussions of Marxist thought are for the most part rather unoriginal. Where they do make more unusual claims, these more often than not seem questionable or wrong. *The Two Marxisms* contains some interesting insights, but on the whole reading it one is surprised that such a large volume should have been dedicated to covering what is — as Gouldner himself admits — heavily trodden ground. The contrast upon which the book is based and which indeed informs much of Gouldner's later work, between Scientific and Critical Marxism, is surely too gross to be of much use. It is no doubt true that in Marx there are positivistic strains of thought which exist uneasily alongside a commitment to dialectics and social critique. Even in Marx's works there are several complicated strands to this relation, and the subsequent development of Marxism is altogether too complex to be subject to this sort of sub-division. The more 'official' versions of Marxism have tended to emphasize the scientific status of Marxist thought. They have also usually been associated with a particular kind of political outlook, emphasizing progressive change rather than dramatic processes of revolution. There are any number of thinkers whom such a categorization does not readily fit, including Lenin. Gouldner tries to fit Lenin's ideas into his scheme by claiming that Lenin began as a Scientific Marxist but increasingly became a Critical one. However, this is not particularly convincing. Threads of each perspective were combined in Lenin's writings from early on. As Gouldner uses the terms, both Scientific and Critical Marxism cover a diversity of views, which in the writings of many authors are combined in such a way as to cut across the classification Gouldner makes.

Gouldner's discussions of Marxism operate almost wholly on a meta-theoretical level. In one sense, given Gouldner's concern to connect his analysis of Marxism with his interpretations of reflexivity, the culture of critical discourse and the role of intellectuals, this is perhaps not too surprising. But since a good deal of Gouldner's later writings consists of a 'coming to terms' with Marxism, a confrontation with the more substantive claims of Marxist thought cannot really be avoided. Gouldner does not provide it. He discusses neither the usefulness of Marx's major concepts, nor the validity or otherwise of the generalizations advanced in Marx's work. How far does Gouldner consider Marx's analysis of modern capitalism to be a defensible one? How far is the apparatus of Marxist economics still relevant to developments today? Apart from one or two passing comments, Gouldner appears to provide no answers to questions such as these. They are hardly of negligible significance in assessing both the intellectual character of Marxism and its practical implications for the modern world. Given that Gouldner's declared sympathies are toward the pole of 'Critical Marxism' we should probably presume that there is not much of the substance of Marx's claims which he believes plausible. But in lieu of a systematic discussion of such views, Gouldner's analyses of Marxism remain rather diffuse and elusive.

Perhaps Gouldner avoided a definite settling of accounts with Marxism in this manner because he was unable satisfactorily to relate his own position to it. Gouldner was a non-joiner *par excellence*. Given a somewhat less jarring style, in the earlier part of his life he would quite readily have been welcomed into the embrace of mainstream American sociology. Having escaped its clutches, he was not thereafter able to affiliate himself closely with any particular 'European' current of thought. The version of 'reflexive sociology' which he advocated has a resonance with some of the ideas he lumped together as 'Critical Marxism'. Yet to accept the designation 'Marxist' seemed to him to compromise the independence of outlook necessary to examine ideas — most notably Marxism itself — in the context of their development. Gouldner himself observed that 'if I am a Marxist at all, I belong to no Marxist *community*, and certainly to no Marxist establishment. If my own view is solicited, I would have to label myself as a — Marxist *outlaw*.'[15] He saw himself as 'demystifying' Marxism, as deconstructing the grounds of its assumptions — a complementary task to that undertaken in relation to academic sociology in *The Coming Crisis of Western Sociology*. Later Gouldner seemed to place in question even this ambivalent relation to Marxism, describing his own standpoint as a 'neo-Hegelian' sociology.[16]

Does this vacillating self-identification signal anything more than simply a reluctance to be labelled? In my view it probably does. In his formulation of reflexive sociology, Gouldner places emphasis upon the importance of understanding the production of knowledge in social science as an active process, in which the position of the knower must

[15] Alvin Gouldner: *The Dialectic* . . . , p. 12.
[16] Alvin Gouldner: *The Future* . . . , p. 5.

be grasped. Such a standpoint may very well be desirable, but it does not absolve the social analyst from the need to establish criteria relevant to judging the substantive validity of claims to knowledge. One searches in vain among Gouldner's later writings for a sustained discussion of this issue. In its absence there is little to save reflexive sociology from becoming embroiled in that self-defeating circularity characteristic of ventures into the sociology of knowledge. Although obviously aware of the difficulty, Gouldner did not appear to discover a satisfactory mode of coping with it. The self-styled Marxist outlaw ended as a 'High Plains Drifter' coming from nowhere and having no identity.

Gouldner's writings on ideology are among the most important and innovative of his later writings. The subject again of course has an intrinsic connection with Marxism. Since Marx, 'ideology' has ordinarily been understood as having derogatory connotations. Ideology is false consciousness or defective claims to knowledge. Gouldner's discussion of ideology by no means escapes the self-same circularity of reasoning just mentioned. However, he quite properly seeks to rescue the notion from inevitable association with distortion. To understand ideology we have to engage in a two-fold endeavour: to see it as an object in a theoretical region, and to see the region within which it is constituted as an object.[17] For Gouldner Marxism is itself an ideology; but this does not mean that it is necessarily thereby discredited. Ideologies stand at the origin of the development of the culture of critical discourse. Ideology presumes the reflexive capability to use speech to talk about speech. Ideologies link the culture of critical discourse to specified courses of practical action devoted to transforming the world. The development of modern mass media are the primary vehicle of the construction and dissemination of ideologies. This view of ideology has a good deal to commend it. Gouldner's writings on these matters are evidently strongly influenced by Habermas. However one might in the end decide to conceptualize ideology itself, there is no doubt that it makes sense to see spheres of modern life being 'opened up' by their exposure to rational argumentation. In other words, areas previously organized by tradition or coercion become increasingly settled by discussion and argument carried on in a publicly available manner.

However, there are definite problems with Gouldner's formulation

[17] Alvin Gouldner: *The Dialectic* . . . , p. 10.

of the notion of ideology, which in the end proves to be rather ambiguous and baffling. Ideology, Gouldner sometimes says, is 'stunted reflexivity'[18]; but what makes it 'stunted'? How is an observer to decide about this without reference to a standpoint which itself might be regarded as ideological in the same sense? The question is not really answered by Gouldner at all. While he flirts with the solution of a Habermas-style ideal speech situation, in the end he rejects this. Ideology, he says on other occasions, is a 'limited form of rationality'.[19] What 'full rationality' would be is never disclosed. I do not think it possible to produce a coherent concept of ideology following Gouldner's approach (although in this respect his view is no different from that of the majority of those who have written about the problem). We can only develop a viable notion of ideology if we either treat the notion as a 'neutral' concept; or alternatively if we link it specifically with exploitative domination. The first tactic seems to me essentially uninteresting, because then 'ideology' is no different from general descriptive terms such as 'idea-system' or 'symbolic system'. I therefore prefer to adopt the second sense. According to such a standpoint, modes of signification are ideological when they are pressed in the service of sectional interests via the use of power. Ideology in this sense is by no means limited to the modern period, or to what Gouldner calls the culture of critical discourse. But this culture nevertheless has very definite consequences for the nature of modern society. As Thompson points out, Gouldner's approach to ideology is both too general and too specific.[20] It is too general in the sense that, by understanding ideology in relation to projects animated by rational discourse, Gouldner obscures that very relation between ideology and domination which should be regarded as fundamental. Gouldner's notion on the other hand is too specific because it sees ideology as essentially a modern phenomenon, something that has emerged over the past two or three hundred years.

Gouldner's concept of the culture of critical discourse is interesting and important, even if it adds little to what Habermas has written in identifying the 'public sphere'. However, to associate this closely with ideologies, as Gouldner does, seems at best misleading. Gouldner

---

[18] Ibid., p. 48.
[19] Ibid., p. 50.
[20] John B. Thompson: *Studies in the Theory of Ideology*. Cambridge: Polity Press, 1985, p. 88.

links the culture of critical discourse to Bernstein's elaborated codes. Such codes are regarded as distinct from the contextualized modes of discourse involved in day-to-day talk and conversation. Even were it the case — which is dubious — that the notion of an 'elaborated code' is acceptable, one has to see that day-to-day talk and 'high discourse' tend closely to influence one another. The ideas which intellectuals develop are often taken from lay notions; while lay discourse in turn is continually penetrated by concepts and modes of discourse originating in 'decontextualized' communication. This again has implications for what is to count as 'ideology'. It is one thing to emphasize that ideology is essentially involved with language and communication; it is another to link it specifically to a particular form of formalized discourse. The forms of talk involved in day-to-day life might very well be the most profound source of ideology — where 'ideology' is understood as concerning the connections between signification and domination.

Marxism, the culture of critical discourse, intellectuals — these are the persisting concerns of Gouldner's later writings. Yet perhaps it is the intellectuals who brook most large. This again can be traced back to Gouldner's preoccupation with reflexivity. A distinctive feature of modern culture, as Gouldner had come to see by the time of writing *The Coming Crisis of Western Sociology*, is its propensity for self-examination through the mobilizing of discourse. One of his main criticisms of mainstream sociology is precisely that it ignores the reflexivity of its own position. In the concluding sections of the book, Gouldner shows himself acutely aware of the limitations of any form of social analysis which does not chronically turn its modes of study back upon itself — hence the elaboration of 'reflexive sociology'. Understood in this way, the social sciences become one aspect of a general expansion of reflexively-based culture, a culture elaborated and extended by the intellectuals. Similarly, Gouldner's analysis of ideology tends to focus upon intellectuals, since ideology is defined in terms of the culture of critical discourse which they perpetrate.

It would seem, therefore, that Gouldner's analysis of the role of intellectuals in modern culture should form the strongest element of his later work. However, far from such being the case Gouldner's account of the role of intellectuals in modern societies is almost embarrassingly weak. As he employs it, the term 'intellectual' is a vague category. Very often it seems to mean all those who have been through some sort of process of higher education. Sometimes Gouldner distinguishes 'intellectuals' from 'intelligentsia', with the former being a much narrower concept than the latter. But this distinction is by no means continuously observed in what he has to say, and on occasion he seems even to associate 'intellectuals' with those who have experienced any sort of formal education whatsoever. Such casual terminological usage might not matter much were it not for the enormous importance which Gouldner wishes to attribute to intellectuals in the overall organization of modern societies. If one is going to make use of the term 'intellectual' at all, surely it should be confined to a fairly narrow and distinguishable stratum: those who are professional specialists in the innovative articulation of discourse and who are able to propagate this in a 'public' fashion. This differentiates intellectuals, as 'cultural leaders', from the vast army of professionals and office workers engaged in some sense in either 'knowledge production' or 'symbolic labour'.

Gouldner regards the intellectuals as a 'New Class' but wilfully avoids what 'class' is to be taken to mean here. His comment on this makes plain his unease when using 'class' to refer to intellectuals, although such a usage is essential to the theses he develops. There are many commentators, he says, 'who will be dismayed' that he should call the New Class a 'class' and who will claim that such cannot be the case. 'If I might say so', he goes on, 'my attitude towards this question is rather more Marxist than theirs . . . I remind them that, since Marx did little to define 'class' formally and connotatively, I feel similarly free not to make a scholastic issue of this matter.'[21] Class, he goes on to add, refers in a general way to categories of individuals sharing the same relationship to the means of production. No more precise formulation is offered. Gouldner's conception of the New Class obviously shares something in common with the ideas of authors — such as Djilas and others — who have employed the same term, usually in relation to the East European societies rather than the West. Even when restricted to these societies the idea that a New Class has come into being is, to say the least, debatable. Rather than being based primarily upon control of the means of production, the Party elites in such societies seem to derive their pre-eminent position much more from bureaucratic power. Gouldner supposes that the position of the New Class depends upon possession of cultural capital. But does 'capital' have much meaning in a society in which large segments of social and economic organization are taken out of the

[21] Alvin Gouldner: *The Future* . . . , p. 8.

market? Gouldner's argument on this point seems particularly confused. In the East European societies, he says, the expansion of the administrative apparatus of the state extends the domain over which the New Class holds sway.[22] Yet power which derives from participation in a governmental apparatus is clearly not market power and the notion of 'cultural capital' seems largely irrelevant to it. If such is not the case, then the notion of 'capital' has become so attenuated as to be of little analytical value.

According to Gouldner, the New Class is coming to power everywhere, not only in the East. But how and why? What are the processes bringing about the ascent of the New Class? On these matters also Gouldner is vague. The main thread of his argument seems to be that in a society in which scientific, technical and other forms of knowledge become central to production, those who specialize in the creation and sustaining of such knowledge will thereby eventually become dominant. This does not follow at all. In order to demonstrate such a thesis, it would be necessary to carry out a range of tasks which Gouldner does not even attempt. These would involve an extended analysis of the institutional transformation of modern societies, East and West. If it were the case, for example, that there were emerging some form of 'post-industrial' society, in which definite types of realignments of class power could be demonstrated, then the thesis of the arrival of a New Class might appear plausible. Since Gouldner nowhere confronts these issues in any detail, his arguments are unconvincing. More than this, I would be inclined to assert quite bluntly that they are wrong. There is no New Class coming into being, much less coming into power, in modern societies. The production of knowledge and information no doubt is coming to be more and more significant. The education system, and processes of mobility within it, are not just expressions of the class system defined in terms of property ownership and economic power. The notion of cultural capital, particularly as Bourdieu has formulated it, might be a useful one. But the way to develop these observations and notions is not through the sort of account Gouldner offers.

Alvin Gouldner was by any token one of the major figures in sociology in the period since the Second World War. No one can remain unimpressed by the extraordinary range of his later writings. The project he pursued seemed in the end to defeat him. It may very

---

[22] Ibid., p. 61.

well be that some of Gouldner's earlier writings, more modest in scope though they are, will stand the test of time more robustly than the ambitious works of his later years.

12

The perils of punditry:
Gorz and the end of the
working class

The working class, Marx once commented, will become the gravedigger of capitalism, administering the last rites of the system that is the origin of its oppression.[1] Today, however, if not exactly in the best of health, capitalism is certainly still with us, while the proletariat — or so many would claim — is fading away. Its demise is not the outcome of its subjection to capital, but the result of technological changes eroding traditional, blue-collar manufacturing work. Capitalism remains to preside over the burial of the working class, not the other way round. The thesis that the working class is becoming progressively more marginal to modern capitalism has been elaborated in contrasting ways by different authors. André Gorz's *Adieux au Proletariat*, however, is rather unusual.[2] Most of those who have waved goodbye to the working class have been associated with liberalism or the political Right. They have, as it were, bid farewell to an unwelcome presence. Gorz stands firmly on the Left. Moreover only a relatively short while ago he still believed that the labour movement could bring about the revolutionary transformation of capitalism.[3] His recent

---

[1] This essay was formerly published in German and appears in English for the first time here.

[2] André Gorz: *Adieux au proletariat*. Paris: Galilée, 1980; translated as *Farewell to the Working Class*. London: Pluto, 1982.

[3] André Gorz: *Strategy for Labour*. Boston: Beacon, 1964.

work is thus of some especial interest, and I shall use it in this essay as a stimulus to reflection about the position of the working class in contemporary capitalist societies.

1

Gorz begins with a sweeping critical indictment of Marxism. His arguments are familiar enough when emanating from the Right, but are usually resisted by those towards the other side of the political spectrum. Marx did not derive his interpretation of the historic mission of the working class, Gorz points out, from the empirical study of class relations. Marx's views were founded upon a transmuted version of Hegelianism, merged with ideas borrowed from French socialist thought of the early nineteenth century. History was regarded by Hegel as having an inherent *telos*, inaccessible to the human agents who are the makers of that history; the dialectical process transcends the intentions of individual human beings. Marx took over this conception, substituting the triumph of the proletariat for the self-realization of Spirit. 'It is not a question', Marx wrote, 'of what this or that proletarian, or even the whole proletariat, at the moment *regards* as its aim. It is a question of *what the proletariat is*, and what, in accordance with this *being*, it will historically be compelled to do. Its aim and historical action is visibly and irrevocably foreshadowed in its own life situation as well as in the whole organization of bourgeois society today.'[4] What if the working class seems not to be revolutionary? Well, something must be inhibiting the development of its militant consciousness. The fault does not lie with the theory.

Gorz is not content with any such notions, and proceeds to attack other aspects of Marx's ideas linked to them. In Marxist thought, the specific objectives which the working class pursues in its struggles across the face of history have a general relevance to society as a whole. The workers, as Marx put it, are nothing but they can become everything. The spread of capitalism strips workers of whatever skills they used to possess, reducing them all to a common level. But this very process makes them a 'universal class'. Since workers are no

[4] Karl Marx and Friedrich Engels: *The Holy Family*, in *Collected Works*, vol. 4. London: Lawrence & Wishart, 1975, p. 37. This passage is quoted by Gorz on p. 16 of his book.

longer tied to particular work processes, they have the capacity to master and control them all. Gorz calls this the 'myth of collective appropriation'. The capacity of workers to become a 'universal class' is not the same as its actuality. The facts of the matter are that the maturation of capitalism has created a fragmentation of labour, such that workers have no chance of grasping the character of production as a whole. Marxist theory has in any case always been vague in respect of who exactly was to bring about the collective appropriation of the means of production, and who would actually co-ordinate productive activity in the new society projected for the future. We should not really be surprised, Gorz says, to find that the socialist societies today are infused by 'an almost mystical cult of the proletariat',[5] associated with an emphasis upon disciplined labour, while real power is held by minority cadres within party organizations. These lines of development emerge very easily from both the main tenets of, and the ambiguities within, Marxist thought.

In Marx's view, as Gorz represents it, the emancipatory potential of the working class is founded upon the surplus production which industrial capitalism makes possible. Modern industry generates productive forces that create far more wealth than is necessary to meet basic human needs. In surplus production we see foreshadowed an area of freedom from the constraints of enforced labour; work will become an end in itself, governed only by the fulfilment which it offers to the producer. This was regarded by Marx as essential to the revolutionary capabilities of the proletariat: sooner or later the workers will realize that they are the means of liberating humanity from its servitude to nature. But once again the subsequent evolution of capitalism has confounded these expectations. The adoption of Taylorism by management has effectively quashed any consciousness workers might have had of their sovereign creativity. The factory is today no longer an economic unity, but is part of integrated production processes which may span several continents. The sites of production themselves have long ceased to be the main centres of the formation of policy and the enactment of decisions. The idea that workers can 'take over' production, in such a context, has become anachronistic. Even the formation of workers' councils in industry would be of little importance. In an era of technically-organized global production processes, the only power workers in localized production settings

[5] André Gorz: *Farewell*, p. 32.

could possess would be negative power — the capability in some degree to block managerial initiatives.

As Gorz puts it:

> Grass-roots workers' power can thus be seen to be a material impossibility within the framework of the existing structure of production. All that is actually possible is the power of trade unions, that is the power of the institutional apparatus to which workers delegate representative power. Trade-union power is not, however, the same thing as workers' power, any more than the power of parliament is the power of the sovereign people. Unions possess power *as institutions* that are relatively autonomous from their mandators. They become autonomous as a result of the mediatory power conferred on them by their institutional role. There is no point in reproving individual trade unionists for this fact. They sometimes experience the contradiction as a source of anguish or misery. Not they individually are at fault but the technical and social division of labour, the mode and relations of production, the size and inertia of the industrial machine which, because they rigidly predetermine both the results and the phases of the work process, leave no more than marginal space for workers' control in and over production.[6]

If this sounds like a heavy dollop of Weberianism, so it is. Gorz goes on to argue that, in the modern world of large-scale bureaucratic organizations, no one effectively holds power. The personal power of 'capitalists, directors and managers of every kind' is just an 'optical illusion'. Those who run industry are only administrators, as imprisoned within the framework of capitalist production as workers are. Much the same applies to the modern state. Sovereignty is not held by any particular individuals, but is exercised impersonally. Power does not belong to them, or derive from them, but is an outcome of the system as a whole.

Unlike Weber, however, Gorz is not prepared to forego the liberative ideals of socialism. The project of socialism, as Marx conceived of it, is as dead as the revolutionary proletariat. Yet the very trends that have helped to undermine this project have created new possibilities of social transformation. Workers cannot hope to seize power within either the sphere of industry or the state. 'The point now', Gorz argues, 'is to free oneself *from* work by rejecting its nature, content,

6 Ibid., pp. 51 — 2.

necessity and modalities'.[7] But repudiating work means disavowing the traditional format of the labour movement. The issue is no longer that of the achievement of power by the working class, as Marx thought, but attaining the freedom to reject the role of worker altogether. This is not a framework within which the concept of class has any part to play. On the contrary, the developments within capitalism outlined above have replaced the working class with what Gorz calls 'a non-class of non-workers' or the 'neoproletariat'. This 'non-class' is specifically created by processes of economic change witnessed within capitalist enterprise today. It is composed of those categories of people who either become permanently unemployed, or whose intellectual abilities are rendered irrelevant by the technical organization of labour. The old working class, Gorz says, is no more than a privileged minority. Most of the population belong to the post-industrial neoproletariat: if they are in work, they are in occupations which are poorly unionized, lack a definite class identity, and are low in job security. Those in such circumstances are usually over-qualified for whatever work they can find, and they lack any involvement with the tasks they carry out. In the longer term, as a consequence of the introduction of micro-technology, many of these individuals will join the ranks of the chronically unemployed.

Since it is not a class, and has no organizational coherence, the neoproletariat is not a replacement for the working class in Marxist theory: it does not have a mission guaranteed by history. But this apparent weakness is a source of strength. For those in the new 'non-class' have no reason to accept the productivist ethos of either capitalism or socialism, and tend to seek sources of satisfaction completely outside the realm of work. Work, Gorz claims:

> has become a means towards the extension of the sphere of non-work, a temporary occupation by which individuals acquire the possibility of pursuing their main activities. This is a critical mutation announcing the transition to post-industrial society. It implies a radical subversion of the ideology, scale of values and social relations established by capitalism. But it will only eliminate capitalism if its latent content is revealed in the form of an alternative to capitalism that is able to capture the developing cultural mutation and give it political extension.[8]

[7] Ibid., p. 67.
[8] Ibid., p. 81.

Such an alternative will not have much in common with socialism as traditionally understood. Socialists have always found it difficult, Gorz says, to come to terms with pluralism — with the recognition that there are a diversity of ways in which human beings might choose to live their lives. However, diversity of life-styles — outside of the sphere of production — is likely to be a major value pursued by the majority of the population in the coming decades. We are moving, Gorz claims, towards a 'dual society'. In one sector, production and political administration will be organized to maximize efficiency. The other sector will be a sphere in which individuals occupy themselves with the manifold pursuits in which fulfilment or the pursuit of enjoyment lead them to engage. The sphere of necessity will be as confined as possible, increasingly marginal to the activities in which people define their identity and seek self-realization.

The two sectors in the dual society, Gorz adds, will not be entirely separate from one another. In so far as individuals discover satisfactions in pursuits outside work, they are likely to be stimulated to resist any gratuitous extension of the hierarchical organization of labour. This applies to the state as well as the economy. The state, Gorz says, cannot be abolished, but the scope of its operations can nonetheless be substantially reduced. Just as it is impossible in any meaningful sense to democratize industry, so it is also in the case of the state. State power can only be limited by fostering the autonomy of individuals in civil society. The activities of the state will thus have to be rigidly circumscribed. A certain degree of centralized planning is a necessary task of government, as is the co-ordination of systems of transportation, communication, policing, and so on. Yet the realm of 'politics' will no longer have to do with struggles to achieve power. Rather, it will be concerned with designating and controlling the objectives of government. Politics, for Gorz, 'is the specific site at which society becomes conscious of its own production as a complex process and seeks . . . to master the results of that process'.[9] Good government is government which confines itself to technical problems of administration, leaving the population otherwise free to busy itself with matter of its own choosing.

This scenario, Gorz proposes, is already practicable. For we have reached a stage, in the industrialized societies, at which the productive forces are overdeveloped rather than the reverse. Current developments

[9] Ibid., p. 117.

in micro-electronics will push things further. It used to be believed —
and, indeed, it was until recently the case — that technical progress
involved more and more costly expenditure upon machinery. This is
no longer so. The new technology makes it possible not just to
economize upon labour, but upon labour and capital at the same time.
We are at the beginning of a process of technical transformation that
will have a massive impact upon the nature of industrial activity —
leading especially to higher levels of automated production. In these
circumstances, more investment in industry does not create more
jobs, but fewer. Automation is becoming every bit as important in
office work as in manual labour. Gorz quotes a study which estimates
that about a third of the office employees in French banks and
insurance companies are in fact redundant, but for political reasons
have not been dismissed. Opportunities in the tertiary sector will
certainly not compensate for the elimination of blue-collar jobs.

Among the logical responses to such a situation are a radical
shortening of the average working day, and extensive introduction of
the practice of job-sharing. Employers are nearly always opposed to
these measures. Why? There is no sound economic reason, according
to Gorz, but there are powerful ideological ones. Contemporary
capitalism is founded upon the performance principle, the renunciation
of pleasure in favour of the sober and dutiful enactment of labour
tasks (one of the many places in his work where what Gorz has to say
carries more than an echo of Marcuse). Unemployment, seen by most
employers and workers alike as a negative phenomenon, is a force
aiding in the discipline of those who are in employment. But this has
really now become an archaic economy of time. The self-management
of time is the key to overturning this traditionally-established ethic.
The point is not just to allot people more 'free time', but to empower
them to take it, thus breaking the passivity characteristic of a great
deal of what passes for 'leisure'. An active 'time policy' is a
revolutionary demand, because it calls for a dislocation of the guiding
morality of capitalism. Revolutionary it may be, but utopian it is not
— or so Gorz claims. It is already the case in Germany that substantial
numbers of employees choose not only the hours at which they begin
and stop work but, within certain limits, the amount of time they
work per month. A range of other possible systems can be envisaged:
'retirement advances' given at any age in return for a postponement of
retirement from the labour force; sabbatical leaves, such as are at
present found only in a few settings, most notably universities; and
'time savings-accounts', whereby individuals who have 'accumulated'

a certain amount of work over a given period will be able to reduce the hours they work subsequently, without loss of earnings. 'Such goals', Gorz concludes, 'constitute a radical negation of capitalism.' An economy 'in which production is subordinated to capital's need for profits' can be replaced by 'an economy (originally known as socialism) in which production is subordinated to needs'[10] — a view which hence turns out to be not so completely different from at least certain elements in Marx after all.

Gorz's book is declaredly an essay, not claiming to be either precise or comprehensive in its treatment of the themes raised. Thus there is little point attempting to provide a critique of the detail of his arguments. Gorz has a knack of expressing ideas in a provocative fashion and by his attacking style stirs the reader to response. I will concentrate my discussion upon three topics:

1)   The apparent declining importance of working-class occupations within the industrialized economies.
2)   The likely impact of the new technology upon pre-existing class relations.
3)   The prospects for socialism, as ordinarily conceived.

Of course, I shall not be able even to cover any of these themes in an exhaustive way.

2

Let me approach the first issue by contrasting Gorz's views with those coming from quite another quarter — the recent work of Himmelstrand and his co-authors, written in the context of Sweden.[11] Himmelstrand's analysis is an attempt to endorse just those phenomena which Gorz declares now obsolete: a process of socialist reform led by the labour movement. Moreover, it is a defence of a Marxist interpretation of such a process. Himmelstrand specifically denies that the working class has either shrunk in relative size, or that it has become 'incorporated' within the existing order. Sweden is among the most materially prosperous, egalitarian, and technologically advanced

---

[10] Ibid., p. 122.
[11] Ulf Himmelstrand *et al.*: *Beyond Welfare Capitalism*. London: Heinemann, 1981.

societies in the world. It is also one which has experienced nearly half a century of government by a professedly Labour party, the Social Democratic Party. Just this fact, according to Himmelstrand, makes it possible in Sweden to progress 'beyond welfare capitalism' to socialism. 'Socialism', as Himmelstrand understands it, does not refer to the nationalization of industry or to centrally-planned production. It means, in his eyes, real control by workers over processes of production — exactly that which Gorz dismisses as incapable of attainment. Moreover, this is not just a prospect which someone with an eye to the future might see as desirable, it is on the agenda now.

A transition to socialism, Himmelstrand emphasizes, would presume the active engagement of the bulk of the working class. It would be a 'revolution through reform', but one very much closer to traditional conceptions of socialist politics than anything envisaged by Gorz — or, to be more accurate, the Gorz of today. According to Himmelstrand, the working class is not declining in size but actually increasing. The unemployment rate in Sweden is low (3 per cent in 1985). There is no talk in Himmelstrand's book of an increasingly populous neoproletariat of the unemployed or partly employed. Himmelstrand writes instead of what he terms the 'extended working class' — the large mass of the labour force — who are presumed to hold overall interests in common in a socialist transformation of society. The extended working class comprises all those involved in routinized labour, including lower white-collar and service workers. He tries to show that, according to various indices of class consciousness, union organization and political activity, the proletariat — in the shape of the extended working class — is not only alive but kicking. Conditions exist for the development of struggles which will go beyond the usual trade union negotiations towards a more radical programme of social reconstruction. Proposals for a system of wage-earners' funds — officially sanctioned now by the Social Democrats — provide a focus for active struggle to bring about economic democracy. In Himmelstrand's view, Sweden could demonstrate a 'third way' of social development, moving beyond liberal democracy while skirting the totalitarian consequences of socialism based upon centralized planning. This at least he shares in common with Gorz: a recognition that the state socialism of Eastern Europe has generated repressive political regimes while at the same time being economically rather less than a dazzling success.

How is it possible that there should be such large differences of viewpoint between two authors, each writing about current developments in the class structure of the industrialized societies? One answer to this question takes us back to theories of the so-called 'new working class' of about two decades ago. The proponents of such theories held that the 'new working class' — workers in technical and scientific occupations — could become a revolutionary vanguard of the labour movement. Those who made these claims were French, and their ideas were mainly based on materials drawn from France. Workers in these occupations in other countries seemed far from revolutionary, and it is apparent that the conception of the 'new working class' was an over-generalization from what, even in France, proved to be a fairly transient set of circumstances.[12] Perhaps something similar is the case comparing Gorz and Himmelstrand? The latter's work is explicitly concentrated upon Sweden, and he does not claim that his conclusions can be directly applied elsewhere. Gorz on the other hand clearly does intend his analysis to have very general application: and yet perhaps it is excessively influenced by trends that are more marked in some countries than in others. I shall come back to this later, because it is of some considerable importance.

To begin with, the issue must be tackled of whether or not the working class is disappearing (as Gorz says) or expanding (as Himmelstrand claims) within the occupational system of Western societies. The view that working-class occupations are diminishing in relative importance has for some while been a lynch-pin of theories of post-industrialism. Gorz uses the adjective 'post-industrial' rather loosely, and it is not clear how far he accepts that the presumed transition from industrialism to post-industrialism depends upon the sort of changes in the occupational system which Bell emphasizes. Bell's ideas have achieved a good deal of prominence in the literature of class analysis, and it is certainly worth considering one of his main themes, even if it is nowhere directly discussed by Gorz. This is the contention that the relative diminution of working-class occupations is brought about by changes which expand the role of services. The production of primary and secondary goods, Bell argues, requires a progressively diminishing input of labour; the tertiary, or service sector, by contrast, undergoes a considerable enlargement.[13]

12 See Anthony Giddens: *The Class Structure of the Advanced Societies.* London: Hutchinson, 1973, chpt. 11.
13 Daniel Bell: *The Coming of Post-Industrial Society.* London: Heinemann, 1974.

Bell accepts that the term 'services' covers a range of different things — including transportation, utilities, banking, insurance, travel, entertainments and so on. And defined in this embracing fashion the trend towards the growth of service occupations at first blush seems undeniable. In the United Kingdom, over the lengthy period from 1841 to 1971, the proportion of the active labour force working in the tertiary sector, if this includes transportation and utilities, rose from 32 per cent to fully 60 per cent. The proportion working in the secondary or manufacturing sector has in fact barely changed at all over this period, amounting to some 35 per cent at the beginning and end dates. The chief difference is a very large decline in the numbers of those working in agriculture and mining — from 25 per cent to 4 per cent.[14]

However, as Gershuny has emphasized, we have to consider rather carefully what 'services' are.[15] 'Goods' are evidently durable objects, made by workers with the aid of machines, sold or distributed to consumers. Services, on the other hand, are non-material facilities, consumed at the moment of their acquisition. We have to stress the latter phrase in this sentence, because goods also supply a service, in so far as they meet needs of consumers. Goods and services alike cater for needs, and in many instances the same needs can be met by either. Someone who wants their washing done regularly may send their dirty linen out to a laundry, or alternatively they may buy a washing-machine and do the task at home. Bell's thesis, and that of others who have adopted similar ideas, is that provision for needs (which expand as the phase of industrialism draws to a close) is more and more met by services than by goods. His main source of support for this contention is the demonstration of the relative growth of the tertiary or service sector. This does not in and of itself vindicate his case, because it says nothing about the actual consumption of services — what they are used for, and by whom. Many services may be consumed as part of overall processes of production, even if service workers are not themselves 'proletarians' — engaged in the direct manufacture of goods.

Pursuing this observation empirically is not a simple matter, but there are various ways of approaching the problem. The most

[14] Jonathan Gershuny: *After Industrial Society?* London: Macmillan, 1978, pp. 60—1.
[15] Ibid., chpt. 4.

straightforward, and telling, method is to classify employment by industrial sector, so that all occupations are categorized in relation to the final product with which they are involved. Gershuny has carried out an analysis of this type, indicating that those involved in provision of services for final consumption make up less than half the service workers in the labour force. The growth in the tertiary sector is probably not primarily to be explained in terms of the expansion of 'services and amenities'. A high proportion of the growth in service employment is due to the contribution those in such employment make to the production of goods for final consumption.[16] It is, in other words, in large part an expression of the complexity of the division of labour. The co-ordination and technical organization of modern industry, geographically dispersed and incorporated in an international division of labour, involves a high proportion of employees distant from the direct manufacture of goods but nevertheless integral to their production and consumption.

Of course, a sectoral analysis of occupational change is one thing, and the identification of changes in conditions of work another.[17] A higher proportion of occupations may be involved in manufacture than is presumed by the advocates of the post-industrial society thesis. Nonetheless there still may have come about major changes in the nature of labour-tasks, since the 'office' has grown in relative importance compared with the 'shop-floor'. Bell, Richta and others have proposed that workers at the middle levels of the class system tend to gain in autonomy as a result of socio-economic change. But equally prominent in the recent literature is an opposing view: that work is becoming 'de-skilled' rather than the reverse. On this point at least there is agreement between Gorz and Himmelstrand, both of whom accept that down-grading rather than up-grading is the order of the day within the sphere of work. It is precisely this phenomenon, in fact, which Himmelstrand has in mind when he speaks of the extended working class. Following Braverman, he argues that although people working on the shop-floor constitute a minority of the labour force, the conditions of labour of those working in other than blue-collar

[16] Ibid., pp. 84ff.

[17] See Guy Routh: *Occupation and Pay in Great Britain 1906 — 79*. London: Macmillan, 1980; Erik Olin Wright and Joachim Singlemann: 'Proletarianisation in the changing American class structure', *American Journal of Sociology*, vol. 88, 1982.

occupations are sufficiently similar to them to speak of the continued existence of a majority 'working class'. Braverman's much-debated 'deskilling' theory involves the diagnosis of two convergent trends in the division of labour in the industrialized countries. One is the progressive disappearance, among manual workers, of craft skills; the other, the mechanization of office work. Taken together, Braverman argues, these trends bear out Marx's projection of the proletarianization of the mass of the work force. Braverman's working class is not revolutionary, but it is a unitary phenomenon in respect of the growing similarity of overall conditions of labour. But how has the deskilling notion, to which Himmelstrand makes appeal, stood up to the battering it has received from critics? The answer is surely: not very well.[18] Among the qualifications which have to be made to Braverman's thesis, as originally formulated, are the following.

1) There are major differences both between countries, and sectors of industry within countries, in respect of how far the forms of managerial style emphasized by Braverman — supposedly leading to deskilling — were instituted.

2) Braverman exaggerates the level and variety of craft skills that existed prior to the advent of capitalism, and the range of new skills thrown up by processes of technological change.

3) By neglecting the active resistance which workers are often able to mobilize against threats to their autonomy in the workplace, the deskilling thesis underestimates the capability of workers to influence the definition of what 'skill' is.

4) The deskilling of work is not the same as the deskilling of workers; workers may be able to move out of settings in which the quality of labour task has been undermined into others of a more rewarding kind.

5) It is questionable whether the mechanization of white-collar work has dissolved the range of differentiations which in many contexts have separated the 'office' from the 'shop-floor'.

6) Control over labour, which Braverman tends to focus upon almost exclusively, is only one among a number of other basic concerns

[18] Harry Braverman: *Labour and Monopoly Capital*. New York: Monthly Review Press, 1974. Out of a by now extensive critical literature, see especially the various contributions to Stephen Wood: *The Degradation of Work?* London: Hutchinson, 1982.

of management, and 'management' is not a homogeneous entity.

7)   Braverman treats managerial control as a zero-sum relation, in which the more power that accrues to managers over industrial design, the less there remains for workers. But this assumption is not valid logically, and there seem good grounds to object to it empirically.[19]

Discussion of changes in the distribution of occupations, or even in aspects of the labour process, is obviously not sufficient in and of itself to settle the question of how far the working class is becoming a less or more significant part of the class system of the advanced capitalist societies. A variety of other factors enter into class structuration. However, I think it reasonable to suppose — unpalatable though it might be for those who would discern neat and unambiguous trends — that the working class is neither swelling to compose a gigantic proletariat, nor is it on the verge of disappearing. Although there are no doubt considerable variations between different countries, in Sweden as elsewhere talk of an 'extended working class', based on the deskilling hypothesis, has to be regarded with caution, and is an oversimplification. On the other hand, we do not live in a post-industrial society, if that notion is taken to depend primarily upon transformations in the nature of the work that the majority of the paid labour force carry out.

However, there is another resonance of the idea of post-industrialism in Gorz: this has less reference to sectoral changes leading to the evanescence of working-class occupations than to novel technological developments which presage the shrinking importance of 'industry' or 'work' as such. Here his view of the demise of the working class depends upon an interpretation of the likely impact of micro-electronics upon employment, and it is to this which I now turn.

3

A measure of caution is well advised in approaching pronouncements such as those which Gorz offers. Sociological observers have not proven to be particularly effective pundits in previous generations, and there is no reason to suppose that they have become any more

---

[19] See Stephen Wood & John Kelly: 'Taylorism, responsible autonomy and management strategy', in Stephen Wood, *Degradation* . . . .

acute today than they were in yesteryear. We do not have to go back to Marx to uncover confident predictions which have proved to fall wide of the mark. Look back some fifteen years, to the period at which the Western economies were enjoying a period of steady growth, with levels of employment generally high and inflation low. The sociological literature at that time was replete with views of social development which projected (in the West) the progressive diminution of material inequality, the expansion of welfare, development of education and so on. Many critics on the Left accepted this picture as unquestioningly as their liberal counterparts, while still discerning major failings in the societies of affluence. If today we see slight or even sometimes negative economic growth rates, a contraction of the welfare state in many countries, and large-scale unemployment, we should not leap to the conclusion that these are necessarily now generic features of the industrialized societies as a whole. Many commentators appear to have reached such a view with as little hesitation as those at the earlier period presumed the opposite. This does not mean that they are necessarily wrong, of course; but it suggests that we should not be too ready to infer from the present to an indefinite future.

Let me concentrate here upon unemployment and its relation to automation, since this is a key theme in Gorz's discussion. How far, first of all, are the high levels of unemployment currently displayed by most — although not all — Western countries the result of a world recession which might reasonably be expected to be short-lived? There is no doubt that a number of contingent events, particularly the so-called 'oil crisis' of 1973—4, have played a part in checking the seemingly steady prosperity of the post-Second World War period. But there are assuredly other factors involved. As measured by the conventional indices anyway, growth rates of most Western countries were slowing down some while before OPEC came on the scene. Over the past decade and a half there have come about some major shifts in the location of industrial production, especially manufacture, in the world economy — now well-documented in a range of recent studies.[20] During the same period in which economic growth in the West has slackened, a considerable number of 'less developed' countries have actually experienced a marked acceleration in growth, especially within manufacturing industry. In most of these latter countries, rates

[20] See, for instance, Folker Fröbel *et al.*: *The New International Division of Labour*. Cambridge: Cambridge University Press, 1980.

of unemployment have in fact diminished.[21] It seems at least reasonable to suppose that the relocation of primary production within the global division of labour will continue. In combination with an overall relative decline in world trade, however temporary that might turn out to be, some of the major industries of the West are likely to find themselves increasingly uncompetitive and subject to relative decline.

The joker in the pack, however, is automation, particularly as connected with developments in micro-electronics. Writers of very different persuasions accept that there is a relation between the level and character of automation in a given industry or economic sector, and changes in the rate of employment in that industry or sector. But there is very little agreement indeed over just what the relation actually is. Some hold that automation expands employment opportunities, others that the reverse is the case. A large speculative element is added just because micro-electronic technology is so new.

The idea of automation has been around a long time; Marx's comments on it in the *Grundrisse* are fairly typical of nineteenth-century thinking on the subject. Moreover in the 1950s there were many works written predicting a widespread trend towards the electronic office and the automatic factory, presuming that computers would take over many of the tasks previously done by human labour. Yet the extent of automation during this period was not large. Computers at that time were very expensive to buy and maintain and were prone to mechanical faults. Thus the British catering company, Lyons, introduced a computerized office in 1953, the 'Lyons Electronic Office'. It was claimed that LEO could carry out the equivalent of the labour of some six hundred clerical workers doing payroll calculations, if used for eighty hours per week around the year. The computer cost £100,000 (£700,000 at today's prices), and was expensive to run; the costs of using it seem to have considerably outweighed the savings. A computer of the same output today costs only £8,000; and whereas LEO occupied a whole room, the newer version is only the size of a filing cabinet.

The sheer pace of technological change, packed into a period of a few years, is what is stunning about the development of micro-electronics. The first useful computers, made just after the end of the Second World War, weighed up to thirty tons, occupied a very large

21 Bill Jordan: *Mass Unemployment*. Oxford: Basil Blackwell, 1982, chpt. 4.

floor space, and used as much power as a steam train. A computer of similar output now is circuited onto several pieces of semiconductor material each no more than the size of a shirt button.[22] Shrinking size, expansion of computing power, flexibility of use in different contexts, adaptability to communication networks — to all these have to be added the developments in robotics, of which Gorz speaks. Modern robots are adjuncts or 'peripherals' to computers, enabling the programmed enactment of mechanical tasks.

It is easy in the abstract to think of ways in which the extended use of micro-electronics can generate employment; and of ways in which exactly the contrary effect can occur. Cheaper mass production of existing products might create new demand; new products and/or services might be opened up; sectors of industry in financial difficulty might regain profitability. On the other side of the coin, of course, is the fact that the new technology radically reduces the need for labour in contexts where it permits the introduction of automated processes: large numbers of workers in clerical, sales, and assembly operations will simply become redundant. But all this remains little more than vague speculation if not connected to other aspects of economic — and political — organization.

Gorz, however, concentrates primarily upon automation, and it is worthwhile making a few comments about this. The concept of automation is not as easy to define as might be imagined. Automation is usually understood in the context of a single production setting or type of production setting: the replacement of human labour by mechanized processes. The sense in which labour is 'replaced' is potentially complex. For while technological changes may, for example, reduce the need to use labour in one part of the production process, the very same changes may increase such a need in other parts of that process. Automation is only different from mechanization if the overall effect of technological change in a given industry or area is actually shown to be connected to a net loss in the demand for labour. Thus I shall follow here the general distinction Jordan makes between 'mechanization' and 'automation'.[23] He refers to the former as a situation in which technological change serves to increase output more rapidly than it augments labour productivity. 'Automation' is

[22] Peter Marsh: *The Silicon Chip Book*. London: Abacus, 1981, pp. 107–8 and p. 4.
[23] Bill Jordan, *Mass Unemployment*, p. 99.

involved in any circumstance in which technological innovation increases productivity faster than output: only in such a situation does machinery substitute for human labour. This is a somewhat unorthodox definition, to be sure, but it does help to make sense of the varied relations that may exist between technological change and unemployment.

Understood in this fashion, automation was of only marginal importance in the industrialized economies up to the late 1960s. Levels of employment increased over the period from World War Two to that date, since output grew faster than productivity. The exception was agriculture, where automation proceeded rapidly, transferring large proportions of the labour force from the land. Automation began to make its mark in the 1970s, within the core areas of industrial production. Rather than displacing low-productivity workers (from agriculture) who were absorbed into higher-productivity labour, workers were displaced from high-productivity sectors. Given the background of world slump, the result has been to tend to foster unemployment, with a low level of reabsorption of workers into the labour force. These processes have clearly differed substantially among the industrialized countries and between economic sectors. For example, in spite of the 'oil crisis', the petroleum and natural gas producing industries have remained prosperous; while the production of metals, most notably iron and steel, has fallen substantially in the EEC countries — levels of employment dropping even more rapidly than output.

Automation in some 'successful' economies has been associated with a continued growth in industrial production, but in others — particularly in Britain — is linked to levels of unemployment higher than during the worst years of the 1930s. It does seem more than within the bounds of possibility that rates of unemployment will remain high, or increase further, in at least a certain proportion of the industrialized countries in the foreseeable future — although this is surely not as inevitable as most observers now seem to assume. But it is again important not to over-generalize, or to regard any particular society as necessarily supplying a model of what is likely to happen in others. Moreover, like gross data on occupational distribution, the statistics of unemployment cannot be interpreted just at their face value. The relation between rates of unemployment and the actual level of economic activity in a population may be less direct than most writers are prone to suppose. Demographic factors, for example, such as the changing age distribution of a population, or the inflow and outflow of migrant workers, are obviously relevant; as is the existence of a substantial 'secondary economy'. A rising statistical rate of unemployment in a given country may actually conceal a growth in real levels of paid economic activity — where the latter is the ratio of those working in remunerative labour to the total population.

4

What, then, of Gorz's prognostications about the end of the working class, the imminent decline of the labour movement and the essential irrelevance of socialist politics? Gorz's sketch of the 'neoproletariat', or 'non-class', for the time being remains one of various possible future scenarios, not an accurate designation of the present day. The rate of unemployment in Britain is among the highest among the countries of Western Europe. However, the proportion of those in the active labour force working in manufacture has not declined, but actually risen if we accept Gershuny's analysis. How far these workers constitute a unitary 'class', as I have said, depends upon a variety of considerations. There are major cleavages within, and fuzzy boundaries to, the working class. Differences of skill, strength of unionization, job tenure and other factors are involved in such divisions. There still remain differences, material and ideological, between office workers and manual workers. But the working class can hardly be written off as casually as Gorz appears to do. Two categories of the population are at the moment particularly badly hit by unemployment: women and young people just leaving school. Their work prospects might very easily deteriorate further. Women have been increasingly represented in the labour force in all Western countries over the past forty years, and are disproportionately clustered in routine office work. If offices are increasingly invaded by micro-technology, women workers will almost certainly suffer most. Similarly, those who leave school and find no employment are likely to lack the skills or qualifications which would allow them to enter the labour force at a later date were there an economic recovery. The social consequences of these phenomena are likely to be very considerable, but they do not signal either the disappearance of class or of class politics.

The case of Sweden looks very different from that of either Britain or France, and it is not difficult to see the force of Himmelstrand's arguments, whatever reservations one might have about some of his claims. Sweden, as has been mentioned, not only has a long tradition of Social Democratic government and a very well-developed welfare state. The level of unionization is much higher than in most Western countries, including that of white collar workers. While the notion of an extended working class may be questionable, political alliances are feasible in Sweden which are highly improbable in, say, Britain. Swedish politics since the early 1970s have been dominated by the coalition of the two main labour organizations, one representing mainly manufacturing workers, the other salaried employees. The proposal to introduce workers' investment funds as a mechanism for stimulating greater industrial democracy is part of a programme of change which stands a real chance of being systematically implemented — even if one may doubt that the social change thereby brought about is likely to be as far-reaching as some anticipate.[24] In this connection it is interesting to remark that the institution of workers' advisory councils in Sweden had quite a contrary result to a virtually identical scheme introduced in France. In the latter country the measure was largely received apathetically, while in the former it had the effect of galvanizing demands for worker self-management in industry.[25]

It is worth distinguishing various strands in Gorz's discussion, in addition to the issues I have mentioned so far, and treating them separately. These are: his critique of Marx; his disavowal of the possibilities of any sort of genuine democracy in industry or the political sphere; and his analysis of the diminished significance of work as a medium for fundamental social reform. Gorz's critique of Marx is perhaps somewhat crudely expressed, but the main points he makes are valid enough. Marx surely did pin far too much upon the revolutionary potential of the working class, and upon the transformative significance of class conflict more generally. No one should underestimate the achievements of labour movements in the industrialized countries (or elsewhere for that matter). The struggles of workers' organizations have played a major part in creating modern 'welfare capitalism', and may yet have a good deal of influence, as Himmelstrand and others hold, upon whatever may lie 'beyond' it. But all this is quite distinct from the more adventurous flights of

[24] See my discussion of Himmelstrand *et al.*, in the review symposium in *Acta Sociologica*, vol. 16, 1983.

[25] E. H. Stephens: 'The politics of workers' participation', Yale PhD dissertation, quoted in John D. Stephens: *The Transition from Capitalism to Socialism*. London: Macmillan, 1979.

fancy about the historical role of the proletariat that Marx made an essential ingredient in his writing.

Gorz's dismissive attitude towards economic and political democracy, however, is based upon quite different grounds from his criticisms of Marx. Those who would look for more egalitarian or participatory modes of organization in the institutional 'centres' of contemporary societies appear as mere dreamers. The increasingly systematic and global character of modern production, and of the state, necessarily herald the triumph of technocratic reason over the older forms of liberal and democratic socialist ideals. Although Gorz's remarks on this issue are written in an attitude of tough-minded realism, they must rank among the least compelling of the various diagnoses he offers in his book. Gorz's 'dual society' is more unrealistic and naive than the conceptions of democracy which he rejects. The 'state' is no longer a phenomenon clearly separable from 'civil society', and if there is one trend that does seem to move implacably forward, it is the expanding character of state involvement in even many of the minutiae of daily life. It is less plausible to suppose (as Gorz does, here coming in curious alignment with the contemporary Right) that this process can be reversed than it is to argue that its hierarchical, arbitrary, or impersonal aspects can be countered. State power, like industrial authority, is not necessarily a zero-sum relation; the expansion of the state need not ruthlessly draw power away from those subject to it.

Of course, it would be foolish to be sanguine about the possible extension of either representative or participatory forms of democracy — as perhaps Gorz was in his earlier work. Anyone who supposed that a few homilies about participatory democracy or workers' co-operatives were sufficient to correct the limitations of Marxist conceptions of social transformation would be naive indeed. It is surely evident now that the connections between Marxist thought and totalitarian features of the Eastern European societies are more than just contingent. Moreover, most — although by no means all — forms of Marxism do exhibit that 'productivism' which Gorz, and everyone sensitive to ecological issues, wish to disclaim. It is plain enough that 'unemployment' is regarded both by those who experience it and by ruling groups in West and East almost wholly as a negative phenomenon. Proposals for a 'time policy' that would regard being 'out of work' as a gain rather than a loss for the individual are eminently sensible, even in a context in which most of the population are supposedly 'fully employed' — let alone in the circumstances which Gorz envisages, in which the sphere of 'work' contracts dramatically for almost everyone.

Any sort of political programme based mainly upon such proposals would be a risky and short-sighted undertaking. For the 'high technology, low employment' society might turn out to be chimerical, itself the result of an over-generalization from certain trends of the moment. Gorz's theorizing here tends to perpetuate, in the more straitened times of today, shortcomings characteristic of sociological punditry in the phase of Western affluence.

Index